Mistake of Law

Annemieke van Verseveld

Mistake of Law

Excusing Perpetrators of International Crimes

T·M·C·ASSER PRESS

Springer

Annemieke van Verseveld
Criminal Law Department
University of Amsterdam
Amsterdam
The Netherlands

ISBN 978-90-6704-866-8 ISBN 978-90-6704-867-5 (eBook)
DOI 10.1007/978-90-6704-867-5

Library of Congress Control Number: 2012940540

Published by T.M.C. ASSER PRESS, The Hague, The Netherlands www.asserpress.nl
Produced and distributed for T.M.C. ASSER PRESS by Springer-Verlag Berlin Heidelberg

Printed on acid-free paper

Springer is part of Springer Science+Business Media (www.springer.com)

Ignoring it doesn't work, nor does denouncing it, and there is no disavowing it, never mind denying it. The stain is inescapable and irreversible, and it is ours, and if we have any hope of containing it and living it down it can only come from seeing it whole.[1]

Philip Gourevitch and Errol Morris

[1] Gourevitch and Morris 2008, p. 160.

Preface

Why devote a voluminous book to the issue of mistake of law in international criminal law? Would it not appear frivolous for a person accused, for example, of crimes against humanity to claim that he did not know that what he did was against the law? And even if he was in fact mistaken, why should the law care as long as the perpetrator was aware of what he was doing?

Annemieke van Verseveld brilliantly lays to rest such skeptical queries about the need for her study. In this book, she shows that it is not only worthwhile but even urgently necessary to reflect on mistakes of law. She demonstrates the relevance of her inquiry by showing, in Chap. 6, a host of areas of international criminal law where the applicable law is far from clear. And, based on a comprehensive analysis of four national legal systems (USA, England, Germany, and France) as well as of international criminal law, the author shows that the law in regard to mistakes of law is presently in disarray and lacks a clear direction. Annemieke van Verseveld's concise but thorough treatment of the topic, therefore, is timely and useful. Any practitioner who deals with international criminal law cases should read this book.

But that is not all. The issue of how the law should react to a defendant's claim that he was not aware of the norm he violated raises fundamental questions about the purpose and structure of the criminal law. Does the intent required for conviction of a crime include knowledge of the relevant criminal prohibition, or of the moral wrongfulness of one's conduct? Should the perpetrator's mistake of law affect his culpability rather than the required *mens rea*? Or can such mistakes simply be ignored, in accordance with the maxim *ignorantia iuris neminem excusat*?

Annemieke van Verseveld shows that the correct answer to this question can only be found by taking into account the structure of the criminal law as a whole. Some legal systems content themselves by distinguishing between objective and subjective elements of crime and adding an assortment of "defenses". Such legal systems—and the author shows that international criminal law, at its present state, is one of them—have great difficulty in dealing with (honest) misconceptions of the criminal law because they face the choice between ignoring such mistakes altogether or acquitting the perpetrator for lack of *mens rea* even where he could easily have avoided his error. Other legal systems offer the prospect of a more differentiated approach. When a system distinguishes between the wrongfulness of a person's conduct (which comprises objective and subjective elements) and that person's individual blameworthiness, it becomes possible to acknowledge that a perpetrator has intentionally committed a crime and yet might be excused because it was not well possible for him to learn about the relevant law.

Annemieke van Verseveld prefers the second approach and, on its basis, drafts a concise and comprehensive provision which would resolve, or at least strongly reduce, the doctrinal problems that mistakes of law presently pose to any legal system, and especially to international criminal law. The charm of her approach lies in its flexibility: it is a matter of criminal policy on what conditions and to what extent a law maker is willing to grant an excuse to the perpetrator who knew very well what he did but failed to know that his acts were legally (or morally?) prohibited. Of course, it remains open to discussion whether the "unavoidability" of any mistake of law—the parameter chosen by the author—provides the correct yardstick for measuring the perpetrator's blameworthiness, how that yardstick relates to any general theory of blameworthiness, and when exactly a mistake of law can be deemed "unavoidable". But the virtue of this book is that its author has clearly identified the issues that matter, and has done away with much of the undergrowth that has so far impeded a rational debate.

Even if this book did not provide for such remarkable progress in the debate of a thorny issue, it would be an excellent work of scholarship. Annemieke van Verseveld has immersed herself in five different legal systems and offers the reader masterful summaries of each system's treatment of the mistake of law problem. Moreover, she presents a remarkably detailed and insightful discussion of the relevant case law, including hard-to-find decisions of various courts purporting to apply international criminal law in the aftermath of the Second World War, as well as an analysis of the relevant provisions of the Statute of the International Criminal Court. At the same time, Annemieke van Verseveld offers profound new insights into the most difficult questions of criminal law theory.

This book is a great achievement. Congratulations!

Cologne, May 2012

Thomas Weigend
Professor of Criminal Law
University of Cologne, Germany

Acknowledgments

First and foremost, I wish to thank Professor Harmen van der Wilt (University of Amsterdam) and Professor Simon Stolwijk (University of Amsterdam). Harmen van der Wilt wrote the initial research proposal for this study and he has been a source of inspiration in every conceivable way. Our conversations about the research always enlightened me, although I must admit that the implications of his sharp comments would sometimes only dawn upon me days later. Simon Stolwijk, I wish to thank for continually making the time to talk about issues at hand and for his keen and lucid observations.

I owe much gratitude to Professor George P. Fletcher (Columbia University, New York), whose thought-provoking work continues to stimulate me infinitely. To have had the opportunity to participate in his seminars on criminal law at Columbia University is a great privilege. I am greatly indebted to Professor Thomas Weigend (University of Cologne) for his profound and thorough assessment of the penultimate manuscript of this book and to Professor Terry Gill (University of Amsterdam) for his elaborate comments, particularly on Chap. 6. I am indebted to the Netherlands Organisation for Scientific Research (NWO) for granting me a scholarship which made my stay at Columbia University possible. For its financial support, I also wish to thank the Amsterdam Center for International Law.

Colonel Dr. Paul Ducheine (University of Amsterdam) and Major Eric Pouw (Netherlands Defence Academy), I would like to thank for their insightful comments from a military perspective on earlier drafts of Chap. 6. Judge Howard Morrison (International Criminal Tribunal for the Former Yugoslavia), I am incredibly grateful for making language corrections to the manuscript. Much gratitude is due to all my colleagues at the criminal law department of the University of Amsterdam. I owe a special word of thanks to Tom Blom, Göran Sluiter, Henna Redan, Maike Steen, and Geranne Lautenbach. I wish I could have expressed my gratitude to Bert Swart. I will remember him as a colleague of rare kindness and wisdom, his presence will be deeply missed.

My dear friends Melanie Jansen and Jarinde Temminck Tuinstra, I thank for their endless support. Joke Bulte, I wish to thank for always showing an interest. My dear sister, thank you for being so thoughtful and always wishing me luck. My dear parents, I cannot thank you enough for your infinite love and support. This book is dedicated to you. Hendrik Jan, my dearest, without you, your love, creative mind, patience, and passions, I would be nowhere. Mia, m'n schatje, wat ben jij lief, jij bent alles.

Amsterdam, February 2012 Annemieke van Verseveld

Contents

Chapter 1
Introduction

1.1 Torture At Abu Ghraib

The disclosure of pictures of American soldiers abusing prisoners in the Abu Ghraib prison in Iraq caused a worldwide wave of shock and disbelief.[1] The pictures showed a wide range of scenes of abuse: naked Iraqi prisoners in stress positions, lying in a pile on top of each other, with a hood over their head standing on a box with electric wires attached to their hands, driven into a corner under attack of a prison guard dog, its teeth right in the face of the terrified prisoner. In some of the pictures, next to the abused prisoners, American soldiers can be seen, posing for the camera, smiling, giving the thumbs up. The most notorious of these is probably the picture of Pfc. Lynndie R. England holding one end of something that looks like a dog leash, a prisoner lying on the floor at the other end of it.[2]

The next shock and feeling of disbelief probably came when some of the soldiers, back in America and being prosecuted for these crimes, said that they were just doing their jobs, following orders, not knowing to have done anything wrongful, that they had acted under mistake of law. How is it best to respond to any defence of mistake of law in such serious cases? Is this a palatable defence? Considering allegations of such a grave nature the irrebuttable presumption that everyone knows the law seems more than justified.

If it is completely irrelevant that these soldiers were mistaken about the wrongfulness of their behaviour, their defence can be denied at the outset. But is a mistake truly irrelevant to the determination of culpability? Does the fundamental principle of *nulla poena sine culpa* not require that we respond to these pleas? Assessing first of all the credibility of it: were or might these soldiers have been truly mistaken? And, second, if we assume they were, the question arises whether they should have known better? Should the ultimate question be whether or not

[1] See e.g. Hersch 2004b; Gourevitch and Morris 2008, pp. 262–264.
[2] Some of these pictures have been published in Strasser 2004, pp. 103–106. *See also* website Standard Operating Procedure: http://www.sonyclassics.com/standardoperatingprocedure/.

A. van Verseveld, *Mistake of Law*, DOI: 10.1007/978-90-6704-867-5_1,

they are to blame for their wrongful conduct, which would also entail a determination of culpability with regard to their mistakes?

The purpose of this study is to investigate the scope and content of the defence of mistake of law in international criminal law. Can a mistake of law exculpate the perpetrator of an international crime? And if so, what would be the circumstances under which the defence should apply? And, are those circumstances covered by the current international codification of mistake of law?

1.2 Outlining the Issue

Acting under mistake of law means that one is unaware of the wrongfulness of one's conduct. The postulate "every man is presumed to know the law" has long been the basis for the rule *ignorantia legis non excusat*, ignorance of the law does not excuse. However, for over half a century this postulate has been questioned because of its harsh outcomes in respect of a blameless defendant. As a result, the presumption is now widely recognised as no longer being irrebuttable.[3] Many legal systems have found ways to respond to the issue of mistake of law, for example by providing for a defence of mistake of law or interpreting certain crime definitions as to require knowledge of the law. A successful defence of mistake of law is generally limited to those defendants who made a reasonable mistake or could not avoid the mistake.

It could be argued that international crimes are of such a grave nature that the presumption that everyone knows the law should be irrebuttable. The more serious the alleged crime, the less reasonable or unavoidable the mistake. On the other hand, the fact that not all norms of international criminal law, including justifications, have fully crystallised and the fact that perpetrators are likely to be less familiar with international crimes than with domestic crimes, may warrant non-exclusion of the defence of mistake of law *a priori*.

1.3 The Occasion

The Statute of the International Criminal Court (ICC Statute) specifically provides, for the first time in the history of the codification of international criminal law, for the defence of mistake of law. This codification has been a starting point for this research. It marks an important step in the development of international criminal law (ICL). As soon as we take a closer look at the relevant provisions, however, the problem of the "unlike parents"[4] of ICL, public international law and criminal

---

3 An important exception is the UK, *see* Sect. 2.2.2.2 *infra*.

4 Weigend 2008, p. 472.

law, becomes apparent. The ICC may be expected to interpret the Statute as a treaty, while from a criminal law perspective a recourse to general principles or reasoning from the rationale of a provision seems warranted. And ICL does not only have these 'unlike parents', but on top of that, the criminal law 'parent' appears to have a 'split personality', containing aspects of common law and civil law. Often ICL tries to reconcile its two personalities. This implies that ICL cannot be studied as a *sui generis* system of law; understanding and interpreting its provisions requires a comparative law perspective. However, as will become apparent from the current study, the domestic approaches are on occasion irreconcilable. Here, ICL must either develop an approach *sui generis* or must choose the domestic approach that it perceives best in the interests of justice.[5]

Common law and civil law apply a different 'structure of offences'.[6] The structure of an offence forms the basis of attribution, which includes the issue of defences, and thus the issue of mistake of law. The 'structure of offences' may be an issue on which common law and civil law appear irreconcilable. The current study aims, through its investigation into the scope of mistake of law, to contribute to the development of a more systematic approach to the structure of international offences.

1.4 Methodology and Limitations

A starting point for this research has been the provision on mistake of law in the ICC Statute and the legal literature that has commented upon it. The provision can be found in Article 32(2) ICC Statute. This article has the character of a compromise, since the Statute came about by treaty negotiations between States with different legal systems. It is the outcome of negotiations in which a certain interpretation of the issue of mistake of law prevailed. In order to fully comprehend this outcome it is of paramount importance to investigate the meaning of mistake of law in the national criminal law systems of the countries that have had an influence on the drafting process of the Statute. I have compared the approach to mistake of law in the common law systems of the United States of America (USA) and the United Kingdom (UK) and the civil law systems of Germany and France.[7] I have consulted legislative sources, case law and legal literature. A case law study of 'international' trials aimed at construing theoretical foundations

---

[5] I am aware of the danger this term holds for it can refer to various, not always compatible interests: justice for the victims or the affected community, justice for the defendant, justice of (general or specific) prevention.

[6] *See also,* Ambos 2007.

[7] In this study I did not include the Dutch approach to mistake of law. Although recognized as an excuse, mistake of law has remained uncodified in the Netherlands. The scope of this unwritten excuse is comparable to the German provision on mistake of law. My choice for including the German approach is among other reasons based on the fact that Germany has a richer tradition of legal doctrine than the Netherlands.

underlying decisions regarding pleas of mistake of law and to discern practical examples of situations in which the defence may be applicable. A study of the elements of international crimes as defined by the ICC Statute and the Elements of Crimes has offered more insight into areas where mistake of law could be relevant. There has been consultation with several military lawyers to validate whether the examples I chose to discuss are realistic scenarios in practice.

The comparative law study and the case law study are limited. I justify the choices made on the basis of the aim of this study, which has not been to determine the customary law status of mistake of law, but to determine, mainly on the basis of a theoretical account, what the scope of mistake of law under international law should be and whether this scope is covered by the current international provision.

1.5 Definitions

In this study, the concept of international crimes refers to war crimes, crimes against humanity and genocide, as defined in the ICC Statute. These crimes are crimes of intent and not crimes of negligence; they concern intentional and knowledge-based behaviour.[8]

In this study, mistake of law does not encompass mistakes concerning issues of procedural criminal law (mistake of formal law) but rather mistakes about the substantive wrongfulness of the act, i.e. a mistake about the underlying norm protected by the specific criminal law (mistake of substantive law). Someone may be totally ignorant of the underlying norm, he may be mistaken about the scope of the norm or about an element of the crime definition or the mistake may concern a ground of justification (putative justification); these are all relevant instances of mistake of law. In relation to international crimes, a mistake about the prohibition as such is, given the grave nature of these crimes, highly unlikely. The most relevant mistakes of law will therefore be mistakes about normative (as opposed to factual) elements of the crime definition and mistakes about justifications. A special place in international criminal law is reserved for mistakes about the justification of superior orders. Many international crimes are committed in the context of a military organisation. A mistake about the lawfulness of a superior order constitutes a mistake of law. The battlefield reality arguably requires a differentiated approach towards mistaken subordinates. The putative justification of superior orders is therefore treated separately from other examples of putative justifications.

A common referred to distinction is that between mistakes of law and mistakes of fact.[9] According to this distinction mistake of fact is generally a good defence and mistake of law is (generally) not. The mistake of a hunter who shoots

[8] Schabas 2004, pp. 108–109. The only exception is command responsibility. *See also*, Ambos 2002b, p. 1031 and Fletcher 2007, p. 108.

[9] *See e.g.*, art. 32 ICC Statute.

someone's dog mistaking it for a wolf, is a mistake of fact. If the hunter, however, believes his hunting permit also allows him to shoot someone's dog, he acts under a mistake of law. In most legal systems, the fact that mistake of fact excludes criminal responsibility is far more acceptable than mistake of law excluding criminal responsibility. This is mainly so because a mistake of fact is more likely to negate the required intent. The distinction between mistake of fact and mistake of law, however, is not always as obvious as in the example of the mistaken hunter.[10] Mistakes about purely descriptive elements are mistakes of fact. A mistake concerning a legal or normative element, however, may variably qualify as a mistake of fact or as a mistake of law.[11] Basing the relevance of a mistake on a disputable distinction is arbitrary. Further, the distinction is most of the time beside the point. The paramount issues concern which mistakes are irrelevant, which mistakes will exculpate per se and which mistakes will only exculpate when reasonable or unavoidable.[12] These issues cannot be answered by applying the distinction between mistake of fact and mistake of law, even if such distinction was unproblematic. The answer as to whether (un)reasonable mistake exculpates can be found by determining whether the mistake negates the required intent. If a mistake negates the required intent, any mistake, reasonable or unreasonable, will exculpate. If the mistake concerns an element extrinsic to the required intent, a reasonableness standard may be applied.[13] Both mistakes of fact and of law can be relevant and irrelevant to the required intent. The determination as to whether or not a certain element belongs to the required intent is unfortunately by no means an easier task than determining whether an element is an element of fact or law.

Since all international crimes are crimes of intent, whether the object of a mistake is part of the intent or not is determinative of whether every mistake exculpates or only a reasonable or unavoidable mistake. Hence, the distinction between mistake of fact and mistake of law is not helpful in determining the relevance of a mistake (although mistake of fact generally negates the required intent and mistake of law generally does not). In this research I use this distinction, nevertheless, to indicate whether a certain case, issue or example belongs to the topic of this research, mistake of law. Mistake of law, as indicated, involves ignorance or mistake as to the wrongful nature of the conduct.

---

[10] *See also* Roxin 2006, p. 308, Rn. 58.

[11] *See also* Sliedregt 2003, p. 303.

[12] Reasonable' is a common law term, 'unavoidable' a civil law term. *See also* Vogeley 2003, p. 91.

[13] *See* Chaps. 2 and 3 *infra*.

1.6 Structure of the Book

As stated, a starting point for this research has been the provision on mistake of law in the ICC Statute. As will become evident from the discussion in Chap. 4 about the contents of Articles 32 and 33, and the various comments thereto, although codification of such an important part of the general part of international criminal law is to be welcomed, the ICC articles are not as comprehensive and sound as they at first sight may seem. The articles, being the result of treaty-negotiations, necessarily have the character of a compromise. The codification of the defence is by all appearances influenced by national understandings of the defence and by previous (inter)national prosecutions of international crimes. Research into national and international regulations and case law is necessary in order to understand the scope and meaning of the ICC provisions.

The comparative law study of Chap. 2, comparing the common law systems of the USA and the UK and the civil law systems of Germany and France, aims at demonstrating the implications of these distinctive systems for the defence of mistake of law. This chapter shows a distinctive approach in the common law systems and the civil law systems in their structure of offences. The common law concept of offences can be characterised as a twofold structure: offences (which consist of *mens rea* and *actus reus*) and defences. The Germanic civil law structure of offences is threefold: the crime definition (*mens rea* and *actus reus*), the wrongfulness of the act (absence of justification) and the culpability of the perpetrator (absence of excuse).[14]

Further theorising about the issue in Chap. 3 it will become evident that the structure of offences which is followed has implications for the prospects of solving the complex issue of mistake of law. Reasoning from the conclusions of Chap. 3, Chap. 4 demonstrates the problematic implications of the current codification of mistake of law; the question arises whether the ICC provision at all addresses the issue of mistake of law. Chapter 5 shows that the case law concerning pleas of mistake of law and superior orders contains many examples of conceptual misconceptions. In Chap. 6 the theoretical analyses of Chaps. 3 and 4 are tested by an investigation into the scope of the current provision on mistake of law in relation to the elements of international crimes as defined by the ICC Statute and by sketching some scenarios which are unduly not covered by the current international provision on mistake of law. It demonstrates that what is at stake is not merely a theoretical argument, as there are situations conceivable which, under the current provision on mistake of law, could lead to unjust convictions. In the final chapter, Chap. 7, it is pleaded that mistake of law should be an excuse available to perpetrators of international crimes.

---

[14] Ambos 2006, pp. 664–665. Fletcher uses the terms bipartite and tripartite structure, *see e.g.*, Fletcher 2007, pp. 43–55.

References

Ambos K (2002b) Other grounds for excluding criminal responsibility. In: Cassese A, Gaeta P, Jones JRWD (eds.) The Rome Statute of the International Criminal Court: a commentary, vol I. Oxford University Press, New York, pp 1003–1048

Ambos K (2006) Remarks on the general part of international criminal law. J Int Crim Justice 4:660–673

Ambos K (2007) Towards a universal system of crime: comments on George Fletcher's *Grammar of criminal law*. Cardozo Law Review 28(6):2647–2673

Fletcher GP (2007) The grammar of criminal law. American, comparative, and international, volume one: Foundations, vol 1. Oxford University Press, New York

Gourevitch P, Morris E (2008) Standard operating procedure. The Penguin Press, New York

Hersch SM (2004b) Torture at Abu Ghraib. The New Yorker 10 May 2004

Roxin C (2006) Strafrecht allgemeiner Teil, Band I, Grundlagen, der Aufbau der Verbrechenslehre. 4th edn. C.H. Beck, Munchen

Schabas WA (2004) An introduction to the International Criminal Court, 2nd edn. Cambridge University Press, Cambridge

Sliedregt Ev (2003) The criminal responsibility of individuals for violations of international humanitarian law. T.M.C. Asser Press, The Hague

Strasser S (ed) (2004) The Abu Ghraib investigations, The official reports of the independent panel and the Pentagon on the shocking prisoner abuse in Iraq. Public Affairs, New York

Vogeley S (2003) The mistake of law defense in international criminal law. In: Yee S (ed) International Crime and Punishment. University Press of America, Inc, Oxford, pp 59–99

Weigend T (2008) Intent, mistake of law, and co-perpetration in the *Lubanga* decision on confirmation of charges. J Int Crim Justice 6:471–487

Chapter 2
The Theory of Mistake of Law in National Criminal Law Systems

2.1 Introduction

This chapter explores different approaches towards mistake of law in national criminal law systems of the common law and the civil law tradition. There are indications that the provision on mistake of law in the ICC Statute is mainly determined by the common law tradition[1] in which ignorance of law is generally held to be no defence. A comparative law perspective allows us to understand the scope of this international provision and, in Chap. 4, to give a theoretical account of which approach could be followed in international criminal law.

There is, obviously, common ground between the common law and civil law systems. Both systems require "knowledge of facts underlying the *actus reus* as an essential element for criminal liability" and "ignorance of the law is treated differently from ignorance of facts".[2] The way in which both systems deal with issues relating to mistake of law, however, is different. In civil law systems mistake of law is a defence under exceptional circumstances; in common law systems it is generally held to be no defence, a rule that is applied rigidly in English law.[3] The first part of this chapter focuses on the common law systems of the United States and the United Kingdom, the second part focuses on the civil law systems of Germany and France. The third part briefly discusses the approach to the defence of superior orders in these national systems. The international codification of the mistake of law defence directly links the two defences. In the national systems under discussion too, the defence of superior orders is a *specialis* of mistake of law. A successful plea of superior orders requires the subordinate to have been unaware of the unlawfulness of the order.

---

1 *See* Fletcher 2007, p. 108. *See also* Scaliotti 2002, p. 12; Sliedregt 2003, p. 307; Ambos 2004, p. 806; Ambos 2007, pp. 2670–2671 (but see pp. 2667–2671 where the author argues that it cannot be said that the drafters of the Rome Statute decided the question of which system, common law or civil law, should be applied).

2 International Committee of the Red Cross 1999, p. 9.

3 International Committee of the Red Cross 1999, p. 9.

A. van Verseveld, *Mistake of Law*, DOI: 10.1007/978-90-6704-867-5_2,

The purpose of the comparative law analysis in this chapter is not to find the most common approach towards mistake of law. The four systems under scrutiny on the contrary provide us with four distinct approaches; I am seeking to identify the approach which in my opinion is best suited to be applied in international criminal law.

2.2 Mistake of Law in the Common Law Systems of the USA and the UK

2.2.1 Introduction: Ignorantia Legis Non Excusat

In the common law systems of the United States and the United Kingdom the adherence to the principle that ignorance of the law should be no excuse has been remarkably persistent.[4] Smith speaks of an "almost mystical power held by the maxim over the judicial imagination".[5] The reasons to adhere to this principle have been mainly utilitarian, referring to social welfare considerations and the necessity to maintain objective morality.[6] However, while the *ignorantia legis non excusat* rule is still applied in common law countries, to avoid unjust results, courts have in some cases interpreted a statutory element of a crime to require knowledge of the law.[7] These are *ad hoc* solutions, however, and a general rule on when a statutory element requires knowledge of the law cannot be inferred from it. In the next section I explore the statutory provisions and case law that form the basis of the general finding that *ignorantia legis non excusat* is still to a large extent the general rule in common law systems.

2.2.2 The Exceptions to the Rule

2.2.2.1 American Law

First, I will discuss the relevant provisions of the American Model Penal Code (MPC), an authoritative text on common law concepts. The MPC is not binding on the States, but it has had a large influence on the statutes and case law of many different States.[8] The provisions relevant to the scope of the defence of mistake of

---

[4] Smith 1985, p. 16.

[5] Smith 1985, p. 16.

[6] Vogeley 2003, p. 61. *See also* Fletcher 1998, p. 154.

[7] *See also* Vogeley 2003, p. 59.

[8] *See* Robinson and Grall 1982–1983, pp. 683–685. *See also* Lensing 1996, p. 7 and Nill-Theobald 1998, p. 136.

law are: §2.02(9), §2.04(1)(a), and §2.04(3). The first provision states the general rule *ignorantia legis non excusat*:

> §2.02(9) MPC Culpability as to Illegality of Conduct
> Neither knowledge nor recklessness or negligence as to whether conduct constitutes an offence or as to the existence, meaning or application of the law determining the elements of an offence is an element of such offence, unless the definition of the offence or the Code so provides.

The provision states that no legal knowledge is required. Vogeley refers to this provision stating that it holds that "knowledge of the law defining the offense is not itself an element of the offense".[9]

The Code subsequently provides in §2.04(1)(a) MPC:

> §2.04 MPC Ignorance or mistake
>
> (1) Ignorance or mistake as to a matter of fact or law is a defence if:
>
> (a) the ignorance or mistake negatives the purpose, knowledge, belief, recklessness or negligence required to establish a material element of the offence.

According to §2.04(1)(a) the defendant is not liable when the mistake negates the mental element required to establish a material element of the offence. Under §2.02(9) knowledge of the criminal nature of the act is generally no element of an offence. This means that only when the legislator has provided for consciousness of unlawfulness as an element of the required intent, will a mistake of law exculpate the defendant. Hence, these provisions, that focus on the intent and internal components of the offence, show great deference to the legislator. Fletcher criticises this deference; it shows too much faith in the capabilities of the legislator to solve theoretical and philosophical problems, such as issues of mistake.[10]

The defence of mistake of law is thus only available in the exceptional circumstance where knowledge of the prohibited nature of the conduct itself is an express element of an offence.[11] This circumstance is exceptional, because most crime definitions do not contain the requirement that the defendant acts with the intent or knowledge to violate the law.[12]

Smith therefore correctly holds that the scope for the application of Section 2.04(1) MPC "to mistakes of fact is far wider than it is for mistakes of law, for the simple reason that the mental element in most crimes does not include any knowledge of the existence and scope of the proscription defining the offence. All turns on what the statute itself says, or at least on the degree of *mens rea* that

---

[9] Vogeley 2003, p. 94. This issue is related to the distinction between conduct rules and decision rules (*see* Sect. 3.2.4 *infra*; the (statutory) crime definition is a decision rule, the underlying norm is a conduct rule).

[10] Fletcher 1998, p. 155.

[11] Vogeley 2003, p. 66.

[12] Husak and Hirsh 1993, p. 158.

the court is prepared to read into it, and in general, a court is reluctant to read into a statute a requirement that the defendant should be familiar with the law".[13]

Moreover, by requiring the mistake to negate the required mental element, the American legislature has complicated the means to normatively assess the mistake. If the required mental element is 'intent', any mistake, reasonable or not, will bar a finding of this mental element.[14] I will return to this issue in the section on English law.

The next exception to the general rule *ignorantia legis non excusat* in the Model Penal Code is §2.04(3), which provides:

§2.04 MPC Ignorance or Mistake

(3) A belief that conduct does not legally constitute an offence is a defence to a prosecution for that offence based upon such conduct when:

(a) the statute or other enactment defining the offence is not known to the actor and has not been published or otherwise reasonably made available prior to the conduct alleged; or
(b) he acts in reasonable reliance upon an official statement of the law, afterward determined to be invalid or erroneous, contained in (i) a statute or other enactment; (ii) a judicial decision, opinion or judgment; (iii) an administrative order or grant of permission; or (iv) an official interpretation of the public officer or body charged by law with responsibility for the interpretation, administration or enforcement of the law defining the offence.

The MPC here provides for a defence in case of mistake of law, when the law was unavailable to the defendant or when he has relied on an official statement or interpretation of the law from a person or agency charged with defining the offence.[15]

With regard to §2.04(3)(a), concerning the case where the statute has not been published, I believe Husak and von Hirsch are correct when they hold that "the rationale for exoneration should be based on the principle of legality rather than on the defendant's lack of culpability. [...] The rationale for a defence in such cases is analogous to that which prohibits retroactive or vague legislation".[16] An important difference between this provision and the principle of legality is, however, that the provision in respect of mistake of law requires that the defendant believed in the

[13] Smith 1985, p. 5.

[14] *See also* Vogeley 2003, p. 66. For application of the same rule in English law *see* Ormerod 2008, p. 315 (also explaining that where the law requires negligence, only a reasonable mistake can afford a defence). Since almost all international crimes require intent, the current discussion is limited to the consequences of the negate mental element requirement for intentional offences. *See also* Ambos 2002b, p. 1031. It should be noted that in a civil law system which applies a threefold structure of offence, a mistake which negates the required intent cannot be normatively assessed either; any mistake, reasonable, or not, will bar the finding of intent. On the distinction between twofold and threefold structures of offences, *see* Chap. 3 *infra*.

[15] *See also* Vogeley 2003, p. 66.

[16] Husak and Hirsh 1993, p. 166.

lawfulness of his conduct. If the defendant, on the basis of the principle of legality, cannot be held criminally liable for his conduct, then, what the defendant actually believed is irrelevant.

With regard to the exception in case of reasonable reliance on an official statement of the law, §2.04(3)(b), Fletcher notes that the types of legal advice that may be relied upon are circumscribed tightly: official statements of law, afterwards determined to be invalid, or erroneous. This excludes reliance on advice by counsel and unofficial advice from law enforcement personnel, and also total ignorance of the law, however reasonable.[17]

The provisions in the MPC show a tendency towards an extensive application of the principle *ignorantia legis non excusat.* Smith sums up the classical justifications for persisting in this maxim: problems of proof, to admit the defence would be to encourage ignorance, allowing the defence could undercut the rule of law and ignorance of the law is itself culpable.[18] The American system thus, as a general principle, rejects the mistake of law defence. In practice, however, according to Vogeley, "the defence is often employed to avoid unjust results".[19]

Unjust results can be mitigated by a variety of devices. An example of such a device is manipulating the distinction between mistakes of fact and mistakes of law. An unjust result may be mitigated by treating a mistake about an issue of law "collateral" to the penal law as a mistake of fact, negating the mental element of the crime.[20] As Grace noted, both mistakes of fact and mistake of noncriminal law "usually involve a mistake concerning circumstances relevant to the prohibited nature of the activity".[21]

Further, unjust results can be effectively mitigated by interpreting terms like 'wilfully' or 'knowingly' to incorporate a requirement of knowledge of unlawfulness. The case law discussed below can be distinguished according to whether the crime definition requires the particular intent of 'wilfulness',[22] or requires the

[17] Fletcher 1978, p. 755.

[18] Smith 1985, pp. 16–21. *See also* Kahan 1997, p. 133 (referring to a decision of the NY Court of Appeals, 507 N.E.2d at 1073)(according to Kahan the argument against the mistake of law excuse, that it would encourage ignorance, is false).

[19] Vogeley 2003, p. 97.

[20] *See* Kahan 1997, p. 132 (referring, for example, to United States v. Anton, 683 F.2d 1011, 1018 (7th Cir. 1982)).

[21] Grace 1986, p. 1394.

[22] Cheek v. U.S. 1991 (attempting to evade income taxes and failing to file income tax returns); Ratzlaf v. U.S. 1994 (structuring financial transactions to avoid currency reporting requirements); U.S. v. Rogers 1994 (conspiracy to evade and violate reporting and return requirements for currency transactions); U.S. v. Obiechie 1994 (engaging in the business of dealing in firearms without a license); U.S. v. Curran 1994 (causing election campaign treasurers to submit false reports to the Federal Election Commission); Bryan v. U.S. 1998 (conspiring to engage in and actually engaging in the sale of firearms without a license).

defendant to have acted 'knowingly',[23] or does not contain such a particular intent element.[24]

The term 'wilfully' has sharply divided the US Supreme Court.[25] In *Cheek v. U.S.* (1991),[26] the Supreme Court held that in tax cases the element of 'wilfulness' "requires the Government to prove that the law imposed a duty on the defendant, that the defendant knew of this duty, and that he voluntarily and intentionally violated that duty".[27] This means that a good faith mistake, whether reasonable or not, will negate the element of wilfulness.[28] In *Bryan v. U.S.* (1998),[29] where the defendant was charged with 'wilfully' dealing in firearms without a federal licence, the Supreme Court held that the 'wilful' requirement was met by the defendant's knowledge that his conduct violated some law.[30] Hence, any good faith mistake, even an unreasonable one, will negate the "wilfully" mental element, which requires knowledge that the conduct violated some law, but not knowledge of which specific law was violated.[31]

In *Lambert v. California* (1957)[32] the Supreme Court held that applying a registration act, which requires former felons to register as such with the local police, "to a person who has no actual knowledge of his duty to register, and where no showing is made of the probability of such knowledge" violates the due process clause of the United States Constitution.[33] The defence of mistake of law was successful because of lack of fair notice. If the defence had not been available the defendant would have had no "opportunity either to avoid the consequences of the law or to defend any prosecution brought under it".[34] In *Reyes v. U.S.* (1958)[35] the

[23] U.S. v. International Minerals & Chemical Corp 1971 (violating Interstate Commerce Commission regulations relating to shipment of corrosive liquids in interstate commerce).

[24] Lambert v. People of the State of California 1957 (violating the Los Angeles felon registration order); Reyes v. United States 1958 (violation of statute regulating border crossings of narcotic addicts and violators); Long v. State 1949 (bigamy).

[25] Loewy 2000, p. 140.

[26] Cheek v. U.S. 1991 (attempting to evade income taxes and failing to file income tax returns).

[27] Cheek v. U.S. 1991, pp. 201, 610.

[28] Cheek v. U.S. 1991, pp. 202, 611. *See also* Loewy 2000, p. 140 and Kahan 1997, pp. 145–146.

[29] Bryan v. U.S. 1998 (conspiring to engage in and actually engaging in the sale of firearms without a license).

[30] Bryan v. U.S. 1998, p. 193, 1946. *See also* Loewy 2000, p. 140.

[31] *See also* Travers 1995, p. 1304.

[32] Lambert v. People of the State of California 1957 (violating the Los Angeles felon registration order).

[33] Lambert v. People of the State of California 1957, pp. 229–230, 243–244. Loewy 2000, p. 143. *See also* Fletcher 2007, p. 81 ("absent a fair warning of impending sanctions, the state has more difficulty justifying conviction and punishment of the citizens acting in good-faith reliance on the permissibility of their conduct").

[34] Lambert v. People of the State of California 1957 (violating the Los Angeles felon registration order), p. 229, 243.

[35] Reyes v. United States 1958 (violation of statute regulating border crossings of narcotic addicts and violators).

9th Circuit held that *Lambert* does not apply in case of narcotic addicts and narcotic violators neglecting to register at border crossings. According to the Court, other than in *Lambert*, the charged offence concerned an act "under circumstances that should alert the doer to the consequences of his deed".[36] Vogeley notes that "[r]ead narrowly, *Lambert* may apply only to *mala prohibita* crimes involving a regulatory scheme where an individual has no prior notice of a duty to perform an affirmative act".[37] The case law indeed reveals a distinct approach according to the nature of the crimes involved. A distinction is made between *mala in se* crimes and *mala prohibita* crimes, between morally wrong behaviour and regulatory or technical offences. As Artz holds, "the more complex our rules become, the less realistic is the assumption that factual knowledge works as an indicator of the unlawfulness or wrongfulness of the conduct involved".[38] Travers sees potential for a wider scope of the mistake of law defence in case of *mala prohibita* crimes requiring wilfulness as the *mens rea* for violation in recent case law of the Supreme Court. He refers to *Ratzlaf v. United States* (1994),[39] in which the Supreme Court recognised that it has often held that 'wilful' is "a word of many meanings" and "its construction is often influenced by its context".[40] In this case the Court held that in the federal money laundering statute the word 'wilfully' requires the defendant to have knowledge of the unlawfulness of the structuring he undertook.[41]

Travers notes, however, that the current status of mistake of law is that the meaning of wilfulness is unclear in the aftermath of *Ratzlaf, Curran*,[42] *Obiechie*,[43] and *Rogers*:[44] "*Ratzlaf* itself acknowledged that the meaning of wilfulness is variable and context dependent. Consequently, no clear rule emerges from these cases for determining whether this term encompasses violation of a known legal duty".[45]

The meaning the Supreme Court attaches to the word 'knowingly' is also unsettled. In *U.S. v. International Minerals* (1971)[46] for example, the Supreme

---

[36] Reyes v. United States 1958, p. 784. *See also* Loewy 2000, pp. 143–144.

[37] Vogeley 2003, p. 71.

[38] Artz 1986, p. 726.

[39] Ratzlaf v. U.S. 1994 (structuring financial transactions to avoid currency reporting requirements).

[40] Ratzlaf v. U.S. 1994, p. 141, 659.

[41] Ratzlaf v. U.S. 1994, pp. 138, 658 and 149, 663. *See also* Travers 1995, p. 1301.

[42] U.S. v. Curran 1994 (causing election campaign treasurers to submit false reports to the Federal Election Commission).

[43] U.S. v. Obiechie 1994 (engaging in the business of dealing in firearms without a license).

[44] U.S. v. Rogers 1994 (conspiracy to evade and violate reporting and return requirements for currency transactions).

[45] Travers 1995, pp. 1315–1316.

[46] U.S. v. International Minerals & Chemical Corp 1971 (violating Interstate Commerce Commission regulations relating to shipment of corrosive liquids in interstate commerce).

Court held that 'knowingly violates any regulation' does not require knowledge of the regulation itself, 'knowingly' refers to knowledge of the facts.[47] It held that where dangerous products or "obnoxious waste materials are involved, the probability of regulation is so great that anyone who is aware that he is in possession of them or dealing with them must be presumed to be aware of the regulation".[48] If you possess these dangerous products or deal with them, without consulting the applicable regulations, you knowingly risk criminal liability. In *Liparota v. U.S.* (1985)[49], on the other hand, the Supreme Court held that 'knowingly' requires the *Government* to prove that the defendant knew that he was acting in a manner not authorised by statute or regulations. The Court found this construction here appropriate because "to interpret the statute otherwise would be to criminalise a broad range of apparently innocent conduct".[50]

In *Long v. State* (1949),[51] a case concerning bigamy, the Supreme Court of Delaware held that also in cases concerning offences which do not require a particular intent like 'wilfully' or 'knowingly', mistake of law can negate a general criminal intent "as effectively as would an exculpatory mistake of fact".[52] In order to show that the reasons for disallowing the mistake are of a practical nature, the Court distinguished three situations of mistake of law: (1) the ignorance consists in "unawareness that such conduct is or might be within the ambit of any crime; or (2) although aware of the existence of criminal law relating to the subject of such conduct, or to some of its aspects, the defendant erroneously concludes (in good faith) that his particular conduct is for some reason not subject to the operation of any criminal law"; or (3) "the defendant made a bona fide, diligent effort, adopting a course and resorting to sources and means at least as appropriate as any afforded under our legal system, to ascertain and abide by the law, and where he acted in good faith reliance upon the results of such effort."[53] The Court held that the first two situations are justifiably covered by the *ignorantia juris* rule, but that the third situation is "significantly different".[54] The Court's reasoning in relation to the third situation is interesting. The Court reasoned that considerations which justify the rejection of a mistake of law of the first and second categories, namely that mistake of law would encourage ignorance and problems of proof, are absent in case of a mistake of law of the third category.[55] In fact, the Court continues, it is

---

47 U.S. v. International Minerals & Chemical Corp 1971, pp. 563–564, 1701. *See also* Bryan v. U.S. 1998 (conspiring to engage in and actually engaging in the sale of firearms without a license), pp. 192–193, 1945–1946; Loewy 2000, p. 144.

48 U.S. v. International Minerals & Chemical Corp 1971, pp. 565, 1701–1702.

49 Liparota v. U.S. 1985 (unlawfully acquiring and possessing food stamps).

50 Liparota v. U.S. 1985, pp. 426, 2088. *See also* Grace 1986, pp. 1398–1400.

51 Long v. State 1949 (bigamy).

52 Long v. State 1949, pp. 278, 497.

53 Long v. State 1949, pp. 279, 497.

54 Long v. State 1949, pp. 279, 497.

55 Long v. State 1949, pp. 280, 497–498.

"difficult to conceive what more could be expected of a 'model citizen' than that he guide his conduct by 'the law' ascertained in good faith [...] by efforts [...] designed to accomplish ascertainment as any available under our system".[56] The Court then consolidates its finding by holding that it believes that "such circumstances should entitle a defendant to full exoneration as a matter of right, rather than to something less, as a matter of grace".[57] The reasoning of this Court, holding that the defendant is entitled to a mistake of law defence as a matter of principle, to a certain extent resembles the German approach.[58] However, this reasoning has not been followed by any court and its implications are rejected by the Model Penal Code in § 2.04(3) as this provision excludes reliance on advice by counsel.[59]

In general it can be concluded that the American case law recognises an exception to the *ignorantia juris* rule in case of crimes *mala prohibita* which require a particular intent, such as 'wilfully'. Cases of total ignorance do not form part of this exception, except where the defendant did not receive a fair warning concerning the unlawfulness of his behaviour. The case law is however by no means uniform. The American legislature complicates the route by which to arrive at an adequate normative account of a mistake of law, by requiring the mistake to negate the mental element. A mistake negating the required mental element of the crime will do so whether the mistake is reasonable or unreasonable.[60] This may explain the reluctance to accept mistake of law as a defence. In the MPC mistake of law is formulated as a failure of proof defence.[61] But as Jescheck notes, "in truth mistake of law is not concerned with the elements of crime, but rather with the unlawfulness of the conduct in a given situation".[62] Many authors criticise the American instrumentalist approach and argue in favour of a more principled solution, treating the mistake of law not as a 'failure of proof defence', but as an excuse, bearing on the culpability of the defendant.[63]

[56] Long v. State 1949, pp. 281, 498.

[57] Long v. State 1949, pp. 281, 498.

[58] *See* Sect. 2.3.2 *infra*.

[59] Loewy 2000, p. 142. *See also* Fletcher 1978, p. 755.

[60] People v Weiss 1938. *See also* Vogeley 2003, p. 67. This is different in some civil law systems, where a requirement of reasonableness applies to all mistakes, *see* Sliedregt 2003, footnote 402, p. 316. For a further discussion see Sect. 2.2.2.2 *infra*.

[61] *See also* Husak and Hirsh 1993, pp. 157–158.

[62] Jescheck 2004, p. 47.

[63] *See e.g.*, Fletcher 1978, pp. 754–756; Husak and Hirsh 1993, pp. 172–174; Smith 1985, pp. 3+9+21–24; Kahan 1997, pp. 152–153; Grace 1986, pp. 1395+1414–1416; Vogeley 2003, p. 74.

2.2.2.2 English Law

English law applies the maxim *ignorantia legis non excusat* even more strictly than American law. The presumption that every man knows the law is irrebuttable.[64] The English jurisprudence relating to mistake and ignorance of the law is, according to Smith, compared with "American Law (let alone the German) woefully underdeveloped".[65] He brings forward two explanations. The first explanation is the fact that the English Courts lack the power to declare statutes unconstitutional, like American courts can under §2.04(3)(b) MPC.[66] "There is a power to declare subordinate legislation ultra vires and void, in which case one would expect the principles expressed in the Model Penal Code to apply," but there seems to be no authority on the point.[67] As a result, Smith shows, there is very little room for reliance cases (defendants reasonably relying on official advice or (earlier) Courts' interpretations of the law).[68] The second explanation brought forward by Smith is the fact that the English system applies without much difficulty the doctrine of strict liability to a whole range of regulatory offences in which mistake of law is most likely to occur.[69]

The English rule makes a distinction between mistake of fact and mistake of law. Mistake or ignorance of fact may exculpate and mistake or ignorance of law, however, reasonable, does not.[70] This is so because mistake is only a defence when it precludes *mens rea* and mistake of law generally does not negate *mens rea*.[71] Like their American colleagues, British judges have tried to come to just results by manipulating the distinction between law and fact.[72] Here too, these cases mainly concern issues of mistakes about civil laws, rather than criminal law.[73] In addition, there are also cases where the courts have found that for specific situations the legislature had determined that mistake of law should be a defence.[74] An example can be found in the definition of blackmail in the Theft Act of 1968 and the

[64] May 1999, p. 72. *See also* Mitchell 1979, p. 944 (§ 1439c.)

[65] Smith 1985, p. 9.

[66] Smith 1985, pp. 9+14. §2.04(3)(b) MPC does not grant this power to the courts, it refers to the situation where someone has relied on an official interpretation of the law, afterward determined to be invalid or erroneous (for example by a court).

[67] Smith 1985, p. 14.

[68] Smith 1985, pp. 14–16.

[69] Smith 1985, p. 9.

[70] Smith 1985, p. 11. *See also* Ormerod 2008, pp. 132–133.

[71] Ormerod 2008, pp. 317–318.

[72] Smith 1985, p. 13.

[73] Smith refers to the following examples: *Smith*, [1974] Q.B. 354 (mistakes as to the ownership of property); *Tolson*, (1889) 23 Q.B.D. 168 (that the defendant believed herself to be a widow was a defence); *Wheat and Stocks*, [1921] 2 K.B. 119 (mistake as to marital status), Smith 1985, p. 11. *See also* Ormerod 2008, p. 320.

[74] Smith 1985, p. 13.

definition of criminal damage in the Criminal Damage Act of 1971. These definitions read as follows:

21. Blackmail

(1) A person is guilty of blackmail if, with a view to gain for himself or another or with intent to cause loss to another, he makes any unwarranted demand with menaces; and for this purpose a demand with menaces is unwarranted unless the person making it does so in the belief-

(a) that he has reasonable grounds for making the demand; and
(b) that the use of the menaces is a proper means of reinforcing the demand.

Criminal Damage

Section 5 (2) (2) A person charged with an offence to which this section applies shall [...] be treated [...] as having a lawful excuse:

(a) [...]
(b) if he destroyed or damaged or threatened to destroy or damage the property in question [...] and at the time of the act or acts alleged to constitute the offence he believed-

(i) that the property, right or interest was in immediate need of protection; and
(ii) that the means of protection adopted or proposed to be adopted were or would be reasonable having regard to all the circumstances.

Ashworth points out how the individual criminal responsibility on the basis of these provisions is entirely dependent on the actor's beliefs; the demand with menace is warranted if the defendant believes it to be so subject to the statutory requirement, i.e. "reasonable" and "proper" and the actor has a lawful excuse if he damages property in order to protect other property and he believes the means to be reasonable.[75]

Finally, English law provides for an exception to the *ignorantia legis non excusat* principle when the law or regulation has not been published or when it is otherwise practically impossible to discover the terms of a particular law.[76] As argued in the preceding section on mistake of law under the US legal system, the rationale of exoneration in this situation is based on the principle of legality rather than on the individual culpability of the defendant.

Smith argues that, contrary to American law, there seems to be no room for reliance on official authority cases in English law.[77] He finds an explanation for this in the fact that, as mentioned above, there is no power of judicial review of the courts to declare a statute unconstitutional, because of the "English doctrine of

[75] Ashworth 1974, p. 653.

[76] Ashworth 1974, p. 654 (referring to *Lim Chin Aik* v. *R.* (1963)). See also Ormerod 2008, p. 319.

[77] Smith 1985, p. 14.

Parliamentary Sovereignty according to which any measure enacted by Parliament is automatically an unchallengeable valid law".[78] There is little authority on the issue whether a defendant has an excuse when he reasonably relied on a decision of the courts or on advice official authorities entrusted with the interpretation of the law.[79] "Although it is nowhere clearly articulated, the fear seems to be that to permit the defence would be to enable the officials to operate a sort of suspending or dispending power, relieving citizens from their obligations to obey the law".[80] It would run counter to the doctrine of Parliamentary Sovereignty if a defendant could rely on a Court's interpretation of the law, which apparently deviates from the meaning Parliament had in mind. Jefferson holds that "it is not unknown for Parliament to afford a defence to a person who relies on official advice".[81] In practice, however, reliance cases are very scarce.[82]

The draft Criminal Code of 1989 provides, with regard to mistake of law, that:

> Ignorance or mistake as to a matter of law does not affect liability to conviction for offence except (a) where so provided, or (b) where it negatives the fault element of the offence.[83]

In British law the basic rule that ignorance or mistake of law is no defence is preserved in the draft criminal code. Jefferson argues that "parliament of course retains the power to create exceptions" and also preserved is the present rule that mistake of law provides a defence where it negatives a fault element of the offence.[84]

As appeared in the previous section on American law, the problem with the negate mental element requirement, or fault element requirement, is that, if the crime definition requires intent or recklessness, any mistake, even an unreasonable one, excludes the defendant's liability.[85] This is referred to as the 'inexorable logic rule'; if the mental element is lacking with respect to one of the conduct elements specified in the definition of the crime, then as a matter of 'inexorable logic'[86] the defendant should be acquitted even if the mistake was wholly unreasonable.[87] This rule does not allow for a differentiated approach based on reasonableness. The much discussed English case *Morgan,*[88] raises the issue of the consequences of applying the inexorable logic rule in case of a mistake about consent. The House of

---

78 Smith 1985, p. 14.

79 Smith 1985, pp. 14–15.

80 Smith 1985, p. 14.

81 Jefferson 2003, p. 303.

82 Smith 1985, pp. 14–16.

83 Law Com. No. 177, 1989, cl 21.

84 Jefferson 2003, p. 304.

85 *See also* Ormerod 2008, p. 315.

86 Ormerod 2008, p. 314 (referring to Lord Hailsham using this term in Director of Public Prosecutions v. Morgan [1976] AC 182, [1975] 2 All ER 347, p. 361).

87 Ashworth 2006, p. 229.

88 Regina v. Morgan 1975.

Lords in *Morgan* "upheld a conviction but also concluded that any mistake, even an unreasonable mistake as to the victim's consent in rape cases, would preclude liability".[89] The facts of this case are that "the four defendants had overpowered the victim and had forcible intercourse with her. Yet they allegedly had been told by the victim's husband that she would dissemble resistance presumably to gain some perverse satisfaction in being "forced" to submit".[90] The mistake made by the defendants in this case was arguably a mistake about a ground for justification, a mistake about an element extrinsic to the mental element required by the crime definition. In this case the element about which the defendants were mistaken was the consent of the victim. The House of Lords in *Morgan* chose the 'inexorable logic' approach, treating the claim of mistake as a mere denial of the required mental element.[91] The majority of judges thus construed the intent required for rape as the intent to have intercourse against the woman's will.[92] The justification serves as a negative requirement incorporated into the definition of the crime. The majority concluded that non-consent is an element of the prohibited act, according to Fletcher, "without attending to the distinction between inculpatory and exculpatory elements, definition and justification".[93] Fletcher holds that this case shows that reliance on ordinary language and textbook statements of the law fails to constitute a method appropriate to the task of determining when a mistake must be reasonable.[94] In determining this issue one has to make theoretical distinctions between definition and justification and between wrongdoing and attribution.[95] Especially since the penetration in *Morgan* was forcible, it is argued that the consent of the woman should have functioned as a justification.[96] "Using force is *prima facie* wrongful and should put a citizen on notice to examine the grounds for doing so—if, of course, time and circumstance permit".[97] "If the perpetrators were mistaken about the supposed justification for forcible intercourse, their wrongful act might well be excused. But if the focus is on excusing their conduct, it is appropriate to require [...] that their mistake be free from fault".[98]

Duff illustrates how Fletcher's reasoning is based on two premises: (1) the mistake can only exculpate if it was reasonable and (2) lack of the victim's consent

---

89 Fletcher 1978, p. 699.

90 Fletcher 1978, p. 699.

91 Ashworth 2006, p. 229.

92 Fletcher 1978, p. 701.

93 Fletcher 1978, p. 703.

94 Fletcher 1978, p. 703.

95 For a discussion of these theoretical distinctions see Chap. 3 *infra*.

96 Fletcher 1978, p. 705; *but see* Ambos 2007, p. 2661 (arguing in footnote 75 that 'it is more convincing to consider [consent] as part of the definition of the offence since rape is a specific form of coercion and as such implies the overcoming of the victim's free will'). The Elements of Crime to the provision in the ICC statute on the war crime of rape (Article 8(2)(b)(xxii)) confirms Ambos' analysis.

97 Ashworth 2006, p. 230.

98 Fletcher 1978, p. 705.

is not part of the definition of rape, but the victim's consent is a justification for what would otherwise be a wrongful act.[99] The first premise can only be true if the second is. Duff sees it differently; I understand his argument as to imply that the inexorable logic rule should be abandoned. He points out how Fletcher's theory falls apart, because the actor's belief in the victim's consent does in fact negate the intent, since lack of the victim's consent is essential to the wrong that rape constitutes.[100] But according to Duff, this does not mean that the actor should be acquitted if his mistaken belief in the victim's consent was unreasonable.[101]

Both arguments are understandable. Duff and Ambos almost state the obvious, when they hold that lack of consent is specifically what characterises the sexual penetration as rape. This element must form part of the constituent or definitional elements of the offence. The argument Fletcher brings forward in support of his position that the mistaken belief in the victim's consent must be reasonable in order to exculpate the defendant is, however, convincing in that it shows how the wrong suffered by the victim exists independently from the actor's belief. He argues that the fact that the victim has a right to self-defence, shows that the attack is unlawful, no matter whether the perpetrator believes the victim is consenting. Thus, according to Fletcher, how could a right to self-defence exist if the perpetrator's act was not unlawful because his belief in the victim's consent negates his intention required for the fulfilment of the crime definition of rape?[102] Under his scheme of wrongdoing and attribution and the distinction between justification and excuse, a mistaken belief in the victim's consent cannot be but a putative or mistaken justification. This scheme allows for a just outcome, because it provides us with a theoretical basis to only excuse the defendant if his mistake was reasonable. The argument does seem somewhat artificial, however, when one accepts Duff's argument that the lack of consent is exactly what constitutes the wrong in rape. If this must lead to the conclusion that lack of consent is an element of the crime definition and thus of the required mental element, one can only require a mistake about this element to have been reasonable if one abandons the inexorable logic rule.

In a different context Van Sliedregt points out a difference between the Anglo-American requirement of reasonableness of a mistake and some civil law approaches to this requirement. In Anglo-American law a mistake negating the intent or recklessness (as opposed to negligence) is not required to have been reasonable; some civil law systems always require mistakes to have been reasonable, irrespective of the required mental element.[103] I consider that this reasonableness requirement is based on the objective standard applied in most civil law systems in assessing whether the defendant acted in the required mental state.

---

99 Duff 2002, p. 72.

100 *See also* Ambos 2007, p. 2661.

101 Duff 2002, p. 73.

102 Fletcher 1998, p. 162.

103 Sliedregt 2003, footnote 402, p. 316.

Because it is practically impossible to determine what the actual state of mind of the defendant was, his conduct is compared to a reasonable person under the same circumstances. The standard is in this sense also normative, but not to the same extent as the negligence standard. It is not an issue of *should have known*, but rather of *must have known*.[104]

Returning to the issue of mistake about consent in rape cases, I conclude by agreeing with Duff, that the reasonableness of a mistake can be taken into account even if the absence of consent is part of the required intent. The objective test brings one closest to knowing what the actual state of mind of the perpetrator was. The issue is whether the evidence justifies the inference that the perpetrators knew or *must have known* the victim was not consenting. In answering this question the reasonableness of his plea of mistake can and must be taken into account. As seen in Chap. 5, this approach is comparable to the inference of knowledge of wrongdoing, often applied in assessing the credibility of a plea of mistake of law.

Moreover, if it cannot be inferred that the defendants had knowledge (must have known) of non-consent, they must be acquitted. This is the inevitable consequence when a mistaken justification concerns an element of the required intent; this mistake cannot be assessed on the basis of the normative *should have known* standard.

Mistaken or putative justifications will usually concern elements extrinsic to the required mental element. These are probably the most relevant types of mistake of law in the sphere of international crimes. We encounter this issue again in Chaps. 4 and 6.

I return to the discussion of the English approach towards issues of mistake of law, requiring the mistake to negate the fault element required by the crime definition.

As in the American legal debate, to be found amongst British scholars too, there are those who oppose the negate mental element approach and reliance on the legislature to solve the issue of mistake. Ashworth, for example, expresses his dissatisfaction with the provision in the draft criminal code.[105] He calls the provision "traditional, inflexible, and unsatisfactory: it would prevent the courts from developing a wider defence, and would relegate most of these matters to mitigation of sentence".[106] He continues, that exception (b) incorrectly assumes that the legislature has contemplated a uniform approach in using 'knowingly' as part of the definition, and that the use of this term would thus implicate that the legislature provides mistake of law so as to negate the required fault element.[107] The courts' reaction to this issue, whether mistake of law negates 'knowingly', has been far

---

[104] On the application of such an objective standard in Dutch criminal law see de Hullu 2006, pp. 216–217.

[105] Law Com. No. 177, 1989, cl 21: Ignorance or mistake as to a matter of law does not affect liability to conviction for offence except (a) where so provided, or (b) where it negatives the fault element of the offence.

[106] Ashworth 2006, pp. 234–235.

[107] Ashworth 2006, p. 235.

from unanimous. Ashworth holds there "is a need to adopt a clear principle (a duty with circumscribed exceptions) and then to interpret statutory offences in the light of it. The same approach should be adopted where the offence includes a phrase such as 'without lawful excuse' or 'without reasonable excuse'."[108]

The principle that Ashworth proposes is that reasonable mistake of law should exculpate the defendant. He recognises that every citizen has a duty to know the law. This duty cannot be absolute, however, because, Ashworth argues, often there is uncertainty in the ambit of the law and secondly, there is the possibility that the State has not fulfilled its duty to make the law public and knowable.[109] He argues in favour of a general duty to know the law, with the exception that reasonable mistake of law excuses the defendant.[110]

According to Ashworth, this principle would also provide for a just result in reliance cases. The issue would then revolve around the question whether the defendant relied on the advice of the person he reasonably assumed to be the proper authority.[111] Ashworth makes an interesting remark where he states that allowing reasonable reliance to exclude liability in case of mistake of law would "signal the value of citizens checking on the lawfulness of their proposed activities".[112] Thus, contrary to the traditional argument against mistake of law as a defence, that it would encourage ignorance, allowing the defence in reliance cases actually encourages people to seek advice before they undertake action.

2.2.3 Conclusion: An Ad Hoc Approach

Several provisions of the Model Penal Code indicate that the American criminal law system adheres to the principle that ignorance or mistake of law does not excuse.[113] Mistake of law can only be a defence when the mistake negatives the purpose, knowledge, belief, recklessness or negligence required to establish a material element. But, as Van Sliedregt describes, "[t]he knowledge element is […] limited to the world of fact. It does [generally, *AvV*] not extent to awareness of legal rules".[114] Courts try in various ways to diminish the sometimes harsh outcomes of this principle by manipulating the distinction between fact and law or interpreting a particular intent as to require actual consciousness of unlawfulness.[115]

---

108 Ashworth 2006, p. 235.

109 Ashworth 2006, pp. 233–234. For the same argument in relation to international criminal law see Boister 2005.

110 Ashworth 2006, p. 234. *See also* Ashworth 1974, p. 658.

111 Ashworth 2006, pp. 235–236.

112 Ashworth 2006, p. 236.

113 §§ 2.02(1), 2.02(9), 2.04 MPC.

114 Sliedregt 2003, p. 232.

115 *See* Smith 1985, pp. 11+13.

The presumption is that anyone who fulfils the definitional requirements of an offence is aware of the wrongful character of his behaviour. Although the MPC provides otherwise, this presumption seems to be rebuttable, in particular when the behaviour falls under 'regulatory offences' or 'technical crimes', the so-called *mala prohibita* crimes. The regulation in the MPC forces courts to place this rebuttal in the *mens rea* requirement category. The American legislature therefore complicates the means to arrive at an adequate normative account of culpability by requiring the mistake to negate the mental element.

In British law the basic rule that ignorance or mistake of law is no defence is preserved in the draft criminal code.[116] Here the deference to the legislature is even greater than under the American system since there seems to be no room for reliance cases even where the defendant reasonably relied on the advice of the proper official authority.

Overall, the Anglo-American law systems seem for "instrumentalist reasons" to adhere to the maxim *ignorantia legis non excusat*. Therefore, the case law relating to the issue of mistakes about legal norms or about factual issues with legal components never directly assay the issue as a mistake of law.[117] As Fletcher holds, "[t]he question is always framed as a matter of discerning whether the mistake negates the required intent or whether the statute defining the offence supports recognition of the mistake as an excuse".[118]

2.3 Mistake of Law in the Civil Law Systems of Germany and France

2.3.1 Introduction

This section focuses on the civil law systems of Germany and France. The German doctrine has devoted much attention to the theory of mistake. Since the landmark decision of the *Bundesgerichtshof* of 18 March 1952 mistake of law is recognised as an excuse. The codification of mistake of law as an excuse in 1975 is seen as the perfection of the principle of guilt as an indispensable requirement for criminal responsibility.[119]

The recognition of mistake of law as a ground for excluding criminal responsibility in France is more recent; it came with the introduction of the new *Code Pénal* in 1994. Until then, the French criminal law approach towards mistake of law was very similar to the common law approach, adhering strictly to the principle *ignorantia legis non excusat*. As we will see, where the Germans have based their concept of mistake of law as an excuse on well-considered theories analysing

116 Law Com. No. 177, 1989, cl 21.

117 Fletcher 1978, p. 736.

118 Fletcher 1978, p. 736.

119 Jescheck and Weigend 1996, p. 452, § 41.I.1.

the structure of criminal offences, the French have adopted a provision on mistake of law which is common to such provisions in various continental European countries, without knowing precisely how to characterise mistake of law within their existing system of criminal offences.

2.3.2 *Germany: Mistake of Law is an Excuse*

Before the landmark decision of the *Bundesgerichtshof* (Federal Supreme Court) in 1952, the principle *ignorantia legis non excusat* was the basic principle in German criminal law. The German legislator of 1871 had not provided for mistake of law as an excuse, mistake of fact on the other hand led to the negation of the required intent.[120] The German judges and legal theorists ran into the same problems of strict application of the *ignorantia legis* principle as their colleagues in Anglo-American systems.[121] The landmark decision of the *Bundesgerichtshof* of 1952 goes into the disadvantageous implications of absolute presumption of knowledge of the law and the difference between the two opposing theories developed by scholars at the time.

2.3.2.1 Das Recht

Before discussing the landmark decision, it is necessary to pay attention to the German doctrine on the distinction between *Gesetz* und *Recht*, a paramount feature of German law and other continental legal systems. Fletcher draws attention to linguistic differences between the Anglo-American legal world and the continental legal world. Anglo-American legal systems use one single word, namely *law*, where the continental systems use two words to distinguish between law as enacted by the legislature and law as a body of principles. In German *Gesetz* means law as statutory law and *Recht* means law as principle.[122] There is no English word for *Recht*. *Recht* refers to a concept of higher law, it refers to the notion of "Law as Right, as a set of principles justifiable on their intrinsic rectitude".[123] The concept of *das Recht* is a paramount feature of German law, it is therefore of great importance to understand the distinction between *Gesetz* und *Recht*. Theoretically acts can be in violation of *das Gesetz*, but in conformity with

---

[120] Roxin 1994, p. 766.

[121] *See* Sect. 2.2.2 *supra*.

[122] Fletcher and Sheppard 2005, pp. 54–55. Note how in Dutch the defence of mistake of law is called 'rechtsdwaling', meaning mistake about 'das Recht'. And, Enschedé describes how traditionally the Dutch legislature distinguished between 'rechtsdelicten' en 'wetsdelicten', violations of 'das Recht' and violations of the law; these two terms referred to the distinction between crimes malum in se and mala prohibita; Enschedé 2008, p. 159.

[123] Fletcher 1998, p. 140.

das Recht; which means that acts in violation of the law (statute) are not necessarily against *das Recht* (wrongful). Fulfilment of all the elements of a crime as defined does not necessarily mean that the act was *unlawful*, or as Fletcher correctly suggests to translate *rechtswidrig*, *wrongful*.[124] Grounds of justification negate the wrongfulness of the act. The act is against the law, but it is not wrongful. German law requires all criminal acts to be in violation of *das Recht* in order to be punishable. Fletcher compares this feature of German law with constitutional law, as a set of higher principles, in the American system.[125]

2.3.2.2 The Landmark Decision

The defendant in this case, who is a lawyer, is being prosecuted for the crime of extortion. The defendant agreed to represent Mrs W. in a criminal case, without having made a prior agreement about his fee. After the trial proceedings had commenced, the defendant demanded his client Mrs W. to pay 50 DM. He threatened her that he would no longer represent her if she did not pay instantly. When Mrs W. paid the required amount the next morning, the defendant forced her to sign a bank note for a fee of 400 DM.[126] The crime with which the defendant was charged is *Nötigung*, § 240 Strafgesetzbuch (StGB—Criminal Code). The relevant sections of the provision read:

§ 240 Nötigung

(1) *Wer einen Menschen rechtswidrig mit Gewalt oder durch Drohung mit einem empfindlichen Übel zu einer Handlung, Duldung oder Unterlassung nötigt, wird mit Freiheitsstrafe bis zu drei Jahren oder mit Geldstrafe bestraft.*
(2) *Rechtswidrig ist die Tat, wenn die Anwendung der Gewalt oder die Androhung des Übels zu dem angestrebten Zweck als verwerflich anzusehen ist.*[127]

The *Landgericht* (Court of first instance) convicted the defendant. The defendant's belief that he was entitled to act towards Mrs W. the way he did, constituted, according to the *Landgericht*, an irrelevant mistake of law.[128] When the case came to the *Bundesgerichtshof*, this Court asked the advice of the *Grossen Senats für Strafsachen* (Great Senate for criminal law matters) on how to answer the following two questions:

---

[124] Fletcher and Sheppard 2005, pp. 55–56.

[125] Fletcher and Sheppard 2005, pp. 55+59.

[126] Bundesgerichtshof 1952, § 6.

[127] Translation (AvV): § 240 (1) The person who wrongfully forces someone, by using violence or threatening with a significant evil, to do a certain thing or to accept or undergo something, will be punished with a prison sentence up to 3 years or a fine. (2) The act is wrongful, if the use of violence or the threat with a significant evil, relative to the aim of the actor, should be regarded as reprehensible.

[128] Bundesgerichtshof 1952, § 6.

(1) *Gehört bei § 240 StGB zur Schuld nicht nur die Kenntnis der Tatsachen des § 240 Abs 2, sondern auch das Bewusstsein, dass die Tat rechtswidrig ist?* [129]
(2) *Für den Fall der Bejahung der Frage zu 1: Handelt der Täter bei § 240 auch dann schuldhaft, wenn ihm das Bewusstsein der Rechtswidrigkeit (in dem zu 1 bezeichneten Sinne) fehlte, wenn dies aber auf Fahrlässigkeit beruht?* [130]

The first issue addressed by the Court is the meaning of '*rechtswidrig*' (against *das Recht*, or wrongful) in § 240 StGB Section 1. The fact that Section 1 refers to the *rechtwidrigkeit* (wrongfulness) of the threat could imply that *Unrechtsbewußtsein* (consciousness of wrongdoing) is an element of the crime definition. The Court rejects this conclusion; *Unrechtsbewußtsein* is not an element of this specific crime definition, and thus of the required mental element, like factual elements are. Rather, it is an element which is common to all criminal offences. The fulfilment of the elements of a crime definition is only punishable if it is also wrongful. The *Bundesgerichtshof* thus states that the term *rechtswidrig* in § 240 StGB Section 1 does not state anything more than the obvious, namely that not all acts that fulfil the factual elements of a crime definition are also wrongful:

> *so kommt dem keine andere Bedeutung zu als die eines Hinweises auf den für alle Verbrechenstatbestände geltenden Satz, dass die Verwirklichung des Tatbestandes nicht immer rechtswidrig ist.*[131]

Rechtswidrigkeit is not an element of the required intent. When the perpetrator fails to recognise the wrongfulness of his behaviour, this does not mean that he acts without the required intent. The Court points out the difference in this respect between mistake of fact and mistake of law. "Mistake of fact means that the perpetrator did not have the will to fulfil the elements of the crime definition. His intent was not aimed at these factual elements. Because his intent is negated by the factual mistake, he cannot be convicted for the intentional offences. If his mistake was negligent, he can only be convicted if there is a crime of negligence that covers his behaviour. Conversely, a mistake of law, a mistake about the *Rechtswidrigkeit* of ones behaviour, concerns the situation where the perpetrator has fulfilled all the elements of the crime definition. The perpetrator is fully aware of the factual circumstances of his behaviour, but he erroneously believes his behaviour to be lawful." The mistake may have been direct or indirect. In case of direct mistake, the defendant is completely ignorant of the norm in question or ignorant of the legal scope of a norm he is familiar with. An indirect mistake is

---

[129] Bundesgerichtshof 1952, § 3. Translation (AvV): (1) Does culpability for the crime of § 240 German Criminal Code require that, besides knowledge of the factual elements of the crime definition in § 240, Section 1, the defendant was also conscious of the wrongfulness of his act?

[130] Bundesgerichtshof 1952, § 4. Translation (AvV): (2) If question (1) is answered in the affirmative: is the perpetrator culpable of committing the crime of § 240, even though he lacked consciousness of wrongfulness, when his ignorance was caused by negligence?

[131] Bundesgerichtshof 1952, § 7. Translation (AvV): it has no other meaning than to refer to the general rule which applies to all offences, namely that fulfilment of the elements of the crime definition does is not always wrongful.

when the defendant knows the norm in question and its legal scope, but erroneously believes there is a justification for his behaviour in violation of this norm. He may either believe there is a justification, which in fact is not recognised in law or he may interpret an existing ground for justification erroneously.[132]

The next issue before the Court is whether, if not an element of the crime definition, consciousness of wrongfulness is a requirement for criminal responsibility at all, and if yes, does absence of consciousness always lead to an acquittal or only when the ignorance was unavoidable. The Court cannot turn to the criminal code for an answer, because the code, in § 59, only provides for a provision on mistake of fact.[133]

The Court first describes how the *Reichsgericht* (Federal Court of Justice) in deciding issues of mistake has always applied the Roman law distinction between mistake of law and mistake of fact. "Mistake about a law outside the criminal law was treated the same as mistake of fact, thus § 59 applied. [...] Mistakes about criminal laws were considered to be irrelevant."[134] The defendant who fulfils the elements of the crime definition is liable; consciousness of wrongfulness is no requirement for liability.[135]

The Court goes into the criticism on the case law of the *Reichsgericht* expressed by scholars from the very beginning. Because it is logically impossible to distinguish between mistakes about criminal laws and mistakes about laws outside the criminal law, the distinction is arbitrary and leads in cases of unavoidable mistake to punishment of non-culpable perpetrators.[136] After 1945 various appeals courts and the High Court for the British Zone have rejected this case law of the *Reichsgericht*.[137]

The Court explains why it believes the criticism on the approach of the *Reichsgericht* is well-founded:

> *Strafe setzt Schuld voraus. Schuld ist Vorwerfbarkeit. Mit dem Unwerturteil der Schuld wird dem Täter vorgeworfen, dass er sich nicht rechtmässig verhalten, dass er sich für das Unrecht entschieden hat, obwohl er sich rechtmässig verhalten, sich für das Recht hätte entscheiden können. Der innere Grund des Schuldvorwurfes liegt darin, dass der Mensch auf freie, verantwortliche, sittliche Selbstbestimmung angelegt und deshalb befähigt ist, sich für das Recht und gegen das Unrecht zu entscheiden, sein Verhalten nach den Normen des rechtlichen Sollens einzurichten und das rechtlich Verbotene zu vermeiden, sobald er die sittliche Reife erlangt hat und solange die Anlage zur freien sittlichen Selbstbestimmung nicht durch die in § 51 StGB genannten krankhaften Vorgänge vorübergehend gelähmt oder auf Dauer zerstört ist. Voraussetzung dafür, dass der Mensch sich*

132 Bundesgerichtshof 1952, § 8 (translation AvV).

133 Bundesgerichtshof 1952, § 9.

134 Bundesgerichtshof 1952, § 10 (translation AvV).

135 Bundesgerichtshof 1952, § 11.

136 Bundesgerichtshof 1952, § 13.

137 Bundesgerichtshof 1952, § 13.

in freier, verantwortlicher, sittlicher Selbstbestimmung für das Recht und gegen das Unrecht entscheidet, ist die Kenntnis von Recht und Unrecht.[138]

However, the Court contends, not every mistake of law negates the culpability of the defendant. Lack of knowledge is, to a certain extent, repairable. The defendant, as a participant in a legal order, has a duty to ascertain whether his behaviour is in conformity with the law. This duty cannot be fulfilled by mere passiveness; it encompasses an active duty to investigate.[139]

Hierzu bedarf es der Anspannung des Gewissens, deren Maß sich nach den Umständen des Falles und nach dem Lebens- und Berufskreis des Einzelnen richtet. Wenn er trotz der ihm danach zuzumutenden Anspannung des Gewissens die Einsicht in das Unrechtmässige seines Tuns nicht zu gewinnen vermochte, war der Irrtum unüberwindlich, die Tat für ihn nicht vermeidbar. In diesem Falle kann ein Schuldvorwurf gegen ihn nicht erhoben werden.[140]

The Court here refers to the so-called *Garantenstellung*, which implies that the amount of knowledge about the law that can be attributed to an individual depends on their position, education, and the fields of social life in which they are active. If after using all their mental capacities and inquiring extra information where necessary, they have not received any indication that the act is wrong, the mistake (that it later turned out to be) was apparently invincible. Only under these circumstances does mistake of law negate the culpability of the defendant.[141]

The Court then turns to the exact scope of the consciousness of wrongfulness that is required for culpability. On the one hand, the defendant is not required to know the criminal nature of his behaviour, nor the specific legal rule he is violating. On the other hand, consciousness of the moral reprehensibility of his

---

[138] Bundesgerichtshof 1952, § 15. Translation (AvV): "Punishment presupposes guilt. Guilt is blameworthiness. If the defendant is found to be guilty, the defendant is blamed for the fact that he has not behaved lawfully, that he chose to do wrong, although he could have chosen to behave according to *das Recht*. The basis for the culpability reproach is that people are inclined to free, responsible and moral self-determination and are therefore capable to decide for what is Right and against what is Wrong, to behave according to the legal requirements and to avoid doing what is prohibited by law, as soon as he has acquired moral maturity and as long as his capacity of free moral self-determination has not been damaged or disturbed by the in § 51 named diseases. A precondition for the capacity to choose in favour of the Right and against the Wrong is knowledge of Right and Wrong." (See for an explanation of the translation of das Recht with Right, section Das Recht *supra*).

[139] Bundesgerichtshof 1952, § 15.

[140] Bundesgerichtshof 1952, § 15. Translation (AvV): "Hereto it is required that the defendant searches his conscience, to such an extent as required by the factual circumstances of the situation and by the specific circumstances of the defendant's personal and professional life. If he, in spite of having fulfilled the required effort to search one's conscience, lacks understanding of the wrongfulness of his behaviour, the mistake was to him invincible, the act to him unavoidable. In this case he cannot be blamed, he is not reproachable."

[141] Bundesgerichtshof 1952, § 15. This leaves unanswered the position of the defendant who has not inquired about the lawfulness of his behaviour because he was completely ignorant in this respect.

conduct is not sufficient to establish consciousness of wrongfulness. What is required is that the defendant realises or should realise that he is violating the law.[142]

The Court emphasises that the case law of the *Reichsgericht* violated a fundamental principle of criminal law, namely the principle *nulla poena sine culpa*, no punishment without guilt. This case law allowed defendants to be punished for intentional crimes even where the defendant's mistake of law was unavoidable and he could thus not be found culpable in this respect.[143] The supporters of the *Reichsgericht's* approach, however, did not fear violation of this principle, because they considered mistake of law in and of itself culpable.[144]

The fact that the criminal law has changed over time from a field of law only regulating crimes *mala in se* to a field of law punishing many kinds of behaviour including acts which have no moral implications, so-called *mala prohibita*, makes the presumption that everyone knows the law no longer tenable. What is now lawful or unlawful and therewith the presumption that everyone knows the law is no longer self-evident. The possibility of making mistakes increases, including the possibility of irreproachable mistakes.[145]

"The result of the case law of the *Reichsgericht*, as even the opponents must admit, was actually most of the time satisfying. On the one hand the satisfying outcome of the *Reichsgericht* case law, is exactly the result of the flexibility of the distinction between fact and law, which allows the Court to reach a just decision. It is precisely the flexibility of the borders of these concepts that made it possible for judges to stretch them one way or the other in order to reach a judgement consistent with their sense of justice. On the other hand, however, did this flexibility taint the decisions with an appearance of arbitrariness, which made the decisions unconvincing and subject to heavy criticism."[146]

Because of the drawbacks in the case law of the *Reichsgericht*, the Court sets out to find the best approach, which guarantees the applicability of the principle of guilt. The Court discusses two theories responding to the issue of intentionally committed acts under mistake of law that have been highlighted in the legal literature. One theory sees consciousness of wrongfulness as an element of the required intent. Lack of this consciousness negates the intent. If the mistake or ignorance was unavoidable the defendant cannot be punished. If the mistake was avoidable the defendant can be punished for the negligent form of this crime, that is, if the legislature has provided for such liability.[147] The other theory considers unavoidable mistake of law to be an excuse, leaving unimpeded the finding that the

142 Bundesgerichtshof 1952, § 16.

143 Bundesgerichtshof 1952, § 17.

144 Bundesgerichtshof 1952, § 18.

145 Bundesgerichtshof 1952, §§ 19–20.

146 Bundesgerichtshof 1952, § 22 (translation AvV).

147 Bundesgerichtshof 1952, § 26. This can be compared to the 'inexorable logic rule' referred to above, see Sect. 2.2.2.2 *supra*.

defendant acted intentionally. Consciousness of wrongfulness, or the possibility of this consciousness, is an element of culpability apart from the intent-requirement.[148] "The first theory is referred to as the *Vorsatztheorie* or intention theory, because it regards the consciousness of wrongfulness as an element of the required intent. The advantage of this approach is that it makes the distinction between mistake of fact and mistake of law redundant, because both are treated the same, namely according to § 59 StGB. The main disadvantage of this theory is, according to the Court, the fact that the defendant can only be found to have acted intentionally if, at the moment of action, he realised he was doing something wrongful. This is, however, only seldom the case. Most crimes are committed in a stressed frame of mind. This is especially true for the most serious of crimes. This puts the judge in a difficult position, and in order to be able to convict this defendant, in accordance with his sense of justice, he must adopt a presumption of consciousness, which is, in light of the principle of guilt, unacceptable."[149] The theory forces the courts to adopt a presumption of consciousness because otherwise no one could be convicted. The theory thus provides no effective solution at all. A further disadvantage of this theory is that if the legislature has not provided for the negligent crime, the defendant who committed an act under an avoidable mistake of law cannot be punished.[150]

The result of the second solution, which is referred to as the *Schuldtheorie*, is the same in the case of an unavoidable mistake, the defendant is acquitted. The difference between the two theories, however, becomes visible if one takes the case of an avoidable or negligent mistake. Under the theory of guilt, this mistake (like the unavoidable mistake) does not impede the finding of intent and (unlike the unavoidable mistake) this mistake does not negate the culpability of the defendant. The avoidable mistake can only be a ground for mitigation of punishment for the intentional crime. This theory allows for a judgement which is more precise in its reproach towards the defendant. The reproach in case of an intentional offence, committed under avoidable mistake of law, concerns mainly the intention of the actor to commit the wrongful act. In contrast, in the case of a negligent offence, the reproach concerns the fact that the defendant has neglected to take account of his responsibilities ensuing from his conduct in society.[151]

In this landmark decision the Court chose in favour of the *Schuldtheorie*. This theory provides for a result that is congruent with the principle of guilt.[152] It

[148] Bundesgerichtshof 1952, § 27.

[149] Bundesgerichtshof 1952, § 29 (translation AvV).

[150] Bundesgerichtshof 1952, § 30. As indicated earlier, international criminal law does not generally contain crimes of negligence, see Sect. 1.5, Sect. 2.2.2.1 *supra* and see also Sects. 3.3.1 and 3.2.2 *infra*.

[151] Bundesgerichtshof 1952, § 32.

[152] Bundesgerichtshof 1952, § 33.

specifies the reproach on the basis of which the defendant is being punished.[153] The Court concludes that § 240 StGB requires the defendant to have had the required knowledge of the factual elements of the crime definition, as to which knowledge of wrongfulness does not attach, and, in addition, that he could and therefore should have been conscious of the fact that with his extortion he was doing wrong.[154]

2.3.2.3 The Codification

The German legislator followed the preference in doctrine and case law for the *Schuldtheorie*. Since 1975, the German criminal code provides for mistake of law as an excuse. German law distinguishes between *Tatbestandsirrtum* (§16 StGb) and *Verbotsirrtum* (§17 StGB). It separates the issue of knowledge of the factual circumstances of the crime definition (*Kenntnis der Tatbestandsmerkmale*) from the issue of consciousness of wrongdoing (*Unrechtsbewußtsein*).[155] In German criminal law intent is the normal *mens rea* requirement. Consciousness of wrongdoing is an element of criminal liability but not an element of this *mens rea*.

Section 17 StGB, on mistake of law, provides:

> *Fehlt dem Täter bei Begehung der Tat die Einsicht, Unrecht zu tun, so handelt er ohne Schuld, wenn er diesen Irrtum nicht vermeiden konnte. Konnte der Täter den Irrtum vermeiden, so kann die Strafe nach § 49 Abs. 1 gemildert werden.*[156]

What are the different issues involved in the assessment of mistake of law as an excuse? The first issue is to establish whether there is actually a case of mistake of law. If the defendant has *Unrechtsbewußtsein*, is conscious of the wrongfulness of his act, he made no mistake of law. What does *Unrechtsbewußtsein* mean and how do you establish whether the defendant had *Unrechtsbewußtsein*? The second issue evolves around the different types of mistake of law. As will become apparent, the lack of *Unrechtsbewußtsein* manifests itself in various ways. The third issue then is to assess the legal effect of a mistake of law. This is discussed in respect of the requirement of unavoidability, since the legal effect depends on whether the mistake was in fact avoidable or not.

---

153 Bundesgerichtshof 1952, § 34.

154 Bundesgerichtshof 1952, § 39.

155 Nill-Theobald 1998, p. 344. *See also* Jescheck and Weigend 1996, at § 41. I.2.

156 Translation (The American Series of Foreign Penal Codes, Germany, Volume 28 (1987)): A person who commits an act in the mistaken belief that it is lawful acts without guilt, provided he could not have avoided making the mistake. If he could have avoided it, the punishment may be reduced in accordance with the provisions of § 49(1). (Translation AvV:) If the perpetrator, whilst committing the prohibited act, did not know he was acting wrongfully, he acted without culpability if the mistake was unavoidable. If the mistake was avoidable, the punishment may be mitigated in accordance with § 49 (1).

1. *Unrechtsbewußtsein*

Obviously, if the defendant had *Unrechtsbewußtsein*, that is, was aware of the wrongfulness of his behaviour, he made no mistake of law. The question is when someone has *Unrechtsbewußtsein*. What is the required knowledge? Is this knowledge of the legal prohibition, including all its technicalities? Or is knowledge of moral wrongdoing sufficient to establish the perpetrator acted with *Unrechtsbewußtsein*?

Jescheck and Weigend agree, *Unrechtsbewußtsein* is present when the actor knows he is violating a rule of criminal law, civil law or administrative law.[157] They argue that material knowledge of breaking some legal rule is sufficient; knowledge of the immorality of the act, however, does not constitute the required *Unrechtsbewußtsein*. Knowledge of the moral reprehensibility of the behaviour, however, often does lead to the conclusion that the ignorance or mistake (as to the wrongfulness of the behaviour) was avoidable, because knowledge of immorality gives cause to reconsider the lawfulness of the act.[158]

According to Jescheck and Weigend, the defendant will, most of the time, have a clear and correct perspective on the wrongfulness of his conduct. This is especially true in case of *mala in se* crimes and acts that are premeditated.[159] Knowledge of the factual elements of the offence should usually warn the defendant about the wrongfulness of his behaviour or at least encourage him to inquire further about the lawfulness of his conduct. This is referred to as the indicative function of the elements of the offence.[160]

Roxin notes, however, that the actor, only rarely actually contemplates the lawfulness of his behaviour. He correctly holds this does not mean, however, that in these instances the *Unrechtsbewußtsein* is not present. That the defendant is at least latently conscious of the wrongfulness of his behaviour may manifest itself in the way the defendant goes about in the execution of the criminal behaviour. For example, if the defendant tries to avoid being caught in the act, his surreptitious attitude might reveal his state of mind concerning any wrongfulness.[161]

With regard to the object of the *Unrechtsbewußtsein*, Roxin argues that the defendant must be specifically aware of the violation of the protected interest for which he is being held criminally liable. You have to be aware of the wrongfulness of the specific elements of the offence.[162] Mistake of law means that you are

[157] Jescheck and Weigend 1996, p. 454, § 41. I.3. *See also* Roxin 2006, p. 933, Rn. 13. But see, in the context of the Dutch approach to mistake of law, Stolwijk 2009 p. 232, § 27 (holding the required knowledge is knowledge of violating (some) criminal law).

[158] Jescheck and Weigend 1996, p. 454, § 41. I.3. *See also* Roxin 2006, p. 933, Rn. 12.

[159] Jescheck and Weigend 1996, pp. 454–455, § 41. I.3. *See also* Artz 1986, p. 725.

[160] *See also* Artz 1986, p. 724.

[161] *See* Roxin 2006, p. 940, Rn. 28.

[162] Roxin 2006, p. 935, Rn. 16.

mistaken about the norm for the violation of which you are being held accountable.[163]

The Bundesgerichtshof has ruled that the perpetrator cannot have doubts, i.e. he must be certain about the lawfulness of his behaviour. A defendant in doubt has *Unrechtsbewußtsein*.[164] According to Roxin, the contrary is true, a defendant in doubt is not excluded from the mistake of law excuse per se. He discusses what he calls 'the conditional variant of *Unrechtsbewußtsein*'. Conditional consciousness is assumed when the defendant has doubts. He thinks his behaviour is probably lawful, but he takes into account the possibility that he is acting unlawfully.[165] Roxin explains how case law and a trend in legal literature support the rule: if in doubt, do not act. Roxin argues that this view is only correct when the defendant did have the opportunity to resolve his doubts.[166] There is, however, broad consensus that in the situation where the defendant is in irresolvable doubt, he can only be excused if he had the option to chose between two ways of acting, both of which he considered to possibly be unlawful.[167] The example Roxin gives is "a police officer who doubts whether it is his right or his duty to shoot a fleeing offender in order to prevent him from crossing the border. If he shoots, he risks criminal liability for assault; if he does not shoot, he risks criminal liability for dereliction of duty".[168] Roxin holds that in situations like these the defendant is required, to such an extent as time and circumstances permit, to balance the protected legal interests involved and to calculate the likeliness of either of the options to be wrongful. If the defendant than ultimately made the wrong choice, he cannot be blamed, because he could not act other than with conditional consciousness of wrongfulness.[169] Roxin argues this situation should be treated analogous to an unavoidable mistake of law under § 17 StGB.[170] He finds the situation more complicated, however, when, in case of irresolvable doubt, there are no alternatives for the actor, every action might possibly be unlawful. Here too, the case law dictates the doubtful defendant should refrain from acting at all. This is, as Roxin holds, unfair: why should a person who has doubts be treated more severe than the person who does not have any doubts?[171] Roxin holds that both defendants should be treated according to the standard of § 17 StGB; situations of irresolvable doubt should be treated analogous to mistake of law. The main issues in the assessment of his culpability will be whether the defendant thought the act to

[163] Roxin 2006, p. 935, Rn. 16.

[164] *See* Roxin 2006, p. 941, Rn. 29 (referring to BGH JR 1952, 285).

[165] Roxin 2006, p. 941, Rn. 29.

[166] Roxin 2006, p. 941, Rn. 30.

[167] Roxin 2006, p. 941, Rn. 31.

[168] Roxin 2006, p. 941, Rn. 31 (translation AvV).

[169] Roxin 2006, p. 942, Rn. 31.

[170] Roxin 2006, p. 942, Rn. 31.

[171] Roxin 2006, p. 942, Rn. 32.

be lawful, what the conflicting interests were, what the damage of not acting would be to him and what damage acting would cause to others.[172]

2. *Types of mistake of law*

Roxin distinguishes four types of mistake of law: (1) mistake about or ignorance of the norm itself; (2) mistakes about the existence or boundaries of justifications; (3) the wrongful interpretation of an element of the crime definition (*Subsumtionsirrtum*); (4) mistake about the validity of a certain norm.[173] The first type of mistake is not very common in case of the so-called core crimes.[174] International crimes generally belong to this category. The second type, however, is very common to occur even in case of the violation of a core prohibition.[175] The third type of mistake can be either a factual mistake (*Tatbestandsirrtum*), a mistake of law (*Verbotsirrtum*), or an irrelevant mistake about the punishability of the act (*Strafbarkeitsirrtum*). If the defendant does not know the social meaning of a normative element of the crime, this mistake is a factual mistake that will negate the required intent. If however, the defendant, because of a legal misinterpretation of a normative element, thinks his behaviour is allowed, his mistake is a mistake of law. The fourth type, a mistake about the validity of a certain norm, only rarely occurs. Note that only recognised grounds for invalidity can sustain such a mistake of law.[176]

Jescheck and Weigend characterise the distinction between type 1 and type 2 mistakes as direct and indirect mistakes of law. Direct mistake of law is when the defendant has full knowledge of what he is doing but is ignorant of the law he is violating or knows the law but interprets it incorrectly. Indirect mistake of law is when the defendant has full knowledge of the norm he is violating but is convinced that he can rely on a ground of justification. The mistake of law in this case lies either in his wrongful interpretation of the condition of a justification recognised by the legal order, or in his assumption that a justification exists when in fact it does not.[177] The defendant thus makes a *Grenzirrtum* or a *Bestandsirrtum*.[178]

Indirect mistake of law arises when the defendant realises that his conduct violates a certain legal norm, but believes that a ground for justification exists. "The perpetrator fulfils, like in direct mistake of law, the intent requirement of the definitional elements of the offence, but lacks *Unrechtsbewußtsein*. Indirect mistake of law is treated the same as direct mistake of law, both are assessed according to their avoidability."[179]

---

172 Roxin 2006, pp. 942–943, Rn. 33–34.

173 Roxin 2006, pp. 937–940, Rn. 20–26.

174 Roxin 2006, p. 937, Rn. 21.

175 Roxin 2006. p. 938, Rn. 22. For this reason, this type of mistake of law will be discussed in depth in Chaps. 4 and 6 *infra*.

176 Roxin 2006, p. 939, §25.

177 Jescheck and Weigend 1996, pp. 456–457, § 41.II.1. *See also* Bundesgerichtshof 1952, § 8.

178 Jescheck and Weigend 1996, pp. 461–462, § 41.III.1.

179 Jescheck and Weigend 1996, p. 462, § 41.III.2. (translation AvV).

As noted, indirect mistake of law is the type of mistake of law most relevant in relation to international crimes, which justifies further elaboration of this issue in Chaps. 4 and 6.

Another category that will resurface in Chaps. 4 and 6 is the third-type of mistake of law, the *Subsumtionsirrtum*. This mistake concerns a mistaken interpretation of a normative element of a crime definition. To these elements the *Parallelwertungslehre* applies; the required intent in relation to this element is not legal knowledge or knowledge of wrongdoing (no criminal intent is required), but knowledge of the social significance of the circumstances of the act.[180] Ignorance of this social significance negates, as *Tatbestandsirrtum*, the required intent. A mistake concerning a normative element does not negate the required intent, when the defendant understands the social significance of his act. A *Subsumtionsirrtum* occurs when the mistake concerns the legal definition of the element concerned; this mistake is irrelevant, no legal knowledge is required. If the defendant, on the basis of a *Subsumtionsirrtum*, lacks knowledge of wrongdoing (*Unrechtsbewußtsein*), this constitutes a mistake of law (*Verbotsirrtum*).[181] In exceptional cases the social significance of an element cannot be understood without legal knowledge; a mistake in this respect will negate the required intent. Roxin gives the following example of such an exceptional case: if someone is mistaken about the element 'belonging to another', namely he believes the property is his, he does not have the intent required by the offences of theft or destruction of property.[182] However, if the legal or normative element is equal to or constitutes the wrongfulness of the conduct, a mistake will not negate the required intent. If, for example, the crime definition contains the normative element 'wantonly' the defendant who believes his act was not 'wanton' acts with the required intent. His mistake constitutes a mistake of law (*Verbotsirrtum*). If one considers that this mistake is a *Tatbestandsirrtum* instead, the undesired result would be that the wrongfulness of the act would depend on the (mistaken) belief of the perpetrator.[183]

3. *Avoidability*

As is clear from the text of § 17 StGB, German law further distinguishes between avoidable and unavoidable mistake. When a mistake was unavoidable, the defendant cannot be blamed for his act and should thus not be punished. The unavoidable mistake negates the culpability. In case of avoidable mistake, however, the defendant is reproachable. According to Jescheck and Weigend the basis for his culpability lies in his duties as a citizen in a free and democratic society. They explain that because under the rule of law, "a citizen must be led by the desire to act according to the law, the legal order requires him every time to make

[180] Roxin 2006, p. 486, Rn. 101.

[181] Roxin 2006, p. 486, Rn. 101.

[182] Roxin 2006, p. 487, Rn. 103.

[183] Roxin 2006, p. 489, Rn. 105.

an effort to ascertain whether he acts accordingly. This is why, even in cases where the defendant in good faith (subjectively) believes in the lawfulness of his behaviour, he is still blameworthy, when he did not make a reasonable effort to determine the legal implications of his behaviour."[184]

Roxin disagrees with the recognition of such a social duty. Civil disobedience is not the ground for punishing the intentional criminal act, but the fact that the defendant has ignored someone's interest, or the general interest, in an unacceptable way.[185] The reproach aimed at the defendant who committed an intentional crime under mistake of law is not that he intentionally breached the law, but that he missed the opportunity to know about the law. According to Roxin, the rule of § 17 StGB, that unavoidable mistake excludes culpability, follows directly from the principle of guilt. This is so, because the person who has not had the opportunity to obtain knowledge of the *Unrecht* (wrong), cannot be reached by the norm.[186] Roxin argues that this clearly demonstrates that culpability in case of mistake of law exists in the possibility of acquiring knowledge of the wrongfulness, and not, for example, in the violation of an independent duty to search one's conscience or investigate. Not 'neglecting to investigate', but the 'attainability' of knowledge about the norm makes the act culpable.[187] It may be argued that Roxin does not offer a truly different standard than the one promulgated by Jescheck and Weigend; if the norm is objectively attainable you blame the actor for not investigating it.

Roxin further holds that the term used by the legislature, referring to the unavoidability of the mistake, wrongfully suggests that only the absolute inability to know about the wrongfulness of one's behaviour amounts to unavoidability. This suggestion must be wrong because, if absolute inability was required, unavoidable mistake of law would never occur, since the *lex certa* principle (as part of the principle of legality) in Article 103 II Grund Gesetz (GG) guarantees that anyone can in principle know about the law.[188]

With regard to criteria on which the avoidability of the mistake is to be assessed, Jescheck and Weigend contend that the measure should be the same as the one used in determining acts of negligence, so that the same obligation to investigate rests on the defendant. It is important to take as guiding assumption the indicative function of the factual elements of the offence. However, the force of this assumption depends on the crime at hand. Jescheck and Weigend hold that if the act does not only violate a legal norm, but also constitutes a violation of moral values, the mistake is very likely to have been avoidable, because the legal

---

[184] Jescheck and Weigend 1996, p. 457, § 41.II.1. (translation AvV).

[185] Roxin 2006, p. 930, Rn. 8.

[186] Roxin 2006, p. 944, Rn. 35.

[187] Roxin 2006, p. 944, Rn. 35.

[188] Roxin 2006, p. 945, Rn. 38. See for a discussion of the relation between the principle of legality and the defence of mistake of law the discussion of the German Border Guard cases below and Chap. 3.

evaluation corresponds to or emanates directly from the moral consciousness. Further, in cases where the act does not show such a close relation to the moral consciousness, there is, according to these authors, a duty to investigate.[189]

Roxin warns that searching one's conscience does not always lead to the proper knowledge to constitute *Unrechtsbewußtsein.* He recognises that where the behaviour goes against one's conscience this can be an indication that one should conduct further inquires into the lawfulness of the act. However, "most mistakes of law are of such a nature, that searching one's conscience will not help to avoid making it".[190] The proper means to assess the lawfulness of one's conduct are therefore "reflection and inquiries".[191] As Roxin holds, however, a mistake of law by the person who does not apply these means is not necessarily avoidable. The avoidability of the mistake is rather based on three interrelated conditions: (a) the actor had an indication of the wrongfulness, he had a reason to investigate; (b) the actor has not undertaken any effort in this regard, he has not or insufficiently conducted further inquiries; and (c) the mistake is nevertheless only then avoidable when sufficient effort would have provided him with the required knowledge of wrongfulness.[192] With regard to the first condition (a), Roxin contends that only in three situations there is reason for the defendant to conduct further inquiries: (1) if he has doubts; (2) if he does not have doubts, but realises he moves in areas where certain sets of rules apply (e.g. traffic or a specific profession); and (3) when the actor knows his conduct causes damage to another individual or the community as a whole.[193] With regard to the second condition (b), he contends that advice of a reliable lawyer is sufficient.[194] Also if the proper authority tolerates the behaviour and this tolerance implies the authority regards the behaviour as lawful, no further inquiries are warranted. In this respect Roxin refers to the German Border Guard cases.[195] These are discussed in further detail at the end of this section. Finally, with regard to the third condition (c) Roxin argues that "what is decisive is not what a certain lawyer actually said, but what the outcome would have been, on which the actor would have been allowed to rely".[196]

Jescheck and Weigend agree that the avoidability can only be established when further inquiries could actually have provided the defendant the information that his behaviour was wrongful. In case of doubt, they argue, this obligation, however, becomes more pressing; the defendant cannot simply choose the most

[189] Jescheck and Weigend 1996, pp. 458–459, § 41.II.2.b.

[190] Roxin 2006, p. 948, Rn. 46.

[191] Roxin 2006, p. 948, Rn. 46 (referring to BGHSt 2, 201 and BGHSt 4, 5).

[192] Roxin 2006, p. 950, Rn. 52. With regard to (*c*) the avoidability can only be established, when further inquiries actually could have provided the defendant the information that his behaviour was unlawful.

[193] Roxin 2006, p. 951, Rn. 51.

[194] Roxin 2006, p. 954, Rn. 62.

[195] Roxin 2006, p. 957, Rn. 67.

[196] Roxin 2006, p. 959, Rn. 69 (translation Avv).

advantageous option.[197] "In general one could say that the German courts apply high standards to the duties of the defendant: he must apply all his mental capacities and his moral consciousness to reach the correct judgement."[198]

What remains is to briefly discuss the legal effect of mistake of law. As § 17 StGB stipulates, unavoidable mistake of law negates the defendant's culpability. The defendant must be acquitted. Avoidable mistake of law, on the other hand, may only lead to mitigation of punishment.

It may be thought that Roxin's account of the issues involved in assessing the criminal responsibility of a defendant who committed an intentional act under mistake of law, as described above, is very illuminating. First, one has to establish whether the defendant actually had (latent) *Unrechtsbewußtsein*. Conditional *Unrechtsbewußtsein* should be assessed analogous to a mistake of law. The issue in case of mistake of law is whether the defendant could have avoided his mistake. Here one needs to investigate whether the defendant had indications that his conduct might be unlawful and whether further inquiries (for example consulting a lawyer) could have prevented the mistake. It is helpful here to discuss a recent German case in which the defendants argued that they had acted under mistake of law.

2.3.2.4 The German Border Guard Cases

These cases concern the prosecution, after the reunification of East and West Germany, of East German border guards for the deadly use of firearms in preventing East German citizens to cross the border to West-Germany.[199] The East-German border regulation, more precisely § 27 Section 2 of the *Grenzgesetz*, arguably allowed or even required the use of firearms in these situations. The first issue before the West German Courts was therefore whether the prosecution of the border guards violated Article 103, Section 2 of the Grund Gesetz (Basic Law of the FDR, hereafter GG), which prohibits retroactive punishment. Justifications, like provided for in § 27 *Grenzgesetz*, fall under the protection of the prohibition of retroactive punishment.[200] The BGH (Federal Court of Justice) and the BVerfG (Federal Constitutional Court) both, although on different grounds, came to the conclusion that there was no such violation. In Mauerschützen I the BGH held that the GDR law could be interpreted in such a way that it respected human rights,

---

[197] Jescheck and Weigend 1996, p. 459, § 41.II.2.b.

[198] Jescheck and Weigend 1996, p. 459, § 41.II.2.b (translation AvV).

[199] See for example: Mauerschützen 1992; Mauerschützen 1993; Mauerschützen 1995; BVerfGE 95, 96, 24 October 1996 1996 (translation in English in BVerfGE 95, 96, 24 October 1996 1997); Case of K.-H. W. v. Germany (Application no. 37201/97) 2001

[200] Mauerschützen I 1992, pp. 15–16 (Page numbers in references to the German Border Guard Cases here and below are page numbers of the printed document, since I was unable to verify the official page numbering). For an extensive study of the principle of legality and international crimes see Boot 2002.

especially the right to life and the right to freedom of movement. Under this interpretation, which the Court considered to be the correct interpretation, the justification of § 27 Section 2 *Grenzgesetz* was not applicable, the shooting of the border guard was unlawful under GDR law at the time of action.[201] The Court concluded that the prohibition of retroactive punishment protects valid expectations of citizens; the expectation that a State practice of providing for a justification that violates fundamental human rights will also apply in the future is not a valid expectation, therefore it does not deserve the protection of the prohibition of retroactive punishment, according to the Court.[202] However, as Walther convincingly demonstrated, the Court's reference to and interpretation of international human rights law is highly questionable.[203] First of all, she refers to a procedural problem. Although the GDR had ratified the International Covenant on Civil and Political Rights of 1966 (ICCPR) in 1974 and it entered into force in 1976, the GDR legislature did not transform it into national law as required by the GDR constitution.[204] Second, Walther argues, the scope of the human rights of protection of life and the right to leave is unclear, especially where protection of these rights conflicts with national security interests.[205] With regard to the right to life she states that it is clear that the use of firearms with the intent to kill is in violation of Article 6 ICCPR. "There seems to be no general consensus, however, on the limits of *possibly* deadly use of firearms—that is, the lawful use of firearms where border officials are aware of the possibility of a deadly outcome."[206] As to the right to leave, Walther continues "international law guarantees leave something to be desired as well. The right is embodied in the UDHR 1948, as well as in numerous other human rights treaties, including Article 12, clause 2 [ICCPR]. Whether customary international law recognises the right seems to be widely regarded as nonverifiable." The court "largely passed over the [...] thorny definitional problems regarding both the right to the protection of life and the right to leave".[207]

In Mauerschützen II the BGH reaffirmed this human rights approach by holding that the prohibition on retroactive punishment does not prevent the Court from interpreting GDR law in a manner favourable to human rights, even though the State practice deviated from this interpretation.[208]

---

201 Mauerschützen I 1992, pp. 9–14.

202 Mauerschützen I 1992 p. 16. *See also* Walther 1995, p. 104.

203 Walther 1995, pp. 104–105.

204 Walther 1995, p. 104.

205 Walther 1995, p. 105.

206 Walther 1995, p. 105 (referring in footnote 51 amongst other sources, to the "motorcycle case" (1988), a West German case in which the court found lawful the use of firearms where deadly force was a possible outcome (BGHSt 35, 379)).

207 Walther 1995, p. 105.

208 Mauerschützen II 1993, p. 10.

In Mauerschützen III the BGH also affirmed its standing on the issue: "the border guards have not been let down in their expectations of the continuing applicability of the law; [...]. Article 103(2) GG does not protect the expectation of a continuing state practice in this respect."[209] The Court continues, "if the law or state practice is obviously and in an unacceptable way a violation of internationally protected human rights, the responsible authorities and those who act on their orders, are not protected by the prohibition on retroactive punishment."[210] Hence, in Mauerschützen II and III the BGH reaffirmed that the GDR law in question could and should be interpreted in such a manner as to respect internationally recognised human rights. The responsible authorities, and those acting on their orders who rely on the continuation of State practice that was obviously not in accordance this interpretation, deserve no protection from the principle of legality.

The same is stated by the *Bundesverfassungsgericht* (Federal Constitutional Court). This Court also refers to the rule of law basis of the ban on retroactivity:

> The strict ban on retroactivity in Article 103(2) basic law, [...], has its rule-of-law justification in the special situation of trust the penal laws bear when enacted by a democratic legislator bound by fundamental rights. This special position of trust does not apply where the other State, whilst legislating elements of offences for the area of the gravest criminal wrongs, nonetheless excluded punishability through grounds of justification for partial areas by calling, over and above the written norms, for such wrongs, favouring them and thus gravely disregarding the human rights universally acknowledged in the international legal community. [...] In this quite special situation the precept of substantive justice, which also includes respect for the human rights recognized in international law, bars application of such a ground of justification. The strict protection of trust by Article 103(2) Basic Law must then yield. Otherwise the administration of criminal justice in the Federal Republic would fall into contradiction with its rule-of-law premises.[211]

This case was brought before the European Court of Human Rights (ECtHR).[212] This Court affirmed the findings of the national courts that there was no violation of the principle of legality. It was not so much concerned as to how the different national courts had approached the issue; the Court only needed to satisfy itself "that the result reached by the German courts was compatible with the Convention, and specifically with Article 7 §1."[213] The state practice to protect the border 'at all costs' was

209 Mauerschützen III 1995, p. 7 (translation AvV).

210 Mauerschützen III 1995, p. 7 (translation AvV).

211 BVerfGE 95, 96, 24 October 1996 1996, pp. 21–22; BVerfGE 95, 96, 24 October 1996 1997, pp. 76–77.

212 Here I will only refer to the appeal of the border guard, not to the appeal of the government officials/political leaders, which appeals were handled by the ECtHR jointly.

213 Case of K.-H. W. v. Germany (Application no. 37201/97) 2001, § 61.

flagrantly in violation of the GDR Constitution and legislation and also in breach of international obligations of the GDR under international human rights law.[214] This practice was no law in the sense of Article 7 ECHR.[215] The Court concluded that "at the time when it was committed the applicant's act constituted an offence defined with sufficient accessibility and foreseeability in GDR law".[216]

2.3.2.4.1 The German Border Guard Cases: The Principle of Legality

One of the pillars of the principle of legality is the foreseeability of criminal punishment. Where the ECtHR deals with the foreseeability of the conviction it conflates the principle of legality and the defence of mistake of law.[217] The Court was convinced that this foreseeability requirement was met; the border policing regime was so obviously an infringement of basic social norms (GDR law and international human rights), that anyone could foresee that following this policy or these orders would lead to criminal punishment. The Court held that "[a]lthough the applicant was not directly responsible for the above State practice, and although the event in issue took place in 1972, and therefore before ratification of the International Covenant, he should have known, as an ordinary citizen, that firing on unarmed persons who were merely trying to leave their country infringed fundamental and human rights, as he could not have been unaware of the legislation of his own country".[218] And, "in the light of all the above considerations, the Court considers that at the time when it was committed the applicant's act constituted an offence defined with sufficient accessibility and foreseeability by the rules of international law on the protection of human rights".[219]

As several authors have convincingly argued, it is questionable whether this analysis is correct.[220] The main argument against this finding is that in 1972 the practice of shooting border violators was not manifestly unlawful. Ferdinandusse refers to a case in the US, where the issue whether shooting a border violator was unlawful remained undecided for more than ten years.[221] Pellonpää, in his dissenting opinion to the ECtHR case, referred to a 1988 case before the BGH against a West German customs officer who fired in a life-threatening manner at a motorcyclist, who tried to avoid customs control at the border between West Germany and The Netherlands.[222] The customs officer was acquitted, "he was

---

214 Case of K.-H. W. v. Germany (Application no. 37201/97) 2001, §§ 66–67.

215 Case of K.-H. W. v. Germany (Application no. 37201/97) 2001, § 90.

216 Case of K.-H. W. v. Germany (Application no. 37201/97) 2001, § 91.

217 See further the discussion in Sect. 3.3.4 *infra*.

218 Case of K.-H. W. v. Germany (Application no. 37201/97) 2001, § 104.

219 Case of K.-H. W. v. Germany (Application no. 37201/97) 2001, § 105.

220 See e.g. Ferdinandusse 2006, pp. 245–248.

221 Ferdinandusse 2006, pp. 247–248.

222 BGHSt 35, 379 1988.

objectively entitled to suspect that the persons fleeing were serious drug offenders or had a comparable reason for fleeing".[223] Although this case concerns quite a different situation (the GDR policy was to give flight prevention precedence over the right to life and in West Germany shooting to kill persons trying to evade border control "has never been officially supported or condoned")[224] Pellonpää holds that "the applicant seems to have acted in accordance with orders emanating from prima facie "constitutionally competent" organs." He therefore finds "it somewhat unreasonable to require that the applicant should have been able to decide a conflict between those orders and other provisions (such as Section 17(2) of the Police Act), applying methods used in a State based on the rule of law".[225] On the one hand, the Courts (both BVerfG and ECtHR) have held that the border guards cannot invoke the ban on retroactivity, because that principle presupposes the rule of law. On the other, they expect the border guards to know which orders to follow and which orders to refuse, despite the absence of the rule of law. Somehow there is friction in this reasoning.[226]

Leaving aside the issue of the principle of legality, and proceeding from the finding of the German courts and the ECtHR that this principle had not been violated, I will now turn to the next issue before these courts, namely the individual culpability of the border guards.

2.3.2.4.2 The German Border Guard Cases: Mistake of Law

In defence the defendant pleaded having acted on superior orders and/or under mistake of law. The findings of the German courts illustrate the relation between these two defences. Under the defence of superior orders, the defendant has no obligation to investigate.[227] When raising superior orders, Article 5 WStG, the soldier does not have a duty to investigate the lawfulness of the order; in case of doubt, which cannot be resolved, he can obey the order.[228] But if the order was

---

[223] Case of K.-H. W. v. Germany (Application no. 37201/97) 2001, dissent Pellonpää, p. 50. On this case see also Frowein 1990.

[224] Walther 1995, p. 105.

[225] Case of K.-H. W. v. Germany (Application no. 37201/97) 2001, dissent Pellonpää, p. 48.

[226] In this respect I would like to refer to a distinction made by Kelk. He refers to the constitutional dimension of the principle of legality and to the legal protection dimension of this principle. The first dimension focuses on the primary objective of criminal law, punishment according to the law and the second dimension focuses on the legal position of the defendant. Under the second dimension there will be more room for exclusion of criminal responsibility on the basis of the principle of legality. Kelk 2005, p. 98 The discussion by the Courts of the principle of legality seems to have been dominated by the first dimension of this principle, punishment according to the law; the second dimension has remained unexplored.

[227] Under the GDR provision, there was such an obligation; the courts applied the more lenient rule, the FDR provision, Article 5 WStG.

[228] Mauerschützen II 1993, p. 13.

manifestly unlawful, the defendant will not be exculpated if he follows it.[229] The courts found the orders and the border policing regime to be manifestly unlawful; the defence of superior orders was denied. This did not settle the issue of culpability, however, because the determination of the manifest unlawfulness of the order does not preclude the possibility of the defendant having acted under a mistake of law, without *Unrechtsbewußtsein*; the defendant can perceive his action as lawful, even though the order was manifestly unlawful. The courts, however, indicated that where the order or policy is manifestly unlawful, often the purported mistake of law will have been avoidable.[230]

Hence, ultimately the culpability of the defendants depended on the avoidability of their mistake. Could they foresee the inapplicability of § 27 Section 2 *Grensgesetz* and therewith the wrongfulness of their behaviour? As it turned out the Court was very strict in the amount of effort it demanded of the border guards. They were not allowed to rely on the East-German officials, who were the "pillars of the system of *Unrecht*".[231] The Court instead investigated whether the people of Eastern Germany at the time approved of their behaviour.[232] This deviation from the basic rule, that reliance on official authority is sufficient, is according to Roxin, a dubious erosion of § 17(1) and leads to a further expansion of criminal responsibility.[233] How can one ask of these subordinates to know the (international) wrongfulness of their border policing regime, whilst they were deliberately kept in the dark?[234]

Roxin and Arnold et al. argue, reasonably it might be thought, that the unlawfulness of orders was probably less manifest to the defendants than the Courts assumed.[235] The BVerfG admitted that "reservations as to the recognizability of the breach of the criminal law beyond all doubt might arise from the circumstance that the GDR State leadership equipped the ground of justification supposed to cover the behaviour of the border soldiers with the authority of the State, and so conveyed it to the soldiers. It is not then a matter of course that the average soldier could be clear beyond doubt as to the proper boundary of punishable conduct, and it would be untenable under the principle of guilt to establish the obviousness of the breach of the criminal law to soldiers solely with the—objective—presence of a severe infringement of human rights; for then it would have to be shown in more detail why the individual soldier, having regard to his education, indoctrination and other circumstances was in a position to recognize the breach of the criminal law beyond doubt".[236] The BVerfG held that the lower

229 See further Sect. 2.4.2 *infra*.

230 Mauerschützen II 1993, pp. 13–14 and BVerfGE 95, 96, 24 October 1996 1997, p. 72.

231 Roxin 2006, p. 957, § 67.

232 Mauerschützen II 1993, p. 13.

233 Roxin 2006, pp. 957–958, §§ 67–68.

234 *See also* Roxin 2006, p. 958, § 68.

235 Roxin 2006, p. 958, § 68; Arnold et al. 2003, pp. 87–90.

236 BVerfGE 95, 96, 24 October 1996a 1997, p. 78.

courts did not "discuss the facts and circumstances from this viewpoint in the initial proceedings".[237] The Court held, however, that the lower courts addressed the issue of guilt in the proper way by establishing that the killing of an unarmed fugitive was a manifest "infringement of proportionality and the elementary ban on killing [that] must have been perceptible and obvious immediately even to an indoctrinated person".[238]

The Court (being a Constitutional Court) could only perform a marginal test, which it concluded by determining that the lower court had correctly assessed the individual's personal guilt.[239] Nill-Theobald seems to reconcile herself with the conclusion of manifest illegality; she summarises the arguments that support this finding: "it must have been obvious that a state does not have the right to have a person, who only wants to travel from one side of Berlin to the other, shot in order to prevent this border violation. [Another argument is that] the availability of the order to shoot was denied in public and the fact that in case of visiting high foreign officials the border guards were not allowed to shoot, except in case of risk of flight and self-defence".[240] The last argument she mentions concerns the fact that soldiers involved were relocated to other divisions and there was a general secrecy policy applicable to shooting incidents.[241]

Whalter has criticised the BGH for "failing to scrutinize more closely the nature of the actual orders and the defendant's ability to recognize them as wrong".[242] In my opinion, the lower courts on the basis of the facts and circumstances summarised by the BVerfG referred to above, could have, and indeed therefore should have, reached the opposite conclusion, i.e., that the individual border guards could not have foreseen the illegality of their acts and could not have avoided their mistake. The guards acted on orders emanating from state authority, they were deliberately kept in the dark about the wrongfulness of these orders and they were formally commended when they had prevented the flight of GDR citizens by the fatal use of firearms.[243] It can therefore, at least, be seriously doubted as to whether the border guards could have avoided their mistake of law. If there is doubt on an issue of culpability, under the fundamental criminal law principle of guilt, this doubt should be resolved in favour of the defendant. That is the only course consistent with the criminal law standard of culpability.

Walther also criticised the BGH in Mauerschützen I for not considering the GDR criminal law doctrine with regard to mistake of law more seriously. This doctrine treated mistake of law as a lack of intent. As seen earlier in this chapter, and as Walther emphasises, lack of intent is a much stronger defence than lack of

---

[237] BVerfGE 95, 96, 24 October 1996a 1997, p. 78.

[238] BVerfGE 95, 96, 24 October 1996a 1997, p. 78.

[239] BVerfGE 95, 96, 24 October 1996a 1997, p. 78.

[240] Nill-Theobald 1998, p. 130 (translation AvV).

[241] Nill-Theobald 1998, p. 130.

[242] Walther 1995, p. 107.

[243] BVerfGE 95, 96, 24 October 1996a 1997, pp. 66–67

consciousness of wrongdoing, because in case of lack of intent, the unavoidability or reasonableness of the mistake is irrelevant. Even an avoidable or unreasonable mistake as to the infringement of basic social norms will exclude intent in this sense. According to Walther, it is to be regretted that the court very briefly dismissed the applicability of it.[244] This is especially so because the East German law seems more lenient in this respect. On the other hand, as argued before, the (West) German rule on mistake of law in principle delivers outcomes in congruence with the principle of guilt and should therefore be preferred over a rule that allows even unreasonable mistakes to be exculpatory.

2.3.2.5 Conclusion

Generally the fulfilment of the elements of a crime definition leads to consciousness of the unlawfulness (*Unrechtsbewußtsein*). The wrongfulness of the act and the culpability of the defendant are presumed when the crime definition is fulfilled. The defendant can rebut this presumption by bringing forward issues of justification or excuse. Consciousness of unlawfulness is generally not an element of the crime definition. *Unrechtsbewußtsein* is not a part of the *mens rea* in the sense that it has expressly to be proven in every case, or that lack of it leads to absence of intent.[245] However, the fact that someone is unaware of the wrongful nature of his behaviour may indicate that he is not to blame for having committed the wrongful act. If you do not realise that your act is unlawful, criminal sanction is not a factor you can weigh in your decision to commit the act or not. The "perpetrator who does not realize that his conduct fulfils the elements of a crime, has not been warned, and thus, has no reason to investigate the lawfulness (or wrongfulness) of his actions".[246] This explains why *Unrechtsbewußtsein* is an element of criminal responsibility, although not of the required *mens rea*. The *Bundesgerichtshof* and the German legislature chose in favour of the *Schuldtheorie*, because this theory more accurately defines and specifies the reproach directed towards the defendant. In case of an avoidable mistake of law the culpability of the defendant lies not only in the fact that he has fulfilled the elements of a certain crime definition but also, and more specifically, in the fact that he could have chosen for the Right instead of the Wrong, since he could have avoided his mistake of law. But even if a system 'on paper' has found a principled solution to the complex issue of (non)attribution and mistake of law, the wish to vent the general public's indignation over an outrageous state practice may hamper applying this doctrine faithfully in individual criminal cases.

[244] Walther 1995, p. 107; Mauerschützen I 1992, pp. 19–20.

[245] *See also* Jescheck and Weigend 1996, p. 456.

[246] Artz 1986, p. 724.

2.3.3 France: Mistake of Law is a Ground for Excluding Criminal Responsibility

The French approach can be characterised as taking a middle position between the Anglo-American approach and the German approach. The French legal system is a civil law system, but the French system shows more resemblance to common law systems than to civil law systems like that of Germany in that it knows a twofold structure of offences, distinguishing between actus reus (*l'élément matériel*) and *mens rea* (*l'élément intellectuel*).[247] The text of the provision on mistake of law, however, does resemble the German provision. This provision is a novelty of the Code Pénal of 1994.

In the new provision, Article 122-3 Code Pénal, the legislator provides for mistake of law as a ground for excluding criminal responsibility. The provision reads:

> *N'est pas pénalement responsable la personne qui justifie avoir cru, par une erreur sur le droit qu'elle n'était pas en mesure d'éviter, pouvoir légitimement accomplir l'acte.*[248]

French textbooks still emphasise that *ignorantia legis non excusat* is the basic rule. They cannot ignore the new provision, but they seem to wish to avoid discussing mistake of law in any other way than as a rare and limited exception to the still valid basic rule. An example is Pradel, who in his chapter on mistake of law, devotes most of his attention to the old adage *ignorantia legis non excusat*. He describes how the French case law reminds over and again that mistake of law is neither a justification nor an excuse and how mistake of law simply has no influence on the culpability of the defendant.[249] The principle is based on a presumption that everyone knows the law. Pradel describes the justification for this presumption as follows. Social order necessitates this presumption, for if everyone would be allowed to argue mistake of law this would lead to the most serious social disturbances. The presumption is an indispensable fiction in the exercise of repressive law.[250] Moreover, he continues, "from the perspective of the social contract theory, this rule is the counterpart of the principle of legality. If every person has the right to be left alone (by state authority) as long as his behaviour is in accordance with the law, the citizen as a counter duty must make sure he acts in

---

[247] *See* Desportes and Le Gunehec 2007, pp. 379–405 and 406–464. *See also*, Fletcher 2007, pp. 44–45.

[248] Translation (The American Series of Foreign Penal Codes): "A person is not criminally responsible if that person proves that, because of an error of law, he or she was not in a position to avoid believing that he or she was able legally to perform the act", The American Series of Foreign Penal Codes, France 1999 Translation (by Elliott): "A person is not criminally responsible who can justify having believed he or she could legitimately accomplish the act in question, as a result of an unavoidable mistake of law.", Elliott 2000, p. 37. (Note how both sources give a different translation for *'justifie':* 'proves' and 'can justify').

[249] Pradel 2006, pp. 456–457, §495.

[250] Pradel 2006, p. 457, §496.

conformity with the law, and if he neglects to do so he commits a wrong towards the society": mistake of law is culpable in and of itself.[251] Pradel acknowledges that these arguments are not completely convincing. The presumption of knowledge of the law may be unjust with regard to certain persons, for example foreigners, and laws are nowadays so numerous and complex that one can hardly require citizens to have full and perfect knowledge of all these rules.[252] Pradel then continues, however, to discuss how wide the scope of the *ignorantia legis non excusat* principle is: it applies to foreigners as well as to nationals, to misdemeanours as well as to crimes, to mistakes about non-criminal laws and criminal law.[253] A distinction between mistakes about laws outside penal law and mistakes about penal law, sometimes applied by the lower courts, has always been rejected by the French Supreme Court.[254] Pradel concurs with the court's numerous and firm decisions on the point.[255]

Pradel, Desportes and Le Gunehec point out how, traditionally, the presumption of knowledge was absolute, meaning that it was irrefutable, and how the case law was in consequence very strict.[256] According to this case law a mistake of law could never negate the culpability of a voluntarily committed act. Even where there was uncertainty as to the laws ambit or where the mistake of law had been truly unavoidable, the result was the same, mistake of law was irrelevant. Pradel refers to how in the legal debate this case law met with much criticism. He admits that the principle *ignorantia legis non excusat* can lead to very unreasonable and unjust results, and that it seems to be nothing more than a fiction that is hard to defend. He indicates how the French legislature has adopted a provision from foreign countries like in Belgium, Germany and Italy, where unavoidable mistake of law is a ground for acquittal.[257]

---

[251] Pradel 2006, p. 457, §496 (translation AvV).

[252] Pradel 2006, p. 457, §496.

[253] Pradel 2006, pp. 457–458, §497. *See also* Desportes and Le Gunehec 2007, pp. 619–620, §674–1.

[254] Pradel 2006, p. 458, §497. *See also* Desportes and Le Gunehec 2007, p. 620, §674–1.

[255] Pradel 2006, p. 458, §497.

[256] Pradel 2006, pp. 458–459, §498 and Desportes and Le Gunehec 2007, p. 621, §676 (Holding that the presumption has always been absolute: « qu'une erreur de droit ne saurait faire disparaître, quelle que soit la cause dont elle découle, la culpabilité d'une acte volontairement accompli » [that the mistake of law cannot negate the culpability of a voluntary committed act] (Crim. 10 juillet 1903, D., 1903, I, 490 ; 16 mars 1972, B., no. 110), que « l'ignorance alléguée du caractère punissable du fait délictueux ne saurait être une cause de justification » [mistake about the criminal nature of the unlawful act is not a justification] (Crim. 24 juillet 1974, B., no. 267), ou que « l'erreur de droit n'est ni un fait justificatif, ni une excuse, l'ignorance alléguée étant sans influence sur l'intention coupable » [that mistake of law is not a justification, nor an excuse, the alleged ignorance is of no relevance to the culpability] (Crim. 2 mars 1976, B., no. 78). My efforts to gain access to the aforementioned case law have failed; I was therefore unable to consult these cases and must rely on the account of French authors.

[257] Pradel 2006, p. 459, §498.

2.3.3.1 The Provision

The provision, 122-3 Code Pénal, provides for a ground for excluding criminal responsibility in case of an unavoidable mistake of law. Desportes and Le Gunehec distil three cumulative conditions for exculpation from this provision: first, the defendant must have made a mistake of law; second, the mistake (or ignorance) must have been unavoidable; and third, the defendant was certain about the lawfulness of his act (he can have no doubts).[258] This last requirement is not to be found in the provision, however. The authors seem to base this requirement on a principle that we also encountered in the previous section on Germany, adhered to by some authors: i.e., in case of doubt, do not act.[259]

Pradel argues the text of Article 122-3 CP is very strict. The unavoidable mistake concerns two exceptional situations, first where the information supplied by the government is false, or second where official publication is lacking.[260] In these situations the mistake was unavoidable when the following three cumulative requirements are met: (1) the defendant, finding himself in doubt, has sought to clarify his understanding by consulting an authorised person or authority and did not act only on the basis of his own assumptions; (2) this authorised person or authority has given false information; and (3) the defendant believed he was given correct information and had no reason to question the correctness of it.[261] Note that the situation where the defendant, because he was completely ignorant of the (potential) wrongfulness of his act, did not inquire about it is not included in this interpretation of Article 122-3. Note also how the requirements correspond with the American approach to mistake of law in 'reliance cases'. It appears that Pradel is referring to the former French approach to the issue of mistake of law, without scrutinising the new provision, which provides for a more general and principled solution, requiring an assessment of the perpetrator's culpability. The problem is probably that the French system, like the Anglo-American system, does not separate the issue of wrongdoing from culpability. As stated, in their literature the French scholars distinguish between 'l'élément matériel' (*actus reus*) and 'l'élément moral' (*mens rea*).[262] The French do not make the distinction between wrongdoing and attribution.[263] In the French system of criminal offences,

[258] Desportes and Le Gunehec 2007, pp. 622+635, §§677+688+689. *See also* Sect. 2.3.3.2 *infra*.

[259] *See* Sect. 2.3.2.3, (1) *supra*.

[260] Pradel 2006, p. 459, §499. These situations are mentioned in the parliamentary debates that preceded the passing of the new Code. Desportes does not regard these examples as limited, *see* Desportes and Le Gunehec 2007, p. 627, §684. *But see to the contrary* Elliott 2000, p. 37.

[261] Pradel 2006, p. 459, §499.

[262] Fletcher 2007, pp. 44–45.

[263] See for a discussion of this distinction Sect. 3.2.2 *infra*.

consciousness of wrongfulness is part of the *mens rea*, (unavoidable) mistake of law negates the required intent.[264] The new provision in the Code Pénal is, however, like the continental European provisions, modelled after and based on a distinction between wrongdoing and culpability.

This explains why French lawyers have difficulties classifying mistake of law.[265] On the one hand, the new provision requires the mistake to have been unavoidable. On the other, using a twofold structure of offences, lacking any distinction between wrongdoing and attribution, they are forced to place the consciousness of unlawfulness requirement into the intent required by the crime definition. These two 'assignments' are irreconcilable, because the concept of intent does not allow for an 'opportunity to know', which is part of the unavoidability requirement. The concept of intent refers to 'knew or must have known' and the concept of avoidability or culpability to 'should have known'.

The confusion, brought about by applying a provision based on a threefold structure of offences in a civil law system based on a twofold structure of offences, also becomes visible in the requirement in French criminal law that the defendant must prove all issues concerning defences.[266] In case of mistake of law, for example, the defendant must prove his mistake of law, the unavoidability of the mistake and his belief in the lawfulness of his behaviour.[267] Placing the burden of proving defences on the defendant violates the fundamental principle of presumption of innocence. According to Delmas-Marty, however, the position that French law places the burden of proving justifications and excuses on the defendant is nowadays disputed.[268]

2.3.3.2 Avoidable Mistake

Desportes and Le Gunehec discuss the issue of avoidability more fundamentally. They raise the issue of an abstract or a concrete assessment of the avoidability of the mistake. An abstract assessment compares the actor to the reasonable person in the same situation (*le bon père de famille*). A concrete assessment takes into account the personal circumstances of the defendant, his capacities, education etcetera. Desportes and Le Gunehec express their hope that the judges would take a middle position. They point out that a purely concrete analysis would harm the

---

264 Elliott 2000, p. 36 (describing the element of awareness as part of the general intent: "The concept of awareness simply requires the accused to be aware that he or she is breaking the law" and describing the effect of certain defences: "Only in exceptional situations will an accused who has carried out the *actus reus* of an offence be found not to have a general intent" at p. 37). *See also* Desportes and Le Gunehec 2007, pp. 417–418 (§§470–471) + 625 (§683); and Sliedregt 2003, p. 234.

265 Fletcher 2007, p. 45.

266 Fletcher 2007, p. 45.

267 See Pradel 2006, pp. 460–461, §499 and Desportes and Le Gunehec 2007, p. 622, §677–1.

268 Delmas-Marty and Spencer 2002, p. 597.

repressive function of criminal law. According to the authors, two arguments support a more abstract analysis: first, the concept of mistake of law does not exclude everyone's obligation to inquire about the legal implications of his acts and second, this obligation is especially strong if the behaviour constitutes a violation of a fundamental rule like, for example, a rule concerning personal integrity. The level of abstractness or concreteness of the assessment should depend on the type of crime involved.[269]

Desportes and Le Gunehec point out how unlikely it is for a defendant to be successful in a mistake of law defence, when the crime he committed is a so-called crime *malum in se*. In these cases, where the crime not only violates a legal rule, but also a moral norm, the mistake will almost always have been avoidable.[270] According to Desportes and Le Gunehec the mistake (either about the lawfulness of the act or the applicability of a justification) must have been complete, that is to say, the perpetrator should be absolutely sure about the lawfulness of his act, he can have no doubts.[271]

According to Desportes and Le Gunehec, under the new provision, Article 122-3, the old case law on the issue of uncertainty about the correct interpretation of a particular law remains valid. "The result in these cases must be, that because the case law is uncertain, the defendant surely could have doubted the lawfulness of his act, he in any case could not have been sure about its lawfulness, so mistake of law cannot hold."[272] It seems wholly unacceptable to attribute uncertainty of law to the defendant. These situations particularly merit an analysis of the avoidability of the mistake; in case of uncertainty of the law, unavoidable mistake of law will be more plausible.[273]

At the moment there is still very little case law. The lower courts remain divided.[274] The Supreme Court is still very strict; so far it has held that every mistake of law argued before it was avoidable.[275] The new provision is hesitantly welcomed by French scholars. Desportes and Le Gunehec conclude their section on mistake of law remarking that it is still to be awaited what the real effects of Article 122-3 will be, how often it will be applied, if at all. At its first introduction,

---

269 Desportes and Le Gunehec 2007, p. 633, §687.

270 Desportes and Le Gunehec 2007, pp. 626–627, §683–2.

271 Desportes and Le Gunehec 2007, p. 635, §§688+689. *See also* Sect. 2.3.3.1 *supra*. As indicated, Roxin argues, to the contrary, that doubts do not per se exclude the defence of mistake of law, see Sect. 2.3.2.3, (1) *supra*.

272 Desportes and Le Gunehec 2007, p. 635, §689 (translation Avv).

273 See also the discussion of the principle of legality and the issue of whether the requirement of avoidability is absolute in Sect. 2.3.2.3, (3) *supra* and Sect. 3.3.4 *infra*.

274 Pradel 2006, p. 460, §499. Again, I need to follow legal literature in their assessment of the case law since my efforts to gain access to French case law were unsuccessful.

275 Pradel 2006 Desportes and Le Gunehec note there is one example of a successful plea of unavoidable mistake of law (Crim. 24 Nov. 1998). However, they argue, the fact that the case has remained unpublished demonstrates its insignificance, *see* Desportes and Le Gunehec 2007, p. 618, §673–2.

the provision was announced as a 'bomb'. Now, Desportes and Le Gunehec predict, "it may well be only a piece of wet fireworks, nothing to be very afraid of, in fact something that will prevent unjust results", which they welcome as a fortunate change.[276]

2.3.3.3 Conclusion

Although the French provision on mistake of law is very similar to the provision in the German Criminal Code, its implications may be more similar to those of the Model Penal Code provision. The reason for this is that the French penal system can be characterised as a so-called twofold system, a system that in its literature "primarily [relies] on the distinction between *actus reus* and *mens rea* as [its] principle of organisation".[277]

The overall impression generated by the French approach towards mistake of law is that, although the legislature has provided for a provision of mistake of law as a ground for excluding criminal responsibility, the general trend, in legal literature and case law, remains that mistake of law should be treated with suspicion. As we saw with regard to the Anglo-American system, the twofold system seems to induce a general reluctance to accept a defence on the basis of mistake of law.

The French system does, however, seem receptive towards the distinction between justification and excuse. An indication for this proposition can be found in Desportes' and Le Gunehec's reference to mistake of law as a *subjective* ground for excluding criminal responsibility. They discuss the issue of responsibility of co-perpetrators in case one of them successfully argued mistake of law. The authors refer to the possibility of still convicting the co-perpetrators, because mistake of law is a *subjective* ground for excluding criminal responsibility. They note, however, that mistake of law is not a purely subjective ground for excluding criminal responsibility, like, for example, insanity, because it also has an objective aspect to it (in the (absolute) assessment of the avoidability of the mistake).[278] The distinction made between objective and subjective grounds for excluding criminal responsibility may suggest that the French criminal law is on its way to accepting the distinction between wrongdoing and attribution. Nevertheless, the issue of how a normative assessment can be applied to a mistake that negates the required intent remains unresolved.

---

[276] Desportes and Le Gunehec 2000, p. 692 (translation AvV).

[277] Fletcher 2007, pp. 44–45. For a further discussion see Chap. 3 *infra*.

[278] Desportes and Le Gunehec 2007, p. 637, §691.

2.4 Superior Orders

This section discusses the provisions on the defence of superior orders in the legal systems of the USA, the UK, Germany and France.[279] All of these systems require, for a successful plea of superior orders, the defendant to have been unaware of the unlawful nature of the order. Hence, the defence of superior orders requires the subordinate to have acted under a mistake of law, which makes discussion of this defence relevant to this study of the scope of mistake of law. Superior orders are often invoked in criminal proceedings against defendants charged with international crimes. In this section the discussion is limited to the relevant domestic provisions on superior orders; I will return to these provisions in Chaps. 4 and 5, in which the international provisions and (inter)national case law on superior orders will be addressed.

2.4.1 USA and UK

The first edition of Oppenheim's International Law of 1906 states the applicable principle is the *respondeat superior* principle. Only the superior is responsible for the acts committed under his command. The same is stated in the 1914 edition of the British Manual of Military Law and the US Rules of Land Warfare (up until 1940), which was based on the British Manual.[280] When Lauterpacht edited his first edition of Oppenheim's International Law, he confirmed this standing. In his editions of 1940 and 1944, however, Lauterpacht radically changed his opinion. The relevant provision changed to: a subordinate is only obliged to follow lawful orders, if he follows an unlawful order he is responsible for the crimes he thereafter committed; a manifestly unlawful order cannot excuse the subordinate.[281] The British and American Field Manuals changed accordingly.[282] The tremendous scale on which the atrocities of the second World War were committed by subordinates and the idea that all these crimes would go unpunished if the subordinate was allowed to argue 'Befehl ist Befehl', brought about this radical change in the rules on superior orders.

§ 627 of the British Manual of Military Law (1958) reads:

> Obedience to the order of a government or of a superior, whether military or civil, or to a national law or regulation, affords no defence to a charge of committing war crimes but may be considered in mitigation of punishment.[283]

---

[279] For an elaborate overview of the history of the defence of superior orders, see Lippman 2001.

[280] Green 2003, p. 325.

[281] Green 2003 p. 326. *See also* Lippman 2001, pp. 159+174; *see also* Solis 1999, pp. 494+507.

[282] Green 2003, p. 327.

[283] *See also* Sliedregt 2003, p. 333; and Green 2003, p. 334.

Superior orders could only be a ground for mitigation of punishment. Ormerod notes that "there is a cogent argument that the serviceman should have a defence if he did not know that the order was illegal and it was not so manifestly illegal that he ought to have known it."[284] According to Ormerod there are however no English authorities on the point.[285]

The British Manual of the Law of Armed Conflict (2004) refers to Article 33 of the ICC Statute in Section 16.47, noting in a footnote that the Rome Statute moved away from a total denial of the defence of superior orders.[286] Section 16.47.2 still, however, refers to the situation where superior orders do not in themselves provide a defence to war crime charges. The same, i.e. superiors orders are not a separate defence, seems to follow from the Manual of Service Law (2011).[287]

The United States Field Manual, the Law of Land Warfare (FM 27-10 (1956)), para 509 reads:

> *Defence of Superior Orders* a. The fact that the law of war has been violated pursuant to an order of a superior authority, whether military or civil, does not deprive the act in question of its character as a war crime, nor does it constitute a defence in the trial of an accused individual, unless he did not know and could not reasonably have been expected to know that the act was unlawful. In all cases where the order is held not to constitute a defence to an allegation of war crime, the fact that the individual was acting pursuant to orders may be considered in mitigation of punishment. b. In considering the question of whether a superior order constitutes a valid defence, the court shall take into consideration the fact that obedience to lawful military orders is the duty of every member of the armed forces; that the latter cannot be expected, in conditions of war discipline, to weigh scrupulously the legal merits of the order received; that certain rules of warfare may be controversial; or that an act otherwise amounting to a war crime may be done in obedience to orders conceived as a measure of reprisal. At the same time it must be borne in mind that members of the armed forces are bound to obey only lawful orders.

Hence, under this provision, the defendant can invoke superior orders when he did not know, and could not reasonably have been expected to know, that the act ordered to be carried out was unlawful. In case of war crimes, however, superior orders may only mitigate the punishment.

Another relevant US provision is § 916(d) of the Rules for Courts Martial:

> R.C.M. 916 (d) *Obedience to orders*. It is a defence to any offence that the accused was acting pursuant to orders unless the accused knew the orders to be unlawful or a person of ordinary sense and understanding would have known the orders to be unlawful. Discussion. [...] An act performed pursuant to a lawful order is justified. [...] An act performed pursuant to an unlawful order is excused unless the accused knew it to be unlawful or a person of ordinary sense and understanding would have known it to be unlawful.[288]

---

[284] Ormerod 2008, p. 357.

[285] Ormerod 2008, p. 358.

[286] The Manual of the Law of Armed Conflict 2004.

[287] Manual of Service Law 2011, Chap. 12, Section 28.

[288] *See also* Nill-Theobald 1998, pp. 141–142.

§ 2.10 MPC applies a more lenient rule, requiring actual knowledge:

> § 2.10 MPC It is an affirmative defence that the actor, in engaging in the conduct charged to constitute an offences, does no more than execute an order of his superior in the armed services that he does not know to be unlawful.[289]

Robinson favours the MPC approach, providing for the defence unless the defendant *knows* that the order is unlawful. Ignorance or mistake, even if unreasonable or in the case of a manifestly unlawful order, exculpates. This purely subjective standard is justified, according to Robinson, to apply in some cases of mistake as to superior orders.[290] "Specifically, if an order is unlawful because it demands unjustified conduct and if that order precludes the independent exercise of judgment as to the unjustified aspect of the conduct commanded, then the compulsion inherent in military orders and the general societal need for deference to military orders, compels an especially broad mistake excuse when such an unlawful military order is mistakenly obeyed."[291]

To summarise, under US military law there is duty to obey lawful orders, obeying an unlawful order does not constitute a defence, "unless the subordinate did not know and could not reasonably have been expected to know that the act ordered was unlawful".[292] The order, even if manifestly unlawful, can always be a ground for mitigation of punishment.[293]

2.4.2 Germany and France

According to § 5 WStG a soldier is criminally liable for committing a(n international) crime in obedience to superior orders if he has actual knowledge of the unlawfulness of the order or if the order was manifestly unlawful.[294] "With this provision the German legislator has adopted a rule of conditional liability, which is determined by an objective (manifest illegality) and a subjective (positive knowledge) criterion."[295] The fact that a mistake of law is a constituent component to a successful plea of superior orders, could imply that Article 17 StGB (*Verbottsirrtum*) is applicable; the mistake must have been avoidable in order to exculpate. Nill-Theobald strongly opposes this theory. She holds that Article 5(I) WStG explicitly rejects the principle of avoidability, and thus a duty to investigate, as laid down in the general part of the Criminal Code. The rule on superior orders

289 *See also* Nill-Theobald 1998 pp. 143–144; and Sliedregt 2003, p. 332.

290 Robinson 1984, pp. 423–426, § 185(b).

291 Robinson 1984 p. 421, § 185(a).

292 *See also* Green 2003, p. 334; Nill-Theobald 1998, p. 142; Sliedregt 2003, p. 317.

293 *See also* Green 2003, p. 334.

294 § 5(I) WStG.

295 Nill-Theobald 1998, p. 116.

takes account of, and priority to, the duty to obey as a fundamental characteristic of military hierarchy.[296] Where under § 17 StGB the defendant in doubt must try to resolve his doubts, under the rule of § 5 WStG the doubting soldier should obey, because the fact that he has doubts means that the order is not *manifestly* unlawful.[297] The applicable German provisions (§ 11(II) SG and § 5 WStG) do stand for a rejection of the duty of blind obedience which § 47 MStGB provided for.[298]

The recent *Völkerstrafgesetzbuch* of 26 June 2002, provides in accordance with the provision in the ICC Statute, which it implements, for a rule similar to that of § 5(I) WStG, except that the application of this provision is limited to the war crimes enumerated in Articles 8 through 14. Genocide and crimes against humanity are excluded from the scope of this defence.[299]

Article 122-4 of the French Code Pénal (CP) provides also for a conditional liability rule. The subordinate is not responsible unless the order was manifestly unlawful.[300] Desportes notes that in case of a manifestly unlawful order other defences are theoretically still possible, but in practice the defence of mistake of law is excluded, because a mistake about a manifestly unlawful order will almost always turn out to have been avoidable.[301] In case of war crimes, violations of international law, the defence of superior orders is, however, categorically excluded; it may only be a mitigating factor.[302] The same applies, according to Article 213-4 CP in case of crimes against humanity.[303] Pradel also refers to a decree concerning military discipline of 28 July 1975 which provides that "a subordinate should not obey an order to commit a manifestly unlawful act or an act in violation of international customs of war and international conventions".[304] Hence, even in case of a non-manifestly unlawful order, the defence does not apply when the subordinate violated international law. If the subordinate does not obey an order because he mistakenly believes it to be illegal, he may be punished for disobedience.[305] Hence, in case of an unlawful act, not manifestly so, and not amounting to an international crime, the subordinate should obey.

According to Pradel and Desportes, the legislator has, by excluding the defence of superior orders in case of war crimes and crimes against humanity, correctly

---

[296] Nill-Theobald 1998 p. 118.

[297] Nill-Theobald 1998 p. 121.

[298] Case law applying this provision will be discussed in Chap. 5 *infra*.

[299] See § 3 VStGB. On a discussion of the provision in the ICC Statute see Chap. 4 *infra*.

[300] "*N'est pas pénalement responsible la personne qui accomplit un acte commandé par l áutorité légitimie, sauf sic et act est manifestement illegal.*"

[301] Desportes and Le Gunehec 2007, p. 668, § 725.

[302] Pradel, Desportes and Le Gunehec refer to '*l'ordannace du 28 août 1944*', Pradel 2006, p. 300, § 315; and Desportes and Le Gunehec 2007, p. 667, § 724.

[303] *See also* Pradel 2006, p. 301, § 315 and Desportes and Le Gunehec 2007, pp. 667–668, § 724

[304] Pradel 2006, p. 301, § 315.

[305] Article 8 Decree of 28 July 1975, Pradel 2006, p. 301, § 315.

followed the IMT Nuremberg precedent; the fact of a superior order can only mitigate the punishment.[306] Here, not even the manifest illegality rule applies; unless all international crimes can be considered to be manifestly unlawful. The inaccuracy of this hypothesis will be discussed in Chaps. 4 and 6.

2.4.3 *Conclusion*

The British Manual of Military Law (1958) excluded the defence of superior orders in case of war crimes; the superior order could only serve as a ground for mitigation of punishment. The British Manual of the Law of Armed Conflict (2004) refers to Article 33 ICC Statute, but also to the situation where superior orders do not in themselves provide a defence to war crime charges. Under the relevant US provision a reasonable mistake of law as to the lawfulness of a superior order will lead to an acquittal. In case of a manifestly unlawful order the defendant cannot be excused; his sentence may still be mitigated. The standard of manifestly unlawful is most likely to be the standard of a reasonable person, meaning the reasonable soldier in the same circumstances as the defendant.[307]

The German provisions provide also for a conditional liability rule; the subordinate is not responsible for the crimes he committed in obeying superior orders, unless he knew the orders to be unlawful or they were manifestly so. The defence is however, in accordance with the ICC Statute, excluded in case of crimes against humanity and genocide. Under French law, superior orders are in the case of international crimes, including war crimes, only a ground for mitigation of punishment.

To conclude it should be remarked that where a system recognises both mistake of law and superior orders as complete defences, the requirements for the latter defence are more favourable to the defendant; a subordinate is not required to ascertain the lawfulness of the superior order he receives. In case of doubt, the order cannot said to have been manifestly unlawful and the subordinate should obey.

2.5 Conclusion: Comparative Analysis

The Anglo-American courts have tried to mitigate the drawbacks of the *ignorantia legis non excusat* rule by manipulating the distinction between fact and law; mistakes about laws ‘collateral’ to penal law are considered to be mistakes of fact, which negate the required intent. American Courts have interpreted particular

---

306 Desportes and Le Gunehec 2007 p. 667, § 724; Pradel 2006, pp. 300–301, § 315.

307 Green 2003, p. 316.

mental elements, like wilfully and knowingly, to require knowledge of the law. The American legislature has provided for a defence of mistake of law where the law has not been published or where the defendant relied on an authoritative interpretation of the law, that was later determined to be invalid.

Although the MPC provides otherwise, the presumption that everyone knows that law, seems to be rebuttable. The twofold structure of offences places this rebuttal within the required mental element. This seriously complicates the means by which to arrive at an adequate normative account of culpability when the required mental element is 'intent'. Placing the issue of mistake within the mental element of intent leaves no room for requiring the mistake to have been reasonable in order to exculpate any specific act.

Germany has chosen in favour of the *Schuldtheorie*, that is, consciousness of unlawfulness being a separate element of criminal responsibility. The *Unrechtsbewußtsein* is not an element that is related to the intent required by the crime definition, it is an element of culpability. Culpability, according to the principle of guilt an unassailable requirement for punishment, is required in addition to the fulfilment of the elements of the crime definition.

A threefold structure of offences allows for differentiation according to the unavoidability of the mistake. Such a structure is based on the distinction between justifications and excuses, between wrongdoing and attribution, and between decision rules and conduct rules. These distinctions, some of which have been illustrated previously in this Chapter, will be the subject of Chap. 3. Further theorising on the issue of mistake of law in the national context will help us analyse the proper place of this defence in international criminal law in Chap. 4.

The national systems under investigation that allow a defence of mistake of law, provide for a more lenient rule when the defendant made his mistake in obeying superior orders. Where the system does not recognise mistake of law as a defence, the same applies to superior orders, this is no defence and can only lead to mitigation of punishment. Whether or not superior orders should indeed be a separate defence to liability for international crimes is discussed in Chap. 4.

References

Ambos K (2002) Other grounds for excluding criminal responsibility. In: Cassese A, Gaeta P, Jones JRWD (eds) The Rome Statute of the International Criminal Court. A commentary, vol 1. Oxford University Press, Oxford, pp 1003–1048

Ambos K (2004) Der Allgemeine Teil des Völkerstrafrechts. Ansätze einer Dogmatisierung, 2nd edn. Duncker & Humblot, Berlin

Ambos K (2007) Towards a universal system of crime: comments on George Fletcher's *Grammar of Criminal Law*. Cardozo L Rev 28(6):2647–2673

Arnold J, Karsten N, Kreicker H (2003) The German Border Guard Cases before the European Court of Human Rights. Eur J Crime Crim L Crim Justice 11(1):67–92

Artz G (1986) The problem of mistake of law. Brigham Young Univ L Rev 3:711–732

Ashworth AJ (1974) Excusable mistake of law. Crim L Rev 652–662

Ashworth A (2006) Principles of criminal law, 5th edn. Oxford University Press, Oxford

Boister N (2005) Reflections on the relationship between the duty to educate in humanitarian law and the absence of a defence of mistake of law in the Rome statute of the International Criminal Court. In: Burchill R, White ND, Morris J (eds) International conflict and security law. Essays in memory of Hilaire McCoubrey. Cambridge University Press, Cambridge, pp 32–48

Boot M (2002) Nullum crimen sine lege and the subject matter jurisdiction of the International Criminal Court: genocide, crimes against humanity, war crimes. Intersentia, Antwerp

Delmas-Marty M, Spencer JR (eds) (2002) European criminal procedures. Cambridge University Press, Cambridge

Desportes F, Le Gunehec F (2000) Le nouveau droit pénal. Tome 1, Droit pénal général. Enseignement et pratique, 7 edn. Economica, Paris

Desportes F, Le Gunehec F (2007) Droit pénal général, 14th edn. Economica, Paris

Duff RA (2002) Rule-violations and wrongdoings. In: Shute S, Simester AP (eds) Criminal law theory: doctrines of the general part. Oxford University Press, Oxford, pp 47–74

Elliott C (2000) The French law of intent and its influence on the development of international criminal law. Crim L Forum 11:35–46

Enschedé CJ (2008) Beginselen van Strafrecht. Kluwer, Deventer

Ferdinandusse WN (2006) Direct application of international criminal law in national courts. T.M.C. Asser Press, The Hague

Fletcher GP (1978) Rethinking criminal law, Oxford University Press, Oxford (reprinted in 2000)

Fletcher GP (1998) Basic concepts of criminal law. Oxford University Press, New York

Fletcher GP (2007) The grammar of criminal law. American, comparative, and international, volume one: Foundations, vol 1. Oxford University Press, New York

Fletcher GP, Sheppard S (2005) American law in a global context, the basics. Oxford University Press, Oxford

Frowein JA (1990) Im Zweifel für den vielleicht tödlichen Schuß? In: Festschrift für Peter Schneider zum 70. Geburtstag. E. Denninger, pp 112–121

Grace BR (1986) Ignorance of the law as an excuse. Columbia L Rev 86:1392–1411

Green LC (2003) Fifteenth Waldemar A. Solf lecture in international law, superior orders and command responsibility. Mil L Rev 175:309–384

Hullu J de (2006) Materieel Strafrecht. Kluwer, Deventer

Husak D, Hirsch A van (1993) Culpability and mistake of law. In: Shute S, Gardner J, Horder J (eds) Action and value in criminal law. Clarendon Press, Oxford, pp 157–174

Jefferson M (2003) Criminal law, 6th edn. Longman, Harlow

Jescheck HH (2004) The general principles of international criminal law set out in Nuremberg, as mirrored in the ICC statute. J Int Crim Justice 2(1):38–55

Jescheck HH, Weigend T (1996) Lehrbuch des Strafrechts, Allgemeiner Teil. Duncker & Humblot GmbH, Berlin

Kahan DM (1997) Ignorance of the law is an excuse—but only for the virtuous. Mich L Rev 96:127–154

Kelk C (2005) Studieboek Materieel Strafrecht, 3rd edn. Kluwer, Deventer

Lensing JAW (1996) Amerikaans Strafrecht. Een vergelijkende inleiding. Gouda Quint, Arnhem

Lippman MR (2001) Humanitarian law: the development and scope of the superior orders defense. Penn State Int Law Rev 20:153–251

Loewy AH (2000) Criminal law in a nutshell, 3rd edn. West Group, St. Paul

May R (1999) Criminal evidence, 4th edn. Sweet & Maxwell, London

Mitchell S (ed) (1979) Archbold, pleading, evidence and practice in criminal cases, 40th edn. Sweet & Maxwell, London

Nill-Theobald C (1998) "Defences" bei Kriegsverbrechen am Beispiel Deutschlands und der USA: zugleich ein Beitrag zu einem Allgemeinen Teil des Völkerstrafrechts, vol Band S 72. Beiträge und Materialien aus dem Max-Planck-Institut für ausländisches und internationales Strafrecht, Freiburg i.Br., iuscrim edn. Max-Planck-Institut für ausländisches und internationales Strafrecht, Freiburg im Breisgau

Ormerod DC (2008) Smith and Hogan criminal law, 12th edn. Oxford University Press, Oxford
Pradel J (2006) Manuel de droit pénal général. Cujas, Paris
Robinson PH (1984) Criminal law defenses, vol 2. West Publishing Co., St. Paul
Robinson PH, Grall JA (1982–1983) Element analysis in defining criminal liability: the model penal code and beyond. Stanf L Rev 35:681–762
Roxin C (1994) Strafrecht Allgemeiner teil, Band I, Grundlagen, der Aufbau der Verbrechenslehre. C.H. Beck'sche Verlagsbuchhandlung, München
Roxin C (2006) Strafrecht Allgemeiner teil, Band I, Grundlagen, der Aufbau der Verbrechenslehre, 4th edn. C.H. Beck, Munchen
Scaliotti M (2002) Defences before the international criminal court: substantive grounds for excluding criminal responsibility—part 2. Int Crim L Rev 2:1–46
Sliedregt E van (2003) The criminal responsibility of individuals for violations of international humanitarian law. T.M.C. Asser Press, The Hague
Smith ATH (1985) Error and mistake of law in anglo-American criminal law. Anglo-Am L Rev 14:3–32
Solis GD (1999) Obedience of orders and the law of war: judicial application in American forums. Am Univ Int L Rev 15:481–525
Stolwijk SAM (2009) Een inleding in het strafrecht in 13 hoofdstukken, 3rd edn. Kluwer, Deventer
Travers ML (1995) Mistake of law in mala prohibita crimes. Univ Chic L Rev 62:1301–1331
Vogeley S (2003) The mistake of law defense in international criminal law. In: Yee S (ed) International crime and punishment. University Press of America, Inc., Oxford, pp 59–99
Walther S (1995) Problems in blaming and punishing individuals for human rights violations: the example of the Berlin wall shootings. In: Roht-Arriaza N (ed) Impunity and human rights in international law and practice. Oxford University Press, New York, pp 99–112

Miscellaneous

The American Series of Foreign Penal Codes, France (1999). The American series of foreign penal codes, vol 31. France
International Committee of the Red Cross (1999) Paper relating to the mental element in the common law and civil law systems and to the concepts of mistake of fact and mistake of law in national and international law. Preparatory commission for the international criminal court, working group on elements of crimes, PCNICC/1999/WGEC/INF/2/Add.4, New York
The Manual of the Law of Armed Conflict (2004) UK Ministry of Defence, Oxford University Press, Oxford
Manual of Service Law (2011) vol I, 31 January 2011 edn. http://www.mod.uk/DefenceInternet/AboutDefence/CorporatePublications/LegalPublications/ManualOfServiceLaw/

Table of Cases

International Case Law

European Court of Human Rights

Case of K.-H. W. v. Germany (Application no. 37201/97) (2001) ECtHR, 22 March 2001

National Case Law

United States

Bryan v. U.S. (1998) Supreme Court of the United States, 524 U.S. 184, 118 S.Ct. 1939
Cheek v. U.S. (1991) Supreme Court of the United States, 498 U.S. 192, 111 S.Ct. 604
Lambert v. People of the State of California (1957) Supreme Court of the United States, 355 U.S. 225, 78 S.Ct. 240
Liparota v. U.S. (1985) Supreme Court of the United States, 471 U.S. 419, 105 S.Ct. 2084
Long v. State (1949) Supreme Court of Delaware, 5 Terry 262, 65 A.2d 489
People v Weiss (1938) New York Court of Appeals, 276 NY 384, 12 NE2d 514, 114 ALR865
Ratzlaf v. U.S. (1994) Supreme Court of the United States, 510 U.S. 135, 114 S.Ct. 655
Reyes v. United States (1958) United States Court of Appeals, Ninth Circuit, 258 F.2d 774
U.S. v. Curran (1994) United States Court of Appeals, Third Circuit, 20 F.3d 560
U.S. v. International Minerals and Chemical Corp. (1971) Supreme Court of the United States, 402 U.S. 558, 91 S.Ct. 1697
U.S. v. Obiechie (1994) United States Court of Appeals, Seventh Circuit, 38 F.3d 309
U.S. v. Rogers (1994) United States Court of Appeals, Fourth Circuit, 18 F.3d 265

United Kingdom

Regina v. Morgan (1975) 2 W.L.R. 923

Germany

BGHSt 35, 379 (1988)
Bundesgerichtshof, 18-03-1952 (1952) GSSt 2/51 (Lexetius.com/1952,1)
BVerfGE 95, 96, 24 October 1996 (1996) 2 BvR 1851, 1853, 1875 und 1952/94
BVerfGE 95, 96, 24 October 1996 (1997) 18 Human Rights L J (1997) No 1–4, pp 65–78
Mauerschützen I (1992) BGHSt 39, 1, BGH 5 StR 370/92, 3 November 1992
Mauerschützen II (1993) BGHSt 39, 168, BGH 5 StR 418/92, 25 March 1993
Mauerschützen III (1995) BGHSt 41, 101, BGH 5 StR 111/94, 20 March 1995

Chapter 3
Comparing the National Approaches: Theorising About the Issue

3.1 Introduction: Twofold and Threefold Structures

Chapter 2 showed two ways to conceptualise criminal offences. The Anglo-American systems and France use a twofold structure; the civil law system of Germany developed a threefold structure.[1] The twofold system to analyse the internal structure of criminal offences distinguishes between the *actus reus* and the *mens rea* of offences,[2] the objective factual side and the inner or subjective side.[3] The threefold scheme of analysis consists of the following requirements: a criminal act must fulfil the elements of a crime definition, it must be wrongful (absence of justification) and the actor must be culpable (absence of excuse).[4] Under a twofold system the issue of mistake of law is dealt with in terms of the required mental element. The threefold system has separated the issue of mistake of law from the mental element by requiring *Unrechtsbewußtsein* as a necessary element of culpability.

The system of offences to be applied has consequences, procedural and doctrinal, some of which we also already encountered in Chap. 2. The current chapter further analyses the differences between these two approaches and, more importantly, the consequences of those differences. This requires more in-depth discussion of the distinction between *justification* and *excuse, wrongdoing* and *attribution*, *defeasible* and *comprehensive rules*, *conduct rules* and *decision rules*. Other issues under discussion, which also bring to light important consequences of applying one system instead of the other, are: (1) *criminal intent*, (2) *putative justifications*, (3) the meaning of an element of *unlawfulness* or *wrongfulness* in the crime definition and (4) the *principle of legality*.

---

1 Ambos 2006, pp. 664–665. Fletcher uses the terms bipartite and tripartite systems, *see e.g.* Fletcher 2007, pp. 43–55.

2 Fletcher 2007, pp. 42–46.

3 Ambos 2004, p. 759.

4 Fletcher 2007, pp. 49–55.

A. van Verseveld, *Mistake of Law*, DOI: 10.1007/978-90-6704-867-5_3,

3.2 Relevant Distinctions

3.2.1 Justification and Excuse

As discussed in Chap. 2, most civil law systems, based on the Germanic tradition, distinguish between justification and excuse, a distinction long ignored in most common law systems.[5] The distinction is part of the threefold assessment of criminal responsibility. The first question is whether the proven facts fall within the definition of the alleged criminal offence. The second question is whether this behaviour, falling within the crime definition, is also wrongful. This question investigates the applicability of a justification. The third question is whether the defendant is culpable, in other words whether the defendant is blameworthy for committing the wrongful act.[6] The wrongfulness and culpability are presumed when all the elements of the crime definition are fulfilled. This presumption is however rebuttable, on the basis of a claim of justification or excuse respectively.[7]

In most common law systems, where justifications and excuses fall under the common denominator of 'defences', any successful plea of such a defence must lead to the conclusion that no unlawful act has been committed.[8] Fletcher calls this "flat legal reasoning". "All elements are of equal significance. If any element, be it affirmative or negative, is absent, the defendant is not guilty."[9] And here the first important consequence of the distinction between justification and excuse becomes evident. A justification will indeed negate the wrongdoing, but "the question of excusing [only] arises after it is established that the norm is violated".[10] I agree with Fletcher when he argues that "the distinction between justification and excuse is of fundamental theoretical and practical value".[11] The theoretical value lies in the fact that recognising excuses, as distinct from justifications, acknowledges the fundamental principle of criminal law *nulla poena sine culpa*, no punishment without guilt.[12] Another related theoretical and, at the same time, practical value is that the distinction allows for a judgment more closely reflecting reality.[13] In the case of an exculpatory excuse you do not reach the (in the eyes of the victim or general public sometimes painful) conclusion that no wrongful act has been committed, instead it is determined that the defendant is not to blame for his

5 Fletcher 1998, p. 93.

6 *See also* Fletcher 1998, pp. 101–102.

7 *See* Sect. 2.3.2.5 *supra*.

8 *See* Sect. 2.2 *supra*.

9 Fletcher 1985, p. 962.

10 Fletcher 1978, p. 735.

11 Fletcher 1985, p. 955.

12 *See also* Ambos 2006, p. 666. On the applicability of this principle in international criminal law, *see*, *e.g.*, Ibid., p. 671 (referring to the IMT, The Trial of Major War Criminals, vol. 22, p. 469).

13 *See also* Ambos 2007, p. 2660.

behaviour, however wrongful.[14] If an excuse is raised, but rejected, the judgement becomes more precise in its reproach towards the defendant.[15] Under a twofold system, that does not recognise the distinction between justification and excuse, any mistake of law will negate the required intent. If the mistake was avoidable or unreasonable, the defendant can only be convicted for committing the crime negligently, but only if the criminal code provides for such a crime of negligence.[16] Under the threefold structure, however, an avoidable mistake of law does not impede the finding of intent; the defendant can be convicted on the basis of intent. When the court finds that the defendant acted with the necessary intent and the defendant raises the issue of mistake of law, which the court decides was avoidable, the conviction and the reproach towards the defendant is based on the fact that he intentionally committed the prohibited act, while he could have behaved differently.

Perhaps the reluctance in twofold systems to accept mistake of law as a defence also stems from the consequences just described. Accepting a defence, justification or excuse, leads to the conclusion that no criminal act took place. In that case, the (mistaken) impression could rise that the individual's interpretation of the law is decisive; i.e. that the defendant decides what is the law. If he, however unreasonably, believes the act to be lawful, his intent is negated and he has committed no wrongful act.

The importance of the distinction between justification and excuse becomes evident from criticism of the judgement of the Appeals Chamber of the ICTY in *Erdemović*.[17] It has convincingly been argued that had the majority recognised the defence of duress as an excuse, there would have been no issue on the legitimacy of duress as a complete defence in principle, even in case of the killing of innocents.[18] The distinction between justification and excuse turns out to be of overriding importance in assessing the responsibility of a person who under duress killed innocent persons. The distinction enables the maintenance of the position that killing innocents can never be justified, and at the same time acknowledges that under certain circumstances the perpetrator cannot be blamed for his wrongful conduct. It is, under any circumstance, unreasonable to ask of someone to sacrifice his own life. Cassese, in his dissenting opinion in Erdemović, argued that an argument for exculpation can also be based on the fact that, had the defendant refused to shoot the victims, they would surely have been killed by someone else.[19] As Van der Wilt states: "Here the human instinct of self-preservation

[14] *See also* Fletcher 1998, p. 90.

[15] See Sect. 2.3.2.2 (discussing Bundesgerichtshof, 18-03-1952 1952) and Sect. 2.3.2.5 *supra*.

[16] See for a comparable argument Heller 2008, p. 444.

[17] Prosecutor v. Erdemović 1997b.

[18] *See* Fletcher 2007, pp. 90–91; Ambos 2002b, pp. 1044–1047; Sliedregt 2003, pp. 273–274 and 290; and Fletcher and Ohlin 2008, p. 123.

[19] Prosecutor v. Erdemović 1997a, at §§ 44 and 50.

merged with the rational calculation that the sacrifice of one's own life would be senseless anyway."[20]

Dinstein, agreeing with the abolition of the defence in a case of the killing of innocents in English law, argues that duress cannot even be an excuse in these cases, because one person's life cannot be valued more than another person's life.[21] It seems that this reasoning does not account for the rationale of the defence, more specifically, of the excuse of duress. Indeed, a justification entails a balancing of interests; and this balancing of interests can never be applied so as to evaluate whose life is more valuable. One rather than another, let alone a group of other persons. It could even be argued, as Ambos has, that "the commission of the atrocious crimes 'within the jurisdiction of the Court' can never be justified on the basis of a balancing of interests".[22] However, the rationale of excuses is not one of balancing interests. Using excuses the system expresses "compassion for and understanding of the actor's human weakness".[23] The rationale of excuses is that the law cannot expect heroism; it cannot fairly be expected of the defendant to withstand a threat that would be "irresistible for a reasonable person in similar circumstances".[24] The issue, in case of an excuse, is "that the individual culpability or blameworthiness, in the sense of a normative understanding of guilt, is lacking".[25]

Cryer notes that the ICC Statute provides for duress as a complete defence, which also applies to offences that involve the killing of innocents.[26] However, Ambos discusses how Article 31(1)(d) is a mixture of necessity as a justification and duress as an excuse.[27] He distinguishes the separate components which indicate that the defence provided for is a justification (the objective elements) or an excuse (the subjective elements).[28] Van Sliedregt describes that same mixture but seems to favour a reading of Article 31(1)(d) to cover the excuse of duress.[29]

It could be argued that because of this conflation neither defence has in fact been provided for in the Statute. The conflation is particularly illogical because the defences differ in rationale,[30] being equal to the different rationale of justification and excuse. The provision requires the act to have been justified and the defendant to be excused. In a threefold structure this is illogical: if the act is justified, the issue of culpability becomes irrelevant.

---

[20] Wilt 1999, p. 656.

[21] Dinstein 2000, pp. 375–376.

[22] Ambos 2002b, p. 1046. *See also* Ambos 2004, p. 869.

[23] Ambos 2002b, p. 1046; *See also* Eser 2008, footnote 162, p. 888.

[24] Eser 2008, footnote 162, at p. 888. *See also*, Ambos 2004, p. 842.

[25] Ambos 2008b, p. 183; Ambos 2004, pp. 842–843.

[26] Cryer 2005, p. 58.

[27] Ambos 2002b, p. 1036; and Ambos 2008b, pp. 181–184. *See also* Eser 2008, pp. 883–884.

[28] Ambos 2008b, pp. 181–184; Ambos 2004, p. 838.

[29] Sliedregt 2003, pp. 267–291.

[30] *See also* Ambos 2008b, pp. 182–183; and Fletcher and Ohlin 2008, pp. 122–123.

The distinction between justification and excuse in a threefold system has advantages. The issue of intent as defined by the crime definition is treated separately from the issues of justification and excuse. This prevents the blurring of the different protected interests and rationales of the separate elements of the offence. It is a well-thought-out doctrinal distinction—it lays out a map for interpreting different defences; the rationale of either justification or excuse determines the conditions for each defence.[31]

Many of the following distinctions (between wrongdoing and attribution, between defeasible and comprehensive rules, between conduct and decision rules) can be compared to the distinction between justification and excuse, which is therefore perhaps usefully called the 'basic distinction'.

3.2.2 Wrongdoing and Attribution

Another way to describe the basic distinction is to refer to the distinction which the threefold system makes between wrongdoing and attribution.[32] The elements of the crime definition and justifications concern issues of wrongdoing. They determine the wrongfulness of the act. A separate issue is the attribution of this wrongful act to the particular defendant. Excuses determine the capacity of the defendant to have attributed to him the wrongful act. Attribution is about the individual culpability of the defendant, about his blameworthiness. Excuses concern mental states which negate the defendant's individual culpability; they remove the possibility of blaming the defendant for his wrongful act. One should clearly distinguish between this subjective element of criminal responsibility and the mental state required by every crime definition. In a threefold structure, excuses do not negate this mental element in the crime definition.[33] The fact that someone acts under duress, or under a mistake of law, does not exclude a finding that the defendant acted intentionally.

The distinction is also relevant to the assessment of the liability of accomplices; the determination of the wrongfulness of the act applies to all participants; excuses only exculpate the individual defendant that has successfully invoked it.

---

[31] Ambos repeatedly stresses the importance of the distinction, see e.g. Ambos 2008c, p. 272 e.v.; Ambos 2004, pp. 826–829, 868; Ambos 2008b, p. 172, § 82 with further references.

[32] *See also* Fletcher 1978, p. 577. 'wrongdoing' refers to the crime definition and absence of justifications. As we will see below, in order to comprehend the issue of putative justification, it is also important to distinguish between these two concepts (crime definition and justifications).

[33] If this mental element is 'intent'; excuses (and justifications) do negate the mental element of 'negligence'. As indicated before (Sects. 1.5, 2.2.2., footnote 29 and Sect. 3.3.1 *supra*), here, only the theory in relation to crimes of intent will be discussed, since international crimes are generally crimes of intent. *See e.g.* Ambos 2002b, p. 1031 footnote 156 and accompanying text and Ambos 2004, pp. 807–808 and 816.

3.2.3 Defeasible and Comprehensive Rules

Fletcher distinguishes between defeasible and comprehensive rules of criminal liability.[34] Defeasible rules are rules of confession and avoidance. The issue of *mens rea* and *actus reus* is separated from the issue of defences. Defences are separate arguments the defendant brings forward to "circumvent the implications" of his criminal act.[35] Comprehensive rules on the other hand, do not use the concept of defences. Under comprehensive rules of liability an actor is only liable if he fulfilled the crime definition with the required *mens rea*, there are no justifications for his behaviour and he cannot be excused.[36]

Fletcher describes how the general trend in both common law and civil law systems has been from defeasible to comprehensive rules of liability.[37] He explains this trend by referring to "an increasing appreciation of an obvious postulate: The criminal law should punish only the guilty", "those who could fairly be morally blamed for wrongdoing".[38] This concept of guilt refers to more than only the descriptive *mens rea* or mental element required by the definition of the offence (i.e. intention or knowledge). "For this new view of the criminal law to take hold, the notion of "guilt" had to become synonymous with the broader moral meaning of "culpability" or "blameworthiness" for wrongdoing."[39] As discussed in the previous chapter, however, in the common law systems and in France, the transition is far from complete. These systems are still based on a twofold structure distinguishing between *actus reus* and *mens rea* on the one hand and defences on the other. The fact that these systems sometimes put the burden of proof concerning issues of excuses on the defendant confirms the suspicion that the transition to a comprehensive system is far from complete. In systems that are based on comprehensive rules, excuses are part of the rule establishing the culpability of the defendant, which means that they fall within the presumption of innocence. This implies that all doubts concerning issues of guilt must be resolved in favour of the defendant.

3.2.4 Conduct Rules and Decision Rules

The final theoretical distinction that bears discussion in relation to the basic distinction is the one between conduct rules and decision rules.[40] Crime definitions,

[34] Fletcher 1998, p. 96.

[35] Fletcher 1998, p. 97.

[36] Fletcher 1998, p. 97.

[37] As Van der Wilt pointed out to me, however, this trend took place on different grounds: in Germany the trend was based on the development of a principle of individual culpability (see Chap. 2) and the US the basis can be found in the principle of presumption of innocence.

[38] Fletcher 1998, p. 99. See also Husak and Hirsch 1993, p. 159.

[39] Fletcher 1998, p. 99.

[40] *See* Dan-Cohen 1984.

justifications and excuses are decision rules; they are the tools for judges and juries to decide a criminal case. The norms underlying the crime definition and justifications are conduct rules. They dictate how to act under certain circumstances. If the factual circumstances are of a specific nature, the same conduct rules apply to everyone. The crime definition refers to conduct that is prohibited. Justifications form general exceptions to these prohibitions. For example, everyone who is under unlawful attack by another person may defend himself and, even under certain circumstances, take the attacker's life, although the basic rule is that taking another person's life is prohibited. These rules are conduct rules, which means that the actor is required to shape his conduct accordingly. This requires that the actor is aware of the relevant circumstances. If the defendant failed to act according to the conduct rules, a judicial authority may decide nevertheless that the defendant should not be held accountable. According to decisions rules, the judges or jurors decide on the culpability, the blameworthiness, of the defendant.[41] The defendant is not required to have an opinion about these issues; the normative assessment of his behaviour is especially assigned to the judicial authority. Moreover, if a defendant is conscious of the presence of an excuse, for example the defendant knows that he is making a mistake of law, this knowledge is logically inconsistent with the excuse.[42] The defendant can no longer properly claim the excuse, because it is exactly a lack of awareness in this respect that prevents the actor from behaving differently. The excuse of mistake of law particularly encompasses the situation where the actor, *because of* lack of consciousness in this respect is prevented from behaving differently. Or, to put it differently, the rationale of excuses is different. Conduct rules (the underlying norms of the crime definition and justifications) require the defendant to balance interests and will lead him to the right conduct. Excuses (which are decision rules) are meant as a tool for the judicial authority to prevent blameless persons, who nevertheless did not follow the conduct rules, from being held accountable. It is the compelling nature of excuses that makes the commission of the wrongful act excusable. It is not the fact that you made a mistake as to the applicability of an excuse to your situation that will excuse you; such mistakes are irrelevant.[43] A mistake as to the existence of the threat, however, may indeed exculpate. This will be a mistake of fact, extrinsic to the required intent.

Understanding mistake of law and its function as an excuse, and thus understanding the improbability of a mistake of law negating the mental element,

[41] *See also* Fletcher 1978, pp. 491–492.

[42] As seen earlier, however, according to Roxin the fact that someone has doubts about the lawfulness of his intended acts does not mean that he is per se precluded from invoking mistake of law (*see* Sect. 2.3.2.3., 1 *supra*). The point made here is that the defendant will not be excused if he thought to himself: I can commit the act because I will be excused because I made a mistake of law. Justifications on the other hand indeed require awareness of the justifying circumstances.

[43] *See also* Ambos 2004, pp. 820–821 (holding that in this respect (excluding mistake of law as to the applicability of an excuse) article 32(2) first sentence corresponds to national approaches).

requires that one distinguishes between conduct rules and decision rules and between wrongdoing and culpability. The definition of offences generally do not require a criminal intent, knowledge of unlawfulness is no definitional requirement. As Fletcher holds, "[n]orms are designed to guide and influence conduct. The norm itself cannot include a condition about what should happen in the event that the norm was violated involuntarily or by mistake. [...] The norm only includes those elements about which the actor should make a decision in seeking to conform his conduct to the law."[44]

3.2.5 Analysis

To conclude, what is the relevance of the above discussed distinctions? First of all, it shows that a criminal act consists of different elements, both an act requirement and a culpability requirement. The act requirement includes a mental element in relation to the material elements. A defendant can however fulfil the act requirement without being culpable, because issues of culpability do not negate the wrongfulness of the act.[45] Moreover, the issue of excuses only arises after it has been established that a norm has been violated.[46]

Second, justifications contain conduct rules. They require awareness of the underlying norm. Crime definitions and justifications have underlying norms; the norm underlying a crime definition contains a prohibition, the violation of which may be justified by the norm underlying a justification. Like crime definitions, the underlying norms of justifications have an objective and a subjective side. The norms underlying justifications, including their objective and subjective side, are different from the norms underlying crime definitions. Some common law sources seem to overlook this distinction.[47]

Third, the distinction between the crime definition on the one hand and justifications and excuses on the other is relevant for the burden of proof. All elements of the crime definition require proof. Elements of justification and excuse need to be brought forward and substantiated by the defendant, the absence of which again requires proof beyond reasonable doubt.[48]

Finally, the distinction between justification and excuse is relevant to the determination of the individual responsibility of participants in the crime. Justifications negate the wrongfulness of the conduct; none of the perpetrators or participants is responsible, since there is no wrongful act. Excuses on the other

[44] Fletcher 1978, p. 734.

[45] Fletcher 1978, p. 734.

[46] Fletcher 1978, p. 735.

[47] See e.g. Robinson 1984, §184(a), p. 398 en §184(e), p. 412 (the (subjective) requirements of justification are linked to the subjective requirements of the crime definition).

[48] See e.g. May 1999, p. 53; and Fletcher 1998, pp. 94–97+108.

hand are personal; if one perpetrator is excused, his excuse does not negate the culpability of the other participants.

3.3 Other Issues

3.3.1 Criminal Intent

If a mistake of law is related to the required mental element, then 'intent' is always negated by the mistake and 'negligence' is only negated if the mistake was reasonable or unavoidable. So, if the perpetrator cannot be convicted for having acted intentionally because he made an unreasonable mistake, he can still be convicted for the negligent version of the crime. That is, if there is such a negligent variant of the crime.[49] In international criminal law, as Article 30 of the ICC Statute provides, the default mental element is that of intent and knowledge. There are generally no international crimes of negligence, with the exception of command responsibility under Article 28 of the ICC Statute.[50] One of the theoretical issues to be studied in the next chapter and in Chap. 6 is whether the mental element required for international crimes includes a criminal intent.

The comparative law study contained in Chap. 2 indicates that in domestic law systems criminal intent is generally not required.[51] An intent to break the law is not an element of wrongdoing. If it were, in every case proof of such an intent would be required, and all mistakes would bar a finding of wrongdoing. Moreover, the (unreasonable) belief of the individual perpetrator would determine the wrongfulness of the act which may lead to an unacceptable reduction of the protection of the legally protected interest. It is therefore only in very exceptional situations that the legislature provides for such a criminal intent requirement.[52] Since these are exceptional provisions, in a system that only grants exculpatory effect to a mistake of law that negates the required intent, the scope of this defence is therefore limited to the minimum. The twofold systems are bound to such a negate-mental-element-requirement, because they lack the theoretical advantages of a threefold system that is based on *Unrechtsbewußtsein* as a requirement for criminal responsibility outside the required mental element. This is one of the distinctive features of the threefold system that proves its benefits over the twofold approach. The *Unrechtsbewußtsein* as a separate requirement of culpability in fact confirms or even justifies the general rule that no criminal intent needs to be

49 *See e.g.* Fletcher 1998, p. 160.

50 *See also* Ambos 2002b, p. 1031 and Fletcher 2007, p. 108.

51 For the lack of such a requirement in Anglo-American law see also Sliedregt 2003, p. 232 (she calls this neutral intention and refers to §2.02(9) MPC).

52 The ICC Statute arguably only provides in one provision for a criminal intent requirement, *see* Sect. 6.2.1.2.1 *infra*.

proven.[53] An avoidable mistake about the wrongfulness of the intentionally committed act will not relieve the actor of liability; proof of criminal intent would be superfluous. One could also say that recognising unavoidable mistake of law as an excuse is not at variance with the general rule that no criminal intent is required. The issue of criminal conduct, of wrongdoing, is separated from the issue of the culpability of the defendant and this allows for a more precise reproach: if the crime is one of intent, the reproach towards the defendant is that he intentionally committed the prohibited act. The issue of his blameworthiness does not negate this finding of wrongdoing. It contains a separate reproach, namely that he acted in a culpable way when he could have behaved differently.

3.3.2 Putative Justifications

Ambos also demonstrates the relevance of the distinction between wrongfulness and culpability by discussing the situation where the defendant made a mistake about the factual elements of a justification, a situation of so-called 'putative justification'.[54] An example of putative justification is when the defendant seriously injures someone in the mistaken belief that he acts in self-defence against an unlawful attack. He thinks for example that the person is approaching him with a knife, but in fact this person is holding a harmless shiny object. As Ambos holds, the key to the right solution lies in the distinction between wrongfulness and culpability. The defendant's act cannot objectively be justified, because he was in fact not under attack. His act remains wrongful. His reasonable belief in the presence of a fact giving right to self-defence, however, excludes his culpability. Ambos suggests that because putative justification lies somewhere between real justification and real excuse, the most convincing solution is to treat putative justification as lack of intent.[55] All depends of course on your definition of intent. Ambos argues that a putatively justified actor, like an actor who lacks intent, lacks "the subjective element of wrongfulness (comprising both the existence of the elements of the offence and the lacking of all elements of the justification)".[56] As noted earlier, however, the subjective elements of wrongfulness consist of both the subjective element of the crime definition and the subjective element of the justification, and these elements may differ, at least as to their object. Triffterer

---

[53] *See also*, on the application of this rule in Dutch threefold system, Hullu 2006b, p. 345.

[54] Ambos 2007, pp. 2661–2664.

[55] Ambos 2007 p. 2662. *See also* Roxin 2006, p. 629, § 14 H (where he argues in favour of the *eingeschräkten Schuldtheorie*). *See also* a similar proposal by Robinson: Robinson 1984, §184(a), p. 398 and §184(e), p. 412.

[56] Ambos 2007, p. 2662. At another place Ambos describes how he favours this approach because under the ICC provisions (artt. 30 and 32) it is the only way to take account of putative justifications; this mistake of fact does not negate the required intent, as formulated by art. 30, but it is a relevant mistake nevertheless. Ambos 2004, pp. 809–810.

suggests, in relation to Article 32 ICC Statute, to treat a mistake of fact as to a ground for justification as if it were a mistake of fact, although this mistake does not negate the mental element required by the crime definition.[57]

This brings to light the relevant distinction, namely the distinction between mistakes that negate the required intent and mistakes that do not. Both putative justifications and mistakes of law generally do not negate the required intent. This means that, in order to exculpate the defendant, these mistakes (of fact and law) must have been reasonable. Mistakes of fact as to a ground of justification should not be treated as negating the required intent, because they do not negate the wrongdoing.[58] If it were otherwise, any mistake, reasonable or not, would negate the required intent; the (unreasonable) belief of the defendant would determine the wrongfulness of the act. This would lead to an insufficient protection of the legally protected interest.

Ambos' example of putative justification concerns a mistake about the factual elements of a justification. Whether such a mistake should be treated as a mistake negating the required intent is a disputed issue. There is, however, also a mistake of law version of putative justification, which was encountered in Chap. 2.[59] In such a case the defendant mistakenly assumes that a certain ground for justification exists in the legal order, where in fact this justification is not recognised, or the defendant is mistaken in the legal scope of an existing ground for justification.[60] For example, the defendant believes that retaliation is a recognised ground for justification or the defendant thinks he can use deadly force to protect property, while in fact the legal system allows the use of lethal force only in case of warding off an attack upon persons. This situation is different from the putative justification based on a mistake of fact. The latter, like the required intent, relates to elements of wrongdoing. As seen earlier, knowledge of unlawfulness is not an element of wrongdoing, but an element of culpability. Mistake of law as to a ground of justification does not negate the required intent.[61] Putative justification based on mistake of law, is an excuse par excellence.

3.3.3 An Element of 'Unlawfulness' in the Crime Definition

Some crime definitions contain an element of 'unlawfulness'. The definitions of several international crimes in the ICC Statute, for example, contain elements like

---

[57] Triffterer 2008, p. 901. This is also the German approach, see Roxin 2006, pp. 626–627, § 14, Rn 64.

[58] See on the German position to the contrary (i.e. that such a mistake of fact should be treated as a mistake of fact which negates the required intent) Roxin 2006, pp. 626–627, § 14, Rn 64.

[59] This is a so called 'indirect mistake of law' (*Grenzirrtum* or *Bestandsirrtum*), *see* Sect. 2.3.2.3, 2) *supra*.

[60] *See also* Roxin 2006, pp. 632–633, § 14, Rn 79–80.

[61] *See also* Roxin 2006, pp. 632–633, § 14, Rn 79–80.

'unlawful' or 'in violation of fundamental rules of international law'.[62] Does this mean that this element is part of the required intent?

The element of 'unlawfulness' in the crime definition can have different meanings. It is not necessarily the position that the fact that unlawfulness is part of the crime definition automatically means a particular mental state is required in relation to this element.[63] When the legislature has provided for a definitional element of unlawfulness it is meant to limit the scope of the prohibition.[64] In such cases the prohibited conduct may be very common and, usually, lawful. The unlawfulness of the act is the exception and is therefore mentioned in the crime definition.[65] As part of the crime definition, this element requires specific proof.

In some very exceptional cases the required intent covers this element of unlawfulness; here the norm is only, and specifically, violated if the perpetrator acted with the intent to violate the law. In all other cases, knowledge of violating the law is not part of the norm itself; it is irrelevant to the proof that the act was wrongful. The problem is how to establish whether the element of unlawfulness is covered by the required intent. One can search for the purpose of the legislator, or more generally for the rationale of the prohibition.[66] If unlawfulness is part of the crime definition this element is linked to the rationale, the *Typizität*, of the offence.[67] One solution to this problem appears in Chap. 2. Roxin demonstrated that the required intent will be negated when the social significance of a normative element cannot be understood without legal knowledge. When, however, the normative element is equal to, or constitutes, the wrongfulness of the act concerned, a mistake as to this element will not negate the required intent, but will constitute a mistake of law. If such a mistake would negate the required intent, this would lead to the undesired result that the (mistaken) belief of the defendant would determine the wrongfulness of the act.[68]

As noted earlier, criminal intent is generally not required. This means that the element of unlawfulness is almost always a so called 'objective' element. The element is objective to such an extent that it is detached from the mental element. No proof is required as to the mental state of the perpetrator in relation to this objective element. It is exactly with regard to these elements that the issue of culpability and mistake of law may arise.[69] Moreover, allowing the defence of mistake of law in respect of these objective elements only confirms the

---

[62] *See e.g.*: art. 8(2)(a)(vii) (unlawful deportation) and article 7(1)(e) (imprisonment in violation of fundamental rules of international law).

[63] The Dutch scholarly debate on this issue is illuminating; hence, the numerous references to Dutch authors in this paragraph.

[64] Veen 1972, p. 467.

[65] Koopmans 2007, pp. 90–91; Kelk 2005, p. 125.

[66] Kelk 2005, p. 199.

[67] Kelk 2005, pp. 129–130.

[68] Roxin 2006, p. 489, Rn. 105. *See also* Sect. 2.3.2.3 *supra*.

[69] *See also* Hullu 2006, pp. 209–210.

justifiability of the general rule that no criminal intent is required for the finding that a legal norm has been violated.[70]

3.3.4 The Principle of Legality

The principle of legality provides a real limitation on the scope of the mistake of law defence where crime definitions are concerned. A crime is only punishable if any reasonable person can foresee that the act will result in criminal responsibility, even if that means one has to consult a lawyer. On the other hand, a prohibition can be ascertainable, but if the circumstances do not permit even a superficial investigation, the defendant is perhaps not to be blamed for his mistake. This is even more apparent where justifications are concerned. Situations in which a justification arises are generally not situations that allow for (extensive) reflection. This is especially so in cases of international crimes, which are committed in situations of armed conflict and which are likely to seriously affect the opportunities for a participant to consult a competent lawyer.

In the prior discussion of the German Border Guard cases we encountered the 'problem' of the 'dual' use of manifest illegality; both in relation to the principle of legality and in relation to the principle of guilt the same terminology is used, namely the manifest unlawfulness of the act. The German Courts clearly distinguish between the two issues. If there is a violation of the principle of legality, for example criminal punishability was not provided for by law at the time, there is no crime and the question of individual culpability is irrelevant. If the act is punishable, however, the questions of wrongfulness and culpability are not therewith answered and issues of justification and excuse may become relevant. If mistake of law is a relevant excuse then foreseeability under the principle of legality cannot have the same meaning as foreseeability (or avoidability) under the defence of mistake of law. As Roxin noted, avoidability of a mistake of law cannot mean absolute avoidability, because the principle of legality already prevents acts from being punishable that are not, in an absolute sense, foreseeably so.[71] The distinction between the two concepts of foreseeability, under the principle of legality and under mistake of law, is that the first concept encompasses an objective test, i.e. what the individual defendant subjectively thought or knew is irrelevant, and the second concept requires a more normative assessment. Accepting foreseeability under the first principle does not automatically imply that the unlawful nature of the act was foreseen by an individual defendant. This requires a subjective assessment, which is, on the final issue of guilt, than again made objective,

[70] *See also* Hullu 2006, p. 375. *But see* Heller 2008 (who does not regard legal elements as objective). For a discussion of his arguments see Sects. 4.2.2 and 6.2 *infra.*

[71] Roxin 2006, p. 945 Rn. 38, *see also* Sect. 2.3.2.3., 3) *supra.*

in the sense that the actual absence of *Unrechtsbewußtsein* must have been unavoidable or reasonable in order to exculpate the defendant.

The ECtHR also assessed whether the conviction of the German Border Guard was in conformity with the principle of guilt. In fact the Court did so while assessing whether there had been a violation of Article 7 ECHR, which concerns the principle of legality.[72] As Arnold et al. noted, thus far the assessment under this heading had always been one of objective foreseeability.[73] In this case, however, the Court discussed how the principle of guilt requires that the defendant could subjectively have foreseen criminal liability. Like the German Courts, it answered this question in the affirmative. Arnold et al., welcomed this incorporation of the principle of guilt into Article 7.[74] It is true that the Court in this way acknowledged the exculpating effect of lack of *Unrechtsbewußtsein*, which is more than can be said of the international regulation of this defence.[75] But there are strong arguments to justify keeping the two notions of foreseeability separated. The conflation creates confusion. What *is* unlawful seems to be dependent on the personal circumstances and personal capacities of the defendant; it may appear as if the law is not the same for everyone. This confusion is exactly what may cause 'fear' for the defence of mistake of law. This fear is completely unjustified precisely because mistake of law is an excuse, i.e. a personal ground for exculpation. It does not negate the abstracted wrongful nature of the act itself.

Under *Foreseeability of the conviction*, the ECtHR covers both the principle of legality and the individual guilt of the defendant. In defence of the prosecution of the border guard, the Court reiterates the rule of law argument made by the BVerfG; indeed a 'rule of law' state cannot leave these crimes unpunished. This is a strong argument in favour of prosecution but it does not say anything about foreseeability, however, let alone about the subjective foreseeability in the individual case of, for example, the border guard. In fact, the separation of the two principles, of legality and guilt, allows those in a state observing the rule of law to express general indignation about the cruel border policy of a totalitarian state or of a former regime; and further to do justice to the understandable expectations or mistakes of an individual who lived and worked in a state not governed by the rule of law.

3.4 Conclusion

Under a twofold system, defences deny the wrongfulness of the act. Thus, also excuses negate the wrongfulness of the act even though in fact they are not concerned with the wrongfulness but with the culpability of the defendant, i.e. the

72 Case of K.-H. W. v. Germany 2001, § 46.

73 Arnold et al. 2003, p. 85.

74 Arnold et al. 2003, p. 87.

75 Arnold et al. 2003, pp. 86–87.

attribution of the wrongful conduct to the defendant. Under a threefold system, mistake of law does not negate the wrongfulness of the act. All elements pertaining to the culpability of the defendant concern blameworthiness; the issue is, whether the mistaken actor can be excused for having made the mistake. Under a threefold system only unavoidable mistakes are not blameworthy. Under a twofold system, admitting a mistake of law would almost appear to let the (mistaken) defendant determine the law. This 'problem of appearances' does not arise under the threefold system that distinguishes between justification and excuse, between wrongdoing and attribution.

Mistake of law is almost by definition an excuse, expressly because criminal intent is not required. Criminal intent is not required because it would be impossible to specifically prove that the defendant intended to break the law, and proof of legal knowledge can never be a requirement, because then only lawyers, or those proved to have a specific knowledge of the relevant law, can commit crimes. But the most convincing argument as to why criminal intent is not required is that, if it were, a mistake of law, even an unreasonable one, would negate the wrongfulness of the conduct.

That criminal intent is not required does not imply that mistakes of law are irrelevant per se. As we saw in Chap. 2, the German threefold structure adopts a presumption of *Unrechtsbewußtsein* when the defendant has fulfilled the elements of a crime definition. This presumption is rebuttable. If the defendant acted under mistake of law, meaning that he lacked awareness of the wrongfulness of his conduct, and his mistake was unavoidable, he is not culpable.

The distinction between decision rules and conduct rules turns out to be helpful in defining mistake of law. The statutory prohibition, or the crime definition, is a decision rule; it guides the judges or jurors on how to value the defendant's conduct. The conduct rule is the underlying substantive norm of the prohibition or of justificatory norms. Mistake of law is ignorance of, or a mistake as to, the underlying substantive norm.

Mistake of law is an excuse. The relevant question in case of a mistaken defendant is whether or not he could have avoided the mistake, because then he could have avoided committing the wrongful act. As Fletcher says it: "If we leave aside the issue of intention, the primary normative question in assessing accountability is whether the actor could fairly have been expected to avoid committing the wrongful act. This single recurrent question unites the issues of ignorance as to excessive risk-taking, duress, insanity and mistake of law."[76]

The advantageous implications of the threefold system have been discussed. The distinctions applied in this system justify the general rule that no criminal intent is required and allow for a more precise determination of the perpetrator's culpability and thus of the reproach that befalls him. Fletcher has noted how the threefold mode of analysis is gaining growing support among North American lawyers and this

[76] Fletcher 1978, p. 496.

"system is not a German doctrine, any more than Einstein's theory of relativity represents a German (or Swiss or American) science of physics".[77]

References

Ambos K (2002) Other grounds for excluding criminal responsibility. In: Cassese A, Gaeta P, Jones JRWD (eds) The Rome Statute of the International Criminal Court: a commentary, vol I. Oxford University Press, New York, pp 1003–1048

Ambos K (2004) Der allgemeine teil des Völkerstrafrechts. Ansätze einer Dogmatisierung, 2nd edn. Duncker & Humblot, Berlin

Ambos K (2006) Remarks on the general part of international criminal law. J Int Crim Justice 4:660–673

Ambos K (2007) Towards a universal system of crime: comments on George Fletcher's *grammar of criminal law*. Cardozo Law Rev 28(6):2647–2673

Ambos K (2008a) Internationales Strafrecht, 2nd edn. C.H. Beck, München

Ambos K (2008b) May the state torture suspects to save the life of innocents? J Int Crim Justice (6):261–287

Arnold J, Karsten N, Kreicker H (2003) The German border guard cases before the European Court of Human Rights. Eur J Crime Crim Law Crim Justice 11(1):67–92

Cryer R (2005) Superior orders and the International Criminal Court. In: Burchill R, White ND, Morris J (eds) International conflict and security law essays in memory of Hilaire McCoubrey. Cambridge University Press, Cambridge, pp 49–67

Dan-Cohen M (1984) Decision rules and conduct rules: on acoustic separation in criminal law. Harv Law Rev 97(3):625–677

Dinstein Y (2000) Defences. In: McDonald GK, Swaak-Goldman O (eds) Substantive and procedural aspects of international criminal law. The experience of international and national courts. Commentary, vol 1. Kluwer Law International, The Hague, pp 369–388

Eser A (2008) Article 31: grounds for excluding criminal responsibility. In: Triffterer O (ed) Commentary on the Rome Statute of the International Criminal Court: observers' notes, article by article, 2nd edn. C.H. Beck oHG, München, pp 863–893

Fletcher GP (1978) Rethinking criminal law, Oxford University Press, Oxford (reprinted in 2000)

Fletcher GP (1985) The right and the reasonable. Harv Law Rev 98:949–981

Fletcher GP (1998) Basic concepts of criminal law. Oxford University Press, New York

Fletcher GP (2007) The grammar of criminal law. American, comparative, and international, Volume one: Foundations, vol 1. Oxford University Press, New York

Fletcher GP, Ohlin JD (2008) Defending humanity; when force is justified and why. Oxford University Press, New York

Heller KJ (2008) Mistake of legal element, the common law, and article 32 of the Rome Statute. J Int Crim Justice 6:419–445

Hullu J de (2006) Materieel strafrecht. Kluwer, Deventer

Husak D, Hirsch Av (1993) Culpability and mistake of law. In: Shute S, Gardner J, Horder J (eds) Action and value in criminal law. Clarendon Press, Oxford, pp 157–174

Kelk C (2005) Studieboek materieel strafrecht, 3rd edn. Kluwer, Deventer

Koopmans FAJ (2007) Het beslissingsmodel van 348/350 Sv. Kluwer, Deventer

May R (1999) Criminal evidence, 4th edn. Sweet & Maxwell, London

Robinson PH (1984) Criminal law defenses, vol 2. West Publishing Co, St. Paul

[77] Fletcher 2007 pp. 54–55.

Roxin C (2006) Strafrecht allgemeiner teil, band I, Grundlagen, der Aufbau der Verbrechenslehre, 4th edn. C.H. Beck, Munchen
Sliedregt E van (2003) The criminal responsibility of individuals for violations of international humanitarian law. T.M.C. Asser Press, The Hague
Triffterer O (2008) Article 32: mistake of law. In: Triffterer O (ed) Commentary on the Rome Statute of the International Criminal Court: observers' notes, article by article, 2nd edn. C.H. Beck oHG, München, pp 895–914
Veen TWV (1972) Facet-Wederrechtelijkheid. Nederlands Juristenblad, pp 466–469
Wilt HG van der (1999) Commentary to the prosecutor v. Erdemovic appeals judgement. In: Klip A, Sluiter GK (eds) Annotated Leading Cases of International Criminal Tribunals, vol I. Intersentia, Antwerp, pp 654–656

Table of Cases

International Case Law

European Court of Human Rights

Case of K.-H. W. v. Germany (Application no. 37201/97) (2001), ECtHR, 22 Mar 2001

International Criminal Tribunal for the Former Yugoslavia

Prosecutor v. Erdemović (1997a) ICTY Appeals Chamber, case no. IT-96-22-A, 7 Oct 1997, Separate and dissenting opinion of Judge Cassese, ICTY Appeals Chamber, case no. IT-96-22-A, 7 Oct 1997, separate and dissenting opinion of Judge Cassese

Prosecutor v. Erdemović (1997b) ICTY Appeals Chamber, case no. IT-96-22-A, judgement, 7 Oct 1997, ICTY Appeals Chamber, case no. IT-96-22-A, judgement, 7 Oct 1997

National Case Law

Germany

Bundesgerichtshof, 18-03-1952 (1952), GSSt 2/51 (Lexetius.com/1952, 1)

Chapter 4
The Theory of Mistake of Law in International Criminal Law

4.1 Introduction

Chapter 2 reflected on mistake of law in national law systems. This chapter gives a theoretical account of mistake of law in international criminal law. The chapter discusses Articles 32 and 33 of the ICC Statute, the first codification of mistake of law as a ground for excluding criminal responsibility in the history of international criminal law.[1] These provisions could mark an important step in the development of the general part of international criminal law.[2] Article 32(2) refers to the general principle *ignorantia legis non excusat*, ignorance of the law is no excuse. Article 32(2) also indicates the possible exceptions to this principle, namely when the mistake of law negates the mental element required or as provided for in Article 33. Article 33 provides that acting on superior orders does not relieve a person from criminal responsibility unless he was under a legal obligation to obey, he did not know the order to be unlawful and the order was not manifestly unlawful. This article can be read in the light of the fact that many international crimes are committed in the context of the military organisation. A subordinate may find himself confronted with the dilemma of incurring responsibility for disobeying superior orders or incurring responsibility for crimes committed in obedience to

---

[1] The ICC predecessors (the International Military Tribunal (Nuremberg), The International Military Tribunal for the Far East (Tokyo), The International Criminal Tribunal for the Former Yugoslavia and the International Criminal Tribunal for Rwanda) did not provide for a provision on mistake of law and regulated the defence of superior orders merely as a ground for mitigation of punishment.

[2] Sliedregt 2003, p. 315.

A. van Verseveld, *Mistake of Law*, DOI: 10.1007/978-90-6704-867-5_4,

superior orders. It is argued that the reality of the battlefield requires a special defence to be available to the subordinate faced with this dilemma.[3]

Articles 32 and 33, being the result of treaty negotiations, have the character of compromise. A discussion in this chapter of the implications of these articles shows that the general part of international criminal law is still in need of further theoretical development.[4] In the previous chapter there is a theorisation of the problem of mistake of law. As seen, central to this theorisation is the distinction between justification and excuse, between wrongfulness and attribution and between conduct rules and decision rules. The paramount importance of these distinctions reappears in the second section of this chapter on the 'negate mental element requirement' in Article 32(2). In the third section there is a discussion in reference to Article 33 on superior orders. In the final section the issue of how to incorporate a more principled approach to mistake of law in international criminal law is addressed. This principled approach recognises the character of this defence as an excuse, requiring a responsibility assessment based on the perpetrator's culpability or blameworthiness.

4.2 Article 32(2): Mistake of Law

4.2.1 Article 32 Mistake

Article 32 of the ICC Statute provides:

Mistake of fact or mistake of law

1. A mistake of fact shall be a ground for excluding criminal responsibility only if it negates the mental element required by the crime.
2. A mistake of law as to whether a particular type of conduct is a crime within the jurisdiction of the Court shall not be a ground for excluding criminal responsibility. A mistake of law may, however, be a ground for excluding criminal responsibility if it negates the mental element required by such a crime, or as provided for in Article 33.

Article 32 provides both for a rule on mistake of fact and a rule on mistake of law. Article 32(1) provides that, as in most national legal systems,[5] a mistake of

[3] *See also* Sliedregt 2003, p. 339 and Robinson 1984, § 185, p. 421 (where he refers to a slightly different rationale, combining duress and mistake of law: "Specifically, if an order is unlawful because it demands unjustified conduct and if that order precludes the independent exercise of judgment as to the unjustified aspect of the conduct commanded, then the compulsion inherent in military orders, compels an especially broad mistake excuse when such an unlawful military order is mistakenly obeyed").

[4] Ambos 2006, pp. 661–662; Ambos 2008b p. 126.

[5] Cassese 2008, p. 290.

fact which negates the required mental element is a ground for excluding criminal responsibility. This provision, although perhaps redundant because already on the basis of Article 30 ICC Statute there can be no criminal responsibility if the defendant lacks the required *mens rea*, is uncontested. This is different with regard to the provision on mistake of law.[6]

The first sentence of Article 32(2), on mistake of law, could be regarded as referring to the general principle *ignorantia legis non excusat*, ignorance of the law is no excuse.[7] Applicability of this principle in international criminal law is often based on the fact that international crimes are of such a grave nature that the unlawful character must be obvious to everyone. Arguments are often also made along the lines of the distinction between crimes *malum in se* and *mala prohibita*.[8] International crimes are then generally characterised as *malum in se*; i.e. that everyone knows the underlying norms and when these are violated. Ambos, however, holds that, especially among war crimes, there are also *mala prohibita* and that the principle of individual guilt requires a limitation of or at least a flexible approach towards the *ignorantia legis non excusat* rule.[9] Moreover, the existence of justificatory grounds for otherwise unlawful conduct are less likely to be clear[10] than the crime definition itself and here an exception to the *ignorantia legis non excusat* rule seems especially warranted. The second sentence of Article 32(2) indicates the available exceptions, that is, when a mistake of law negates the mental element required, or as provided for in Article 33, the mistake is a ground for excluding criminal responsibility.

4.2.2 Negate the Mental Element

The requirement that the mistake should negate the required mental element in order to exculpate the perpetrator has been subject to much criticism. This requirement, on the one hand, makes the article actually redundant because on the basis of Article 30 there can be no criminal responsibility unless the crime is committed with the required mental element.[11] On the other hand, the 'negate mental element-requirement' restricts a 'mistake of law defence' to an absolute minimum, for the

---

[6] Triffterer 2008, p. 900.

[7] *See also* Sliedregt 2003, p. 308 and Cassese 2008, p. 294. This principle is an outmoded dogma according to Fletcher (1998), p. 154; *but see* Cassese 2008, p. 294 (holding that this principle reflects customary law). This sentence also refers to the irrelevance of mistakes of procedural law. *See* Scaliotti 2002, p. 13. *See also* Triffterer 2008, p. 906, § 32; Ambos 2004, p. 817. In this respect the provision is not problematic; in national systems too this type of mistake of law is always irrelevant, see Chaps. 2 and 3 *supra*.

[8] Ambos 2004, pp. 817–818.

[9] Ambos 2004, pp. 817–818.

[10] Wise 1998, p. 52.

[11] Eser 2002, pp. 891–892. *See also* Werle 2003, p. 134.

article thus fails to recognise mistakes not covered by the mental element criterion, like mistakes about norms of justification or mistakes about the prohibition as such.[12] In requiring a mistake of law to negate the mental element, which essentially focuses on facts, Article 32(2) leaves little room for mistake of law to exclude criminal responsibility.[13] It is helpful to once more refer to the statement by Jescheck that: "[i]n truth, mistake of law is not concerned with the elements of crime, but rather with the unlawfulness of the conduct in a given situation."[14]

As will now be demonstrated, the 'negate mental element requirement' in Article 32, read in conjunction with Article 30, reveals that the structure of crimes in the ICC statute is based on a "twofold system along the lines of the Anglo-American actus *reus/mens rea* versus defences dichotomy."[15]

In Article 30 the drafters of the ICC Statute have provided for a default rule on the mental element required for criminal responsibility for international crimes. The article provides:

Article 30—Mental element

1. Unless otherwise provided, a person shall be criminally responsible and liable for punishment for a crime within the jurisdiction of the Court only if the material elements are committed with intent and knowledge.
2. For the purpose of this article, a person has intent where:
    a. In relation to conduct, that person means to engage in the conduct;
    b. In relation to a consequence, that person means to cause that consequence or is aware that it will occur in the ordinary course of events.
3. For the purposes of this article, "knowledge" means awareness that a circumstance exists or a consequence will occur in the ordinary course of events. "Know" and "knowingly" shall be construed accordingly.

This article, like Articles 32 and 33, is a novelty; for the first time in the history of international criminal law the mental element as a general requirement of individual criminal responsibility has been codified.[16] Article 30 defines the 'mental element' as some degree of awareness of the material or definitional elements of the offence.[17] Material elements refers to the positive definitional elements of crime.[18] As Ambos points out 'material elements' could also have referred to 'substantive' and not

---

[12] *See also* Ambos 2004, pp. 817–819.

[13] Eser 2002, pp. 934–935.

[14] Jescheck 2004, p. 47. In Chap. 6 this premise, that mistake of law generally does not negate the mental element, will be validated by an investigation into the mental element requirements for international crimes in the crime definitions in the ICC Statute and the Elements of Crimes.

[15] Ambos 2006, pp. 664–665.

[16] Werle and Jessberger 2005, p. 35.

[17] Werle and Jessberger 2005, p. 38.

[18] Eser 2002, pp. 909–910. *See also* Sliedregt 2003, pp. 56–57 and 307 and Ambos 2004, pp. 764 + 809.

'procedural' elements, but on the basis of the drafting history and the fact that Article 30 refers to the conduct, consequences and circumstances, 'material elements' must be understood as part of the *actus reus*, the objective elements of the crime definition.[19] The required mental element does not, at least not explicitly, include an element of unlawfulness or *Unrechtsbewußtsein*.[20] In Chap. 2 we saw that in Anglo-American law too, *Unrechtsbewußtsein* is not an independent requirement for criminal responsibility; it is therefore also not explicitly recognised as part of the required mental element.[21]

Some authors welcome Article 30 as an establishment in international criminal law of the principle of individual culpability. They refer to the general principle *actus non facit reum nisi mens sit rea*.[22] In order to hold a person criminally liable, that person should have sufficiently been aware of what he was doing and of the consequences of his actions.[23] Criminal responsibility on the basis of strict liability should be rejected. This is a widely recognised principle, in domestic as well as in international criminal law systems.[24] Werle and Jessberger refer, in relation to this point, to the following statement of the ICTY in the Mucić trial judgement: "It is apparent that it is a general principle of law that the establishment of criminal culpability requires an analysis of two aspects. The first of these may be termed the *actus reus*—the physical act necessary for the offence… The second aspect … relates to the necessary mental element, or *mens rea*."[25]

However, as Jescheck argues, "[a]ccording to the principle of culpability—if we take it to mean more than the requirement of [descriptive][26] *mens rea* in Anglo-American law—means and measures of punishment must be based on a court's conviction that the defendant is personally reproachable for the crime he or she has committed."[27] Under the principle of culpability in this sense, that is the general principle *nullem crimen sine culpa*, criminal punishment requires the blameworthiness of the actor. I therefore do not agree with Piragoff who holds that Article 30 deals with "the issue of moral culpability".[28] On the contrary, Article 30, headed 'mental element', concerns only the requirement of *mens rea* as understood in Anglo-American law,[29] not the moral culpability or blameworthiness of the

19 Ambos 2004, pp. 762–764.

20 Ambos 2004, pp. 759–760 and 806–807. Werle 2003, p. 108. *See also* Ambos 2002b, p. 1042. And *see further* Sects. 2.3.2.2 and 2.3.2.5 *supra*.

21 *See* Sect. 2.2 *supra* and Ambos 2004, p. 759.

22 An act does not make a person guilty of a crime, unless the person's mind be also guilty (Translation by Piragoff) Piragoff 1999, footnote 9, at p. 529. *See also* Robinson 1999, p. 52. *Critical* Ambos 2004, p. 759.

23 Werle and Jessberger 2005, p. 36.

24 Ambos 2008a, pp. 15–16, footnotes 64–66 and accompanying text.

25 Werle and Jessberger 2005, p. 36.

26 My insertion; on this term see Fletcher 1998, p. 99; see also Sect. 3.2.3 *supra*.

27 Jescheck 2004, p. 44.

28 Piragoff 1999, p. 528.

29 This does not include *Unrechtbewußtsein*, knowledge of wrongfulness, see Sect. 2.2 *supra*.

defendant. The principle of guilt, in the sense of a moral meaning of culpability, is, however, a fundamental principle of international criminal law.[30]

On the basis of Article 30 it is argued that the 'negate mental element requirement' in Article 32(2) second sentence, must be interpreted as requiring the mistake of law to negate the awareness of the definitional or physical elements of the offence. In fact, if it were not for Article 30, it could have been argued that 'mental element' in Article 32 comprises the broader meaning of *mens rea*, including *Unrechtsbewußtsein*, consciousness of wrongdoing. However, this broad interpretation seems unlikely, since the drafters, as in common law, do not seem to distinguish between intent and *Unrechtsbewußtsein.*[31] Moreover, a restrictive interpretation of 'mental element' to mean only 'intent' entails the very limited scope of mistake of law that the drafters most likely intended to provide for.[32]

Once more, the 'negate mental element requirement' in Article 32, read in conjunction with Article 30, reveals that the structure of crimes in the ICC statute is based on a twofold structure.[33] As observed in Chaps. 2 and 3, one of the main consequences of a twofold structure of crimes is that it does not separate the issue of intent from the issue of *Unrechtsbewußtsein.* It does not allow for a true weighing of the defendant's culpability or blameworthiness in making a mistake of law.

Criticism of Article 32 is mainly directed against this 'negate mental element-requirement', because knowledge of unlawfulness is hardly ever part of the definitional elements of an offence. Eser holds that here "the Rome Statute disregards growing sensitivity to the principle of culpability, particularly with regard to consciousness of unlawfulness (as distinct from and in addition to the fact-oriented intention)".[34]

Fletcher, discussing the shortcomings of the Model Penal Code (MPC) provision on mistake, which also requires negation of the mental element, gives an elaborate overview of mistakes which are erroneously not covered by this MPC provision. He explains that a mistake of law may negate the mental element (in case of an authoritatively defined intent), may negate the culpability (e.g. in case of a mistake as to the legal requirements for justification), or may be irrelevant (e.g. where it relates to a mistake about a decision rule).[35] Since Article 32(2) also has shortcomings in that it does not contemplate all these possible results of mistakes, it does not allow the judges to find doctrinally correct and just solutions.[36]

---

[30] *See also* Ambos 2003, p. 17 (note 20: IMT "one of the most important [legal principles]... is that criminal guilt is personal") and Ambos 2002b, p. 1045; Eser 2002, pp. 889–890 + 934.

[31] *See also* Ambos 2004, p. 819.

[32] *See also* Ambos 2004, pp. 806–807.

[33] Ambos 2006, pp. 664–665.

[34] Eser 2002, p. 935. *See also* Ambos 2004, p. 819.

[35] Fletcher 1998, pp. 149–167. On the same shortcomings of Article 32(2) *see* Ambos 2004, pp. 816–821.

[36] *See also* Ambos 1999, pp. 29–30.

Some authors, like Clark, try to limit the unjust results of the 'negate mental element requirement' by recasting mistakes of law as mistakes of fact.[37] Chapter 2 showed that this is the way common lawyers try to deal with any unjust results of the requirement.[38] Other authors try to repair the 'negate mental element' issue by suggesting that the court should read an unavoidability test, recognised by many national law systems, into the text of Article 32(2).[39] These authors, referring to a similar requirement in national legal systems, seem to base their contention that the Court could implement such an avoidability test on Article 21(1)(c).[40] This contention may not be correct, as this article allows resort to general principles only where the others sources are unclear. The reports of the Preparatory Committee indicate that the unavoidability test was proposed, but did not make it into the final text. This may suggest that the avoidability test has deliberately been left out.[41] The proposed solution of implementing it nevertheless is, in my opinion, not very satisfying either, for fact is, that the 'negate mental element-requirement' still stands. Applying an unavoidability test on top of the 'negate mental element-requirement' leads to an even more unjustifiable limitation of the scope of mistake of law. Arguably, authors who suggest this solution while referring to the object and purpose of prosecuting international crimes appear to attach greater value to convictions than to just convictions.[42] If the mental element is negated by a mistake of law, then there is no more room to require the mistake to have been reasonable or unavoidable; the conclusion must already be that there is no criminal act because of a successful failure-of-proof defence.[43]

Triffterer states with regard to the negate mental element that if a mistake of law "negates the mental element required, the consequence is as self-evident as for an error of fact. On the other side, the mere belief that certain conduct is not punishable or does not fall within the jurisdiction of the Court does not concern the *material* elements of which the perpetrator has to be aware before he may build the *mens rea* required. As expressed in sentence 2, only in *exceptional* cases *may such*[44] an error negate this element; therefore, para 2 also clarifies, though without precisely expressing, when and where such a consequence can be drawn."[45] In my

---

[37] *See* Clark 2001, p. 310. Boister critically discusses this "orthodox common law" solution, Boister 2005, p. 39.

[38] *See* Sect. 2.2 *supra*.

[39] *See e.g.* Sliedregt 2003, p. 316; Triffterer 2008, p. 908; Ambos 2004, p. 823.

[40] *See e.g.* Ambos 2004, p. 823.

[41] *See*, "The Report of the Inter-Sessional Meeting From 19 to 30 January held in Zutphen, the Netherlands" (A/AC.249/1997/L/9/Rev.1, 1997), *in* Bassiouni 1998, pp. 249–250. *Convinced that this is the case* Heller 2008, p. 440.

[42] Here, I would like to refer again to the distinction made by Kelk between the constitutional dimension of the principle of legality and to the legal protection dimension; see Sect. 2.3.2.4.1, footnote 226.

[43] *See also* Heller 2008, p. 441.

[44] Emphasis AvV.

[45] Triffterer 2008, p. 900. *See also* Scaliotti 2002, pp. 13–14.

opinion, however, *such* a mistake can never negate the mental element or the required *Unrechtsbewußtsein* for that matter. The mistake these authors are referring to is an irrelevant mistake; mistakes about the *punishability* or the procedural issue of the Court's jurisdiction are always irrelevant, there are likewise no exceptions to this rule in national criminal law systems.

According to Triffterer "the Court *may* judge that even in these cases [of wrongful legal evaluation] a mistake of law may negate the mental element required and thus exclude responsibility, because the error was unavoidable".[46] It appears that this statement is incompatible both with a threefold concept of crime and with a twofold concept. As seen in Chaps. 2 and 3 a threefold structure applies a threefold responsibility assessment. Triffterer's statement seems to deny the compulsory order of these steps because, if the mental element is negated, you do not even reach the third step. The first step is a matter of proof; does the defendant's behaviour, including his mental state, fall within the specific crime definition. Only if this is the case, and there are no justifications (the second step) do you reach the issue of the defendant's culpability, in case of mistake of law, the unavoidability of this mistake. Triffterer's analysis is incompatible with the twofold structure because it ignores the 'inexorable logic rule', which holds that every mistake negating the mental element (i.e. intent or recklessness) excludes the finding of a wrongful act, not only reasonable or unavoidable mistakes.[47]

Heller points out an interesting and potentially disturbing issue. He holds that under the current provisions, Articles 32(2) and 30, the scope of the defence of mistake of law is, in opposition to the above expressed views, actually very wide, since most international crimes contain legal elements. Heller discusses how different authors try to solve the issue of legal elements. These authors for example refer to the *Parallelwertungslehre*.[48] The defendant is only required to have been aware of the social meaning of a legal element, not of legal technicalities. Heller rejects this solution, amongst other things because it is a typical civil law, or more precisely German, concept.[49] As Heller holds, and as has been stated earlier in Chap. 2 and the current chapter, Article 32 is based on the common law system. And, Heller contends, a solution to the problem of legal elements should therefore also be sought in the common law. He holds that under common law mistakes of legal elements (MLEs) are not *excuses* but *failure-of-proof* defences, which means that the requirement of reasonableness cannot be applied to mistakes about these elements.[50] This is arguably exactly where the problem lies, but let us first look at the amendments to the Statute that Heller proposes:

---

[46] Triffterer 2008, p. 908.

[47] It should be noted that under the threefold system too any reasonable or unreasonable mistake that negates the required intent excludes the finding of a wrongful act. The only way to assess such a mistake more objectively is to incorporate a 'must have known' standard. *See* Sect. 2.2.2.2 *supra*.

[48] *See also* Sects. 2.3.2.3, (2) *supra*.

[49] Heller 2008, p. 439.

[50] Heller 2008, p. 441.

> First, a fourth paragraph could be added to Article 30: 'Notwithstanding paras 1–3, material elements that contain one or more legal rules need only be committed with negligence. A person acts negligently with regard to a legal rule when that person knew or should have known the definition of the rule'. That change would, as noted above, have the effect of requiring MLEs to be reasonable.
>
> Second, Article 32 could be amended directly. Specifically, sentence 2 in para 2 could be altered to read either; (1) 'A mistake of law may, however, be a ground for excluding criminal responsibility if the person neither knew nor had reason to know of the legal rule'; or (2) 'A mistake of law may, however, be a ground for excluding criminal responsibility if it negates the mental element required by such a crime, provided that the mistake is reasonable'.[51]

The first solution requires knowledge of the legal definition; this solution, which would apply to all legal elements, should be rejected because then only legal experts can commit international crimes. The same objection applies to the second solution if 'to know of the legal rule' refers to knowledge of the legal definition of the rule. If it refers to *Unrechtsbewußtsein*, knowledge of wrongdoing, however, this solution could be supported. It is very unlikely that Heller meant to refer to this meaning, since he searches for a solution in common law, not civil law. The final proposed amendment hardly solves the problem of the irreconcilability of intent and reasonableness.

In sum, the proposed solutions do not solve the complex issues of mistake of law. In fact, Heller fails to discuss other relevant mistakes of law, such as mistake as to the prohibition as such and mistakes as to justifying norms. As seen in Chap. 2, Anglo-American law has not found a principled solution to the issue of mistake of law. Mistake of law was generally excluded as a defence, and only because in some situations this led to unjust results, the solution was adopted to require knowledge of unlawfulness when a crime definition reads 'wilfully' or 'knowingly'. This brought about the difficult issue of where to fit in dogmatically the sometimes desired requirement of reasonableness of a mistake; an issue that has remained unanswered in common law.

True, the solution of the *Parallelwertungslehre* is somewhat artificial too. It does not truly solve the substantive problem either because, as with some legal elements, it can hardly be said that the social meaning can be understood without legal knowledge.[52] This solution, which purports that no criminal intent is required, is however justified because *Unrechtsbewußtsein* is a separate element of criminal responsibility. If, because of lack of legal knowledge about a legal element, the defendant acted with the required intent, but without *Unrechtsbewußtsein*, and his ignorance of mistake of law was unavoidable, the defendant will be acquitted.

In sum, it is reasonable to conclude that, however hard we try to interpret Article 32(2) otherwise, in its current state it does not lead to dogmatically correct and just results. By requiring the mistake to negate the mental element the drafters

---

[51] Heller 2008, pp. 444–445.

[52] See Ambos 2004, pp. 813 + 815.

have only complicated, if not excluded, the means to arrive at an adequate normative account of culpability.

As Boister holds, authors who "take the subjective test for culpability seriously" are dissatisfied with Article 32(2).[53] Many authors who are dissatisfied with Article 32(2) argue that incorporating an avoidability test into the provision will solve the main problems of the current codification. As we saw, this solution is however problematic. Perhaps this means that Jescheck's call for an amendment of the provision should be supported.[54] Before addressing a possible solution in Sect. 4.4, it is instructive to turn to the second exception to the *ignorantia legis non excusat* rule provided for in Article 32(2), the defence of superior order.

4.3 Article 33: Superior Orders

4.3.1 Introduction

Weigend argues that it is unlikely that an 'isolated' mistake of law ever arises in connection with the crimes enumerated in the ICC Statute. He argues that it will be very difficult "to make a court believe that someone did not and could not realise that, for example, maltreating of civilians or prisoners of war, [...] was prohibited by law".[55] He notes that "the only practically conceivable exception might arise when the actor is being ordered to commit an act of this kind by his military or civilian superior".[56]

One can dispute Weigend's assumption as to the obvious illegal character of international crimes, but the fact that many international crimes are committed in the context of the military organisations, makes the defence set out in Article 33 of particular relevance to the scope of the defence of mistake of law. The defence of superior orders acknowledges the fact that a soldier may be faced with the dilemma of incurring responsibility for disobeying superior orders or incurring responsibility for committing crimes in obedience to superior orders.

4.3.2 The Provision

Article 33 provides:

Superior orders and prescription of law

---

53 Boister 2005, p. 41.

54 Jescheck 2004, p. 47.

55 Weigend 2004, p. 332.

56 Weigend 2004, p. 332.

1. The fact that a crime within the jurisdiction of the Court has been committed by a person pursuant to an order of a Government or of a superior, whether military or civilian, shall not relieve that person of criminal responsibility unless:

    (a) The person was under a legal obligation to obey orders of the Government or the superior in question;
    (b) The person did not know that the order was unlawful; and
    (c) The order was not manifestly unlawful.

2. For the purpose of this article, orders to commit genocide or crimes against humanity are manifestly unlawful.

The provision stipulates that in principle acting on superior orders does not relieve a person of criminal responsibility. Only when the three cumulative conditions of the first paragraph are met, can acting on superior orders lead to an acquittal. One of the prerequisites is that the subordinate made a mistake as to the lawfulness of the superior order. The knowledge of unlawfulness referred to in para (1)(b), can be inferred from the available evidence; meaning that the evidence may justify the inference that the defendant knew the order to be unlawful—in other words, the conclusion that he *must have known* the order to be illegal is justified.[57] It could be argued, as Dinstein has, that the logic underlying this requirement of absence of personal knowledge is that of *ignorantia juris excusat*.[58]

For this mistake of law to be relevant it does not have to negate the mental element as stipulated in Article 32(2).[59] The scope of the mistake of law under Article 33 is therefore broader than the scope of mistake of law under Article 32(2); the provision is in this sense more favourable to the defendant.[60] Article 33 allows for the defence to be invoked for example in case of a mistaken justification or in case of mistake as to the prohibition as such. Paragraph 2 of Article 33 excludes the possibility of invoking the defence of superior orders, however, when the acts ordered constitute genocide or crimes against humanity.

4.3.3 Criticism: Departure from Customary International Law

The fact that Article 33 allows the defence of superior orders to exclude criminal responsibility for war crimes is open to criticism. In the debate one can distinguish two schools of thought. There are those who support Dinstein's contention that this provision is at variance with customary international law, which according to him treats superior orders merely as a factual element relevant to other defences,

---

57 *See also* Zimmermann 2002, p. 970.

58 Dinstein 1965, pp. 36–37.

59 *See also* Cryer 2005, p. 60 (referring to opposite view of Dinstein 2000, p. 381).

60 Jescheck 2004, p. 46. *See also* Cryer 2005, p. 59.

specifically duress and mistake (of fact or law) and not as a defence per se.[61] Conversely, there are those supporting Green, who argues that orders which are lawful on their face, and thus not manifestly illegal, constitute a defence per se.[62]

Authors often support their contention that Article 33 is at variance with customary international law by referring to the IMT Nuremberg judgement and the subsequent proceedings under Control Council Law No. 10 (CCL No. 10).[63] On the basis of the statutes applicable to these proceedings superior orders was only a ground for mitigation of punishment.[64] Dinstein for example holds that the rule of Article II(4)(b) CCL No. 10, banning superior orders as a defence, applied whenever the defence was raised, even if it was raised in conjunction with other defences like coercion or mistake, because the article is based on a doctrine of absolute liability. Dinstein holds that this may not be just, but that it is the Law nevertheless.[65]

Gaeta argues that, despite its merits,[66] "Article 33 must be faulted, primarily because it departs from customary international law without a well-ground motivation. This departure is even more questionable given that Article 33 is basically inconsistent with the codification of war crimes effected through Article 8 of the Rome Statute. How would it be possible to claim that the order to commit one of those crimes is not manifestly unlawful or that subordinates cannot recognise its illegality?"[67] Ambos too holds that Article 33 should have excluded the defence in case of war crimes. In his opinion, the legal values protected by international criminal law override the need to maintain discipline in the military organisation.[68]

Other authors, supporting Green's analysis, welcome the codification of superior orders as a defence and regret the article's distinction between war crimes on the one hand and genocide and crimes against humanity on the other.[69] Zimmermann holds that there is no basis in customary international law or in national law systems for this distinction.[70]

---

61 Dinstein 2000, p. 379 and Dinstein 1965, p. 88. *See also* Ambos 2008b, p. 178.

62 Green 1999, pp. 245–282.

63 For a discussion of some of this case law see Chap. 5 *infra*.

64 Article 8 IMT Nuremberg, Article 6 IMTFE and Article II(4)(b) CCL no. 10.

65 Dinstein 1965, p. 169 and pp. 117–118 (where Dinstein explains that the same is the inevitable purport of Article 8 IMT, but this does not conclusively determine the issue of obedience to orders in general international law. Dinstein argues that from the standpoint of general international law, he "think[s] that there is more merit in the initial American proposals, which refuse the standing of a defence per se to the fact of obedience to orders but confer upon the tribunal the right to take this fact into account among the other circumstances of the case within the purview of another defence").

66 Which are, according to her, the fact that Article 33 excludes the possibility of invoking superior orders in case of crimes against humanity and genocide. Gaeta 1999, p. 190.

67 Gaeta 1999, p. 190. (*But see* Dinstein 2000, p. 381 (arguing that even the statement that all crimes against humanity are manifestly unlawful is unjustified because "almost every phrase of in para 1 of Article 7 is defined and explained at some length in para 2".)

68 Ambos 1999, p. 31.

69 *See e.g.* Sliedregt 2003, pp. 325–326.

70 Zimmermann 2002, p. 971.

One could argue that there is no difference in illegality between these three types of international crimes.[71] The distinction is basically political[72]; some states thought their soldiers would never commit crimes against humanity or genocide. Another argument against the distinction could be that war crimes are better known to soldiers than the norms relating to crimes against humanity. It is less obvious that a soldier would make a mistake about the wrongfulness of acts constituting war crimes than crimes against humanity. Finally, Scaliotti holds that "the difficult position in which a subordinate may easily find himself cannot be overlooked. Even in the context of international crimes, justice requires that the situation of submission typical for subordinates be rightly weighed".[73] Besides, there are no reasons why the purpose of the defence, excluding criminal responsibility when the defendant made an honest mistake about a not manifestly unlawful order, would no longer be legitimate in case of crimes against humanity and genocide.[74]

In this discussion, on the applicability of the defence in cases of crimes against humanity and genocide, it should not be overlooked that these crimes require specific knowledge and specific intent respectively. One could argue that once these specific mental elements are established, the plea of the defendant that he acted on superior orders is very likely to be denied on the basis of the (inferred) knowledge of the unlawfulness of the orders or on the manifest illegality of them.[75] Article 33(2) is simply redundant. But it could also, and arguably more convincingly, be concluded to the contrary, i.e. that Article 33(2) is harmful, because the issue of mental element and culpability should be determined by a court on a case-by-case basis and although a defendant is very unlikely to be successful in bringing forward the defence of superior orders in these cases, it should not be excluded a priori.[76]

McCoubrey is very persuasive in his argument that the provision on superior orders in the ICC statute does not, except for the exclusion provided for Article 33(2), constitute a radical change with the Nuremberg legacy.[77] Like other authors[78] he explains how the Nuremberg law was situation specific.[79] According to Wise there is no departure from international customary law since "there is still no special defence; the real ground of exculpation is the broader one that someone who could not reasonably be expected to know that his conduct was illegal, or who

---

[71] *See also* Cryer 2005, pp. 66–67.

[72] *See also* Cryer 2005, p. 63.

[73] Scaliotti 2001, p. 142.

[74] *See also* Cryer 2005, p. 65 (stating that if there are such reasons, these should have been indicated).

[75] *See also* Cryer 2005, p. 65.

[76] Cryer 2005, pp. 65-66.

[77] McCoubrey 2001, pp. 386 + 389–390 + 393–394.

[78] *See amongst others* Garraway 1999, p. 788 and Sliedregt 2003, p. 318.

[79] *See also* Röling 1961, pp. 372–373.

could not reasonably be expected to have disobeyed an order, acts without culpability".[80] In such a case of unavoidable mistake of law, the unblameworthy defendant should go unpunished. Merely mitigation of punishment does not do justice to the lack of culpability in case of an unavoidably mistaken defendant. It seems that Article 33 correctly provides for a ground for excluding criminal responsibility. It might be disputed, though, whether Article 33 allows for a true culpability test, especially since Article 33 does not refer to the unavoidability of the mistake and since the provision excludes the defence in case of certain crimes entirely. I will return to this issue at the end of this section.

4.3.4 Criticism: Manifest Illegality

Besides its alleged departure from customary international law, Article 33 is criticised for the use of the 'not manifestly unlawful-requirement' in para 1(c). When the order is manifestly unlawful, the subordinate cannot invoke the defence of superior order in order to be relieved of criminal responsibility. But when is an order manifestly illegal? According to Zimmermann an order is manifestly illegal, when the unlawfulness is "obvious to a person of ordinary understanding [...]. The unlawfulness is not to be determined with regard to a specific domestic legal order; instead the true test is whether the order was manifestly unlawful under international law: a layman with only basic knowledge of international humanitarian law should have considered the action to be unlawful and constitute a punishable crime."[81] It should be noted that some war crimes fall, per se, outside the scope of the defence of superior orders; for example an order to commit rape, because this is no activity relating to military duties to begin with.

Osiel strongly opposes to the 'manifest illegality' rule. His objections generally concern the uncertainty of the scope of 'manifest illegality'. The rule implicates the existence of a standard of what a reasonable person would recognise as manifestly illegal. Indicators of this standard, like the clarity of the legal prohibition, the moral gravity of the act and the procedural irregularity of the order, prove to be very inadequate as to the establishment of the manifestness of the illegality of an order. Osiel further convincingly demonstrates the inability of the manifest illegality rule to respond to issues of individual responsibility under totalitarian regimes.[82] Besides, sociological and psychological research indicates that "the behaviour of the individual is rarely determined principally by its ethical references". The ICRC therefore argues "we have to make international humanitarian law a judicial and political rather than a moral issue".[83]

---

[80] Wise 1998, pp. 52–53 (see also reference to Wise in Nill-Theobald 1998, p. 80).

[81] Zimmermann 2002, p. 970.

[82] Osiel 1999, pp. 147–150.

[83] International Committee of the Red Cross 2004, pp. 110–111.

Keijzer, however, has argued that the manifest illegality principle "results from the superior's authorization deriving from the power of the legitimate government—the essence of authorization being that the legality of orders may be presumed [...], unless [...] an order can under no circumstances be compatible with the law".[84] Keijzer finds that the manifest illegality principle acknowledges the importance of hierarchy and authorisation within the military organisation. He has argued in favour of a separate provision on the defence of superior orders in order to do justice to the position of subordinates in this military hierarchy; subordinates must be able in general to rely on their superiors.

To conclude, as Cryer has noted, 'manifest' could be interpreted as a subjective criterion, in which case it would resemble the unavoidability (or reasonableness) test as part of the assessment of the individual's culpability. If it is an objective criterion, however, it could be said that it is too narrow and too broad at the same time.[85] Too narrow or lenient, because in case of a non-manifestly but nevertheless unlawful order, all subordinates will be exculpated. This includes subordinates who, because of their personal capacities, should have known about the unlawfulness of the order. The objective test is, at the same time, too broad or harsh, since it accounts for personal capacities as little as for personal incapacities. If the order is manifestly unlawful, the defence is not available and there is no consequential assessment of the individual subordinates' culpability on the basis of mistake of law.

4.3.5 Conclusion: Superior Orders a Separate Defence?

With Article 33 the ICC Statute provides for superior orders as a separate defence. The excuse here provided for is, on the one hand, narrower and, on the other, wider than the defence of mistake of law per se. It is narrower, since it is excluded in case of crimes against humanity and genocide. It is wider for it excuses the subordinate when he has followed an unlawful order that was not manifestly unlawful, if he did not know the order to be unlawful, regardless of whether he *should* have known the order to be unlawful.

Keijzer argued in favour of a separate superior orders defence because the military organisation needs a hierarchical structure in which subordinates can rely on the lawfulness of orders from the legitimate superior authority.[86] He has also argued, however, that the limited responsibility approach as applied in the US, Germany and the Netherlands[87] should be preferred over the full responsibility

---

[84] Keijzer 1977, pp. 238–239.

[85] Cryer 2005, p. 62.

[86] Keijzer 1978, p. 218.

[87] No responsibility for obeying unlawful superior orders unless they were manifestly unlawful, *see also* Chap. 2 *supra*.

approach followed in the UK and France.[88] This is because "in the latter two countries, mistake of law not generally being admitted as a defence and mistake of fact being no defence against a charge of an offence of strict liability (UK) or a non-intentional offence (France), in cases of compliance in good faith with superior orders this may lead to unjust decisions".[89]

It could be argued then, that *if* a system recognises mistake of law (and duress) as an excuse, in its 'proper' meaning, i.e. entailing a culpability assessment,[90] then perhaps the separate limited responsibility provision in case of superior orders should be abandoned. If it is established that a subordinate who obeyed an unlawful order had (or should have had) reason to doubt the lawfulness of the order and had the opportunity and means to resolve these doubts, he should be held responsible for neglecting to do so. Both in cases of 'isolated' mistake of law and in cases of superior orders as a *specialis* of mistake of law the true issue is whether the defendant could have avoided making the mistake and whether he can, therefore, fairly be blamed for his committing the wrongful act. Under such a culpability assessment, the designation 'avoidable mistake' will follow less readily when the defendant acted on superior orders, especially on the battlefield.

4.4 Concluding Analysis

Article 32(2) only provides for a failure-of-proof defence. We must conclude that the mistake of law excuse is not provided for in the Statute. This would mean that the Court could apply this excuse on the basis of Articles 31(3) and 21. Olásolo sees such an opportunity for mistakes of law as to whether a given circumstance constitutes a ground for justification, but not for a mistake of law as to whether a particular type of conduct is a crime within the jurisdiction of the Court "because Article 32(2) RS expressly excludes this as a ground for excuse".[91] But what if we could convincingly argue that the first sentence of Article 32(2) refers to mistake of *procedural* law or a mistake as to the *punishability* of the act? This would then mean that the Statute does not cover, nor reject, mistakes about the prohibition as such. It would be a stretch to argue this was the intention of the drafters because, as seen in Chap. 2, in most common law systems, mistake of law is still looked at

[88] Full responsibility, not a defence per se, but may give rise to a defence on other grounds, e.g. by negating the *mens rea*: mistake or duress, see also Chap. 2 *supra*.

[89] Keijzer 1978, pp. 216–217.

[90] As seen in Chap. 3, it could be argued that the ICC Statute provides for neither excuse. Article 31(1)(d) seems to correct the ICTY Appeals Chamber majority decision in Erdemović (which excluded duress in case of murder charges), but the statute in fact does not provide for a classical case of duress, as the excuse is understood in most civil law jurisdictions. In fact the provisions does not even provide for a moral choice test.

[91] Olásolo 2008, p. 245.

with Argus' eyes. However, this could be a 'way out' for the Court if it is confronted with a credible plea of mistake as to the prohibition as such.

If Olásolo is correct, however, and the drafters expressly excluded this type of mistake of law, adding a new provision to the Statute will be the only solution to correct this unjustified neglect of a fundamental component of the principle of culpability.

The new provision should provide for a principled approach to mistake of law, recognizing the true character of this defence as an excuse. The determinative issue is then whether the mistake was unavoidable. As Fletcher holds "the issue of 'unavoidability' resolves into a normative assessment about whether under the circumstances and in the light of his personal capacities, the defendant could have been expected to be more careful before undertaking the act that turned out to be illegal."[92]

Only by acknowledging the importance of the distinction between justification and excuse, and providing for mistake of law as a valid excuse, can international criminal lawyers be true to the principle *nulla poena sine culpa*, one of the most fundamental principles of criminal law. It is proposed that the following provisional is adopted:

> *Article 32a*
> *Mistake of law or mistake of fact*[93]
> If it is concluded that the defendant acted in the mistaken belief that his conduct was lawful, or that he was mistaken about a fact extrinsic to the required mental element, and if this mistake was unavoidable, the defendant shall not be convicted in respect of such a wrongful act.

This provision also recognises mistakes about facts 'extrinsic to the required mental elements', for example mistakes about justifications which do not negate the required mental element.

If this provision were to be added to the Statute, the first sentence of Article 32(2) should either be removed or be interpreted to refer to mistakes of *procedural* law or mistakes as to the *punishability* of the act. The second sentence, referring to mistakes which negate the required mental element, is not in conflict with the proposed Article 32(a).

The proposed provision would, in my opinion, allow abandoning the separate defence of superior orders. I realise that in national systems a separate defence of superior orders often purports that subordinates have no duty to investigate. This marks the main difference between the defence of superior orders and mistake of law. Where mistake of law, however, entails a true weighing of the individuals culpability, taking into account his personal circumstances, (military) training and education and the circumstances of the case, for instance, whether the subordinate

---

92 Fletcher 1978, p. 744.

93 Arguably it is unnecessary to provide for separate defences of mistake of law and mistake of fact; both mistakes, if relevant and not negating the mental element of the offence, fall under the category of excuses, requiring the mistake to have been reasonable or unavoidable.

had time to reflect or not, a separate defence is no longer necessary to account for the soldier's dilemma. If, nevertheless, the defence of superior orders is upheld, Cryer's suggestion that the manifest illegality test in Article 33 could be interpreted as a subjective test, resembling the unavoidability or reasonableness test, should be supported. Moreover, the proposed provision on mistake of law would also apply to cases of genocide or crimes against humanity committed under superior orders. Only if the mistake as to the lawfulness of the ordered act was unavoidable will the subordinate be excused.

The proposal for the new provision is based on a statement made by Professor Wise, commenting on an early draft of the ICC Statute. Arguably this statement says it all: "With respect to both mistake of fact and of mistake of law, the crucial question should be whether the accused acted in the mistaken belief that his conduct was lawful, and whether the mistake was unavoidable. In the case of such an unavoidable mistake, there is no culpability" and, on principle, should be no criminal responsibility.[94]

References

Ambos K (1999) General principles of criminal law in the Rome Statute. Crim Law Forum 10:1–32

Ambos K (2002b) Other grounds for excluding criminal responsibility. In: Cassese A, Gaeta P, Jones JRWD (eds) The Rome Statute of the International Criminal Court: a commentary, vol I. Oxford University Press, Oxford, pp 1003–1048

Ambos K (2003) Some preliminary reflections on the *mens rea* requirements of the crimes of the ICC Statute and of the elements of crimes. In: Vohrah LCea (ed) Man's inhumanity to man. Kluwer Law International, The Hague, pp 11–40

Ambos K (2004) Der Allgemeine Teil des Völkerstrafrechts. Ansätze einer Dogmatisierung, 2nd edn. Duncker & Humblot, Berlin

Ambos K (2006) Remarks on the general part of International Criminal Law. J Int Crim Justice 4:660–673

Ambos K (2008a) Amicus curiae brief, ECCC, criminal case file no. 001/18-07-2007-ECCC/OCIJ (PTC 02), 27 Oct 2008

Ambos K (2008b) Internationales Strafrecht, 2nd edn. C.H. Beck, München

Bassiouni MC (ed) (1998) The Statute of the International Criminal Court, a documentary history. Transnational Publishers, Ardsley

Boister N (2005) Reflections on the relationship between the duty to educate in humanitarian law and the absence of a defence of mistake of law in the Rome Statute of the International Criminal Court. In: Burchill R, White ND, Morris J (eds) International Conflict and Security Law. Essays in memory of Hilaire McCoubrey. Cambridge University Press, Cambridge, pp 32–48

Cassese A (2008) International Criminal Law, 2nd edn. Oxford University Press, Oxford

Clark RS (2001) The mental element in International Criminal Law: the Rome Statute of the International Criminal Court and the elements of offenses. Crim Law Forum 12(3):291–334

[94] Wise 1998, p. 52.

Cryer R (2005) Superior orders and the International Criminal Court. In: Burchill R, White ND, Morris J (eds) International Conflict and Security Law. Essays in memory of Hilaire McCoubrey. Cambridge University Press, Cambridge, pp 49–67

Dinstein Y (1965) The defence of 'obedience to superior orders' in international law. A.W. Sijthoff, Leiden

Dinstein Y (2000) Defences. In: McDonald GK, Swaak-Goldman O (eds) Substantive and procedural aspects of international criminal law. The experience of international and national courts. Commentary, vol I. Kluwer Law International, The Hague, pp 369–388

Eser A (2002) Mental elements—mistake of fact and mistake of law. In: Cassese A, Gaeta P, Jones JRWD (eds) The Rome Statute of the International Criminal Court: a commentary, vol I. Oxford University Press, Oxford, pp 889–948

Fletcher GP (1978) Rethinking criminal law. Oxford University Press, Oxford (reprinted in 2000)

Fletcher GP (1998) Basic concepts of criminal law. Oxford University Press, New York

Gaeta P (1999) The defence of superior orders: the statute of the International Criminal Court versus customary international law. Eur J Int Law 10:172–191

Garraway CHB (1999) Superior orders and the International Criminal Court: justice delivered or justice denied. Int Rev Red Cross 81(836):785–794

Green LC (1999) Essays on the modern law of war, 2nd edn. Transnational Publishers, Inc, Ardsley

Heller KJ (2008) Mistake of legal element, the Common Law, and Article 32 of the Rome Statute. J Int Crim Justice 6:419–445

Jescheck HH (2004) The general principles of international criminal law set out in Nuremberg, as mirrored in the ICC Statute. J Int Crim Justice 2(1):38–55

Keijzer N (1977) The military duty to obey. Vrije Universiteit Amsterdam, Amsterdam

Keijzer N (1978) Military obedience. Sijthoff & Noordhoff International Publishers, Alphen aan de Rijn

McCoubrey H (2001) From Nuremberg to Rome: restoring the defence of superior orders. Int Comp Law Q 50:386–394

Nill-Theobald C (1998) "Defences" bei Kriegsverbrechen am Beispiel Deutschlands und der USA: zugleich ein Beitrag zu einem Allgemeinen Teil des Völkerstrafrechts, vol Band S 72. Beiträge und Materialien aus dem Max-Planck-Institut für ausländisches und internationales Strafrecht, Freiburg i.Br., iuscrim edn. Max-Planck-Institut für ausländisches und internationales Strafrecht, Freiburg im Breisgau

Olásolo H (2008) Unlawful attacks in combat situations: from the ICTY's case law to the Rome Statute. Martinus Nijhoff Publishers, Leiden

Osiel MJ (1999) Obeying orders. Transaction Publishers, New Brunswick

Piragoff DK (1999) Article 30: mental element. In: Triffterer O (ed) Commentary on the Rome Statute of the International Criminal Court: observers' notes, article by article. Nomos Verslagsgesellschaft, Baden-Baden, pp 527–535

Robinson D (1999) Defining "crimes against humanity" at the Rome Conference. Am J Int Law 93(1):43–57

Robinson PH (1984) Criminal Law Defenses, vol 2. West Publishing Co, St. Paul

Röling BVA (1961) The Law of War and the National Jurisdiction since 1945. A. W. Sythoff, Leiden

Scaliotti M (2001) Defences before the International Criminal Court: substantive grounds for excluding criminal responsibility—Part 1. Int Crim Law Rev 1:111–172

Scaliotti M (2002) Defences before the International Criminal Court: substantive grounds for excluding criminal responsibility—Part 2. Int Crim Law Rev 2:1–46

Sliedregt E van (2003) The criminal responsibility of individuals for violations of international humanitarian law. T.M.C. Asser Press, The Hague

Triffterer O (2008) Article 32: Mistake of Law. In: Triffterer O (ed) Commentary on the Rome Statute of the International Criminal Court: observers' notes, article by article, 2nd edn. C.H. Beck oHG, München, pp 895–914

Weigend T (2004) The harmonization of general principles of Criminal Law: the statutes and jurisprudence of the ICTY, ICTR, and the ICC: an overview. Nouvelles Etudes Penales 19:319–335

Werle G (2003) Völkerstrafrecht. Mohr Siebeck, Tübingen

Werle G, Jessberger F (2005) 'Unless otherwise provided': Article 30 of the ICC statute and the mental element of crimes under international criminal law. J Int Crim Justice 3:35–55

Wise EM (1998) Commentary on Parts 2 and 3 of the Zutphen Intersessional Draft: general principles of criminal law. Nouvelles Etudes Penales 13bis:43–53

Zimmermann A (2002) Superior Orders. In: Cassese A, Gaeta P, Jones JRWD (eds) The Rome Statute of the International Criminal Court: a commentary, vol I. Oxford University Press, Oxford, pp 957–974

Miscellaneous

International Committee of the Red Cross (2004) The Roots of Behaviour in War, Geneva, Switzerland

Chapter 5
Applying the Theory of Mistake of Law: An Analysis of (Inter)national Case Law

5.1 Introduction

This chapter is dedicated to an analysis of selected case law concerning defendants who pleaded mistake before national and international courts in cases concerning international crimes. The main focus is on proceedings that followed the Second World War.[1] To a large extent the case law under discussion reflects the general prerequisites for mistake of law as a defence, already explored in the comparative law and theoretical parts of this book.

Complicating factors in studying the case law, however, have been that cases where the defendant invokes, or seems to invoke, mistake of law often also involve other defences like mistake of fact, duress, (putative) necessity and (putative) self-defence. Putative justifications can in themselves be based on a mistake of law. However, they can also be based on mistakes of fact. Because the different defences are often so intertwined, it is difficult to filter out the arguments and legal reasoning related exclusively to the mistake of law defence. Another complicating factor in the analysis of American case law is that military trials have no judgment; the reasoning underlying the verdict remains unknown.[2]

Still, in the studied case law one recognises the theory of mistake of law and superior orders; important parameters are the unavoidability or reasonableness of the mistake and the manifest illegality of the superior orders. One can also recognise the conclusions of the comparative law analysis of Chap. 2; common law jurisdictions try to uphold the *ignorantia legis non excusat* rule (while allowing reasonable mistakes to mitigate the punishment or sometimes even to acquit the defendant) and civil law jurisdictions recognise an unavoidable mistake of law as an excuse in principle, often rejecting the plea on the facts of the case.

---

[1] See for other sources on the history of the defense of mistake of law and/or superior orders: Ambos 2004; Cassese 2003, 2009; Dinstein 1965; Osiel 1999; Vogeley 2003; Lippman 2001. For an overview of the history of the defence of superior orders in the United States see Solis 1999.
[2] If there is a conviction one, perhaps, can assume that the judges followed the view of the Judge Advocate. *See also* Green 2003, pp. 319–320.

A. van Verseveld, *Mistake of Law*, DOI: 10.1007/978-90-6704-867-5_5,

The case law reveals that at one end of the spectrum of possible verdicts is acquittal on the basis of legal uncertainty, and, on the other, is denial of the defence based on the manifest illegality of the superior order followed by the defendant.[3] The intermediate area, where the law is sufficiently clear but the order was not manifestly unlawful, is of particular interest in determining the scope of the defence of mistake of law.

5.2 The Case Law

The selected case law is mainly derived from the proceedings following the Second World War.[4] It covers other criminal proceedings in the decades thereafter as well, such as some cases related to the wars in Korea and Vietnam and a few more recent cases before the International Criminal Tribunal for the Former Yugoslavia (ICTY) and the ICC.

As Röling describes, the courts after WWII were confronted with the plea of ignorance of the law, because the law of war was mainly based on outdated treaties and the Martens-clause and had therefore not been able '"to follow the technical developments and changed spiritual climate".[5] There existed great uncertainty in the law of war, as recognised in the *I.G. Farben* trial.[6] The legality, under the law of war, of reprisals, "illegal acts done with the purpose to compel the adversary to legal conduct", also explains the plea of mistake of law as put forward.[7] The circumstances under which reprisals were allowed were very hard to discern for ordinary soldiers. First of all, it must have been difficult for them to know the applicable rules and second, they were probably not sufficiently aware of the relevant factual situation.[8] Even up to the present day the issue of reprisals remains far from settled.[9]

The cases in this chapter are discussed in a more or less chronological order. The cases are not divided into those that concern pleas of mistake of law and those in which superior orders were raised. As noted in the first paragraph the different defences are often intertwined, a mistake of law is a prerequisite for a successful plea of superior orders. Moreover, as argued by Dinstein, superior orders are not a

---

3 As seen earlier, the fact that many international crimes are committed within the context of the military organisation makes the defence of superior orders of particular relevance to the determination of the scope of the defence of mistake of law.

4 Swart describes how this case law has been a valuable source for the ad-hoc tribunals in establishing customary rules, Swart 2002.

5 Röling 1961, p. 370.

6 Röling 1961, p. 370; I.G. Farben Trial 1948.

7 Röling 1961, p. 371.

8 Röling 1961, p. 371.

9 Kalshoven 2005 and Kalshoven and Zegveld 2001. See for a further discussion of the uncertainty of the law relating to reprisal Sect. 6.3 *infra*.

defence *per se*, but may be a relevant circumstance in other defences like duress and mistake of law. The focus here is on the latter defence.

5.2.1 Pre-WWII Case Law

The *Dover Castle* case and the *Llandovery Castle* case are the two cases most often referred to when illustrating the general approach to the defence of superior orders prior to the Second World War.[10] Both cases were decided by the Leipzig Court which considered cases of German war crimes committed in World War I. The *Dover Castle* case (1921)[11] concerned the sinking of a British hospital ship by a German submarine. The British ship was clearly identifiable as a hospital ship; the defendant, Commander Karl Neumann, did not contest this. He argued that he was following orders of the German Admiralty, which had declared that it would fire at unannounced hospital ships since it suspected the British to use these ships for military purposes. The defendant believed that the order consisted of a legitimate reprisal.[12] The Court held that the *respondeat superior* rule applied; the subordinate has a duty to obey the orders of his superiors and therefore only the superior giving these orders is responsible. Article 47 of the German Military Code only provided for two exceptions to this rule: when the subordinate goes beyond (the scope of) the order or when the subordinate knows that the act ordered is criminal, the subordinate is liable too. In the case at hand, however, there was no evidence that either of these exceptions applied; the defendant was acquitted.[13]

The *Llandovery Castle* case (1921)[14] concerned a Canadian steamer that was torpedoed by a German U-Boat, because it was believed to be transporting troops and munitions, while in fact it was not. The Commander of the German U-boat, First-Lieutenant Patzig, had ordered the torpedoing of the Llandovery Castle, while aware of being acting against orders, because he believed that the enemy used hospital ships to transport troops and munitions.[15] Shortly after the first attack, which sank the ship in about ten minutes,[16] the survivors in life boats were fired upon and most of them were killed. The defendants in this case, Lieutenants Dithmar and Boldt (Patzig had disappeared), refused to give their account of what happened that day, because they said they had promised Patzig to be silent on the matter. They added that they did not shoot and whatever part they played they

---

[10] *See amongst others* Nill-Theobald 1998, pp. 82–88; Green 2003, pp. 322–324; Lippman 2001; and Sliedregt 2003, p. 318.

[11] Dover Castle case 1921.

[12] Dover Castle case 1921, pp. 706–707.

[13] Dover Castle case 1921, pp. 707–708.

[14] Llandovery Castle case 1921.

[15] Llandovery Castle case 1921, p. 710.

[16] Llandovery Castle case 1921, p. 710.

were acting under superior orders. They said they did not know they were doing something unlawful. However, this last attack, against defenceless survivors was, according to the Leipzig court, universally known to be against the law.[17] The court establishes that the defendants, as naval officers by profession, must have known that killing defenceless people is unlawful.[18] According to Lippman a manifest illegality rule was seemingly added to the subjective knowledge test of the Dover Castle case.[19] One could also conclude from the court's reasoning that "knew" in Article 47 of the German Military Penal Code includes "must have known". The Court held that since they knew that killing defenceless people is not legally authorised they should have refused to obey.[20] The defendants, Lieutenants Dithmar and Boldt, were held responsible for having taken part in homicide. They were sentenced as accessories[21] to 4 years' imprisonment, the fact that they had acted on superior orders was considered a mitigating circumstance.[22]

5.2.2 WWII Case Law

The main case law concerning superior orders is to be found in the proceedings after the Second World War. The trend from *respondeat superior* to the conditional liability of the subordinate was continued. In fact, the Statute of the International Military Tribunal at Nuremberg banned the raising of a defence of superior orders all together; the subordinate was responsible and the fact that he had acted on superior orders could only mitigate his sentence if justice so required.[23] Control Council Law No. 10 drafted for the subsequent proceedings provides the same in Article II (4)(b). The subsequent proceedings and national prosecutions following the Second World War show a mixed result, however, sometimes only allowing mitigation but sometimes also resulting in acquittal or at least a recognition of the existence in principle of a complete defence of mistake of law or superior order.[24]

5.2.2.1 United States

In the *High Command* trial (1948), uncertainty of a rule of international law, namely the use of prisoners of war in the construction of fortifications in non-

[17] Llandovery Castle case 1921, p. 721; Lippman 2001, p. 168.
[18] Llandovery Castle case 1921, p. 722.
[19] Lippman 2001, p. 170.
[20] Llandovery Castle case 1921, p. 722.
[21] Llandovery Castle case 1921, p. 721.
[22] Llandovery Castle case 1921, p. 723.
[23] Article 8 IMT Nuremberg; and Article 6 IMTFE.
[24] *See also* Bantekas and Nash 2007, pp. 58–59 and Garraway 1999.

dangerous areas, was reason for a (partial) acquittal on the basis of mistake of law.[25] "Because international law as to this matter was not crystal clear, and certainly not manifestly unlawful, the subordinates/defendants had the right to rely on their superiors".[26]

The accused, in this case, were former high-ranking officers in the German Army and Navy, and officers holding high positions in the German High Command.[27] One of the issues that arose concerned the responsibility of field commanders for passing on unlawful superior orders. The United States Military Tribunal at Nuremberg (NMT) held that to a certain extent a field commander has a right to assume the lawfulness of orders from his superiors. If he does not know the order to be unlawful, and his mistake is reasonable, that is, the order was not criminal upon its face, he is not liable for passing it on.[28] On the one hand, the Law Reports note that this test is applied as a rule to the plea of superior orders in general.[29] On the other, the Law Reports comment that the Tribunal in the High Command case stands out as an exception in the legal effect it attributes to the plea of superior orders: acquittal as opposed to merely mitigation of punishment.[30]

In the *Hostages Case* (1948), the NMT, indeed, held that the plea of superior orders could only lead to mitigation of punishment, it could never afford a complete defence.[31] The following, however, suggests to the contrary, i.e. that under certain circumstances superior orders is a defence, except in case of a manifestly unlawful order: "We are of the view, however, that if the illegality of the order was not known to the inferior and he could not reasonably have been expected to know of its illegality, no wrongful intent necessary to the commission of a crime exists and the inferior will be protected.[32] But the general rule is that members of the armed forces are bound to obey only the lawful orders of their commanding officers and they cannot escape criminal liability by obeying a command which violates International Law and outrages fundamental concepts of justice."[33] The Tribunal than states, however, that "International Law has never approved the defensive plea of superior order as a mandatory bar to the prosecution of war criminals. This defensive plea is not available to the defendants in the present case, although if the circumstances warrant, it may be considered in mitigation of

25 Von Leeb (The High Command Trial) 1948, UNWCC, vol. XII, pp. 88–89. *See also* Henckaerts and Doswald-Beck 2005, rule 155, § 969, p. 3839.

26 Dinstein 1965, p. 187; Von Leeb (The High Command Trial) 1948, UNWCC, vol. XII, pp. 88–89.

27 Von Leeb (The High Command Trial) 1948, UNWCC, vol. XII, p. 1.

28 Von Leeb (The High Command Trial) 1948 UNWCC, vol. XII, pp. 73–74 and Friedman, vol. II, p. 1433.

29 Von Leeb (The High Command Trial) 1948 UNWCC, vol. XII, p. 74, footnote 1.

30 Von Leeb (The High Command Trial) 1948 UNWCC, vol. XII, p. 98.

31 List (The Hostages Case) 1948, UNWCC, vol. VIII, p. 50.

32 The Tribunal referred to the Llandovery Castle case, List (The Hostages case) (1948), UNWCC, vol. VIII, p. 50; *see also* Dinstein 1965, p. 185.

33 List (The Hostages Case) (1948), UNWCC, vol. VIII, p. 50.

punishment under the express provisions of Control Council Law No. 10".[34] In this case, superior orders was only considered to potentially give rise to some mitigation of punishment, not to an acquittal.[35]

The Judgement in the *Einsatzgruppen* case discussed the superior orders defence both in light of the defence of mistake of law[36] and in light of the defence of duress.[37] The Tribunal concludes both forms of the superior orders defence are absent: there is no ignorance of illegality when one participates in an illegal enterprise and no duress when the subordinate "is in accord with the principle and intent of the superior".[38] Knowledge of illegality is inferred from the circumstances of participating in an illegal enterprise.

Anton *Dostler* (1945), commander of the 75th German Army Corps, was prosecuted by the US Militiary Commission in Rome for "having ordered the shooting of fifteen American prisoners of war in violation of the Regulations attached to the Hague Convention Number IV of 1907, and of long-established laws and customs of war".[39] Dostler's defence was that he believed he was executing a lawful reprisal.[40] Dostler's plea of superior orders failed because in ordering the execution he had acted outside the Führer's orders that "if members of Allied commando units were encountered by German troops they were to be exterminated either in combat or in pursuit. If they should fall into the hands of the Wehrmacht through different channels they were to be handed over to the Sicherheitsdienst without delay."[41] And even if there was a superior order underlying his criminal act, this order could never justify the summary execution of P.O.W.'s.[42] The Military Commission probably rejected his plea, holding that all acts of reprisals are forbidden against prisoners of war (Geneva Prisoners of War Convention of 1929). "No soldier, and still less a Commanding General, can be heard to say that he considered the summary shooting of prisoners of war legitimate even as a reprisal".[43] One could say Dostler was mistaken in a double sense, first of all as to the existence and/or scope of the order, and secondly as to the lawfulness of its presumed contents. The first mistake can be considered a mistake of fact, but when the facts, even if they were as the defendant believed or perceived them to be, would not justify the defendant's behaviour, his mistake was in fact a

[34] List (The Hostages Case) 1948, UNWCC, vol. VIII, p. 52.

[35] List (The Hostages Case) 1948, UNWCC, vol. VIII, p. 52.

[36] US v. Otto Ohlendorf et al. (Einsatzgruppen case) 1948, pp. 473–480 (under the heading "Superior Orders Defence Must Establish Ignorance of Illegality").

[37] US v. Otto Ohlendorf et al. (Einsatzgruppen case) 1948 pp. 480–483 (under the heading "Duress Needed for Plea of Superior Orders").

[38] US v. Otto Ohlendorf et al. (Einsatzgruppen case) 1948, p. 473 and p. 480 respectively.

[39] Dostler trial 1945, pp. 22 and 25–26.

[40] Dostler trial 1945, pp. 26–28.

[41] Dostler trial 1945, pp. 26–27.

[42] Dostler trial 1945, p. 33.

[43] Dostler trial 1945, p. 31.

mistake of law; he was mistaken as to a ground for justification. In such a case, the mistake of fact is subsumed by a mistake of law; the mistake of fact is no longer relevant.[44]

The judgement in the *Sawada* trial (1946) held that the defendants had acted on superior orders; "they exercised no initiative to any marked degree". According to the Commission, though, this did not absolve them from guilt. The fact that they had acted on superior orders only led to a substantial mitigation of their punishment.[45]

The UNWCC notes on this case are interesting for they give an overview of the history of the defence of superior orders in international criminal law, which had been raised in war crime trials more frequently than any other defence.[46] The conclusion is that the defence of superior orders is not successful when the orders are manifestly unlawful or when a man of ordinary sense and understanding knows the order to be unlawful.[47] The discussion is somewhat confused; however, because no distinction is being made between *superior orders—mistake of law* and *superior orders—duress*.[48] The main denominator, however, is arguably, "whether moral choice was in fact possible", i.e. whether the defendant had a moral choice to behave differently.[49] The commission probably did not have *superior orders—mistake of law* in mind when it discussed the moral choice test, but it can be argued that both in case of duress and of mistake of law, the defendant had no moral choice to act differently.

In other trials reported in the Law Reports, so the note summarises, the validity of the plea turned "upon the illegality, the obvious illegality or the knowledge or presumed knowledge of the illegality of the order given".[50] This seems rather obvious, a subordinate following lawful superior orders will not likely face prosecution for criminal behaviour. Thus, the superior orders defence will only be invoked in cases of illegal superior orders; illegality plays a fundamental role. But the test applied, either of illegality per se, or knowledge of illegality or manifest illegality, is precisely the determining factor in relation to the defendant's culpability. The UNWCC lacks precision in its analysis on this point.

The commission further summarises the general legal effect of a successful plea of superior orders. According to the commission, most sources show "a great reluctance to regard superior orders as a complete defence".[51] The general legal

44 See also the Almelo trial, Sect. 5.2.2.2 *infra*.

45 Trial of Sawada 1946, p. 7.

46 Trial of Sawada 1946, p. 13.

47 Trial of Sawada 1946, pp. 14–19.

48 This is confusing because in case of duress, a mistake of law is no requirement.

49 Trial of Sawada 1946, p. 19.

50 Trial of Sawada 1946, p. 16.

51 Trial of Sawada 1946 UNWCC, vol. V, p. 19.

effect has been, according to the commission, mitigation of punishment.[52] Not all the sources that the commission refers to, however, exclude the possibility of superior orders leading to the acquittal of the defendant.[53]

5.2.2.2 United Kingdom

In *Peleus* (1945) the defendants were charged with the killing of the survivors of a sunken steamship, the Peleus.[54] The defence argued that the defendants should be acquitted because they were unaware of the illegality of the order they followed. The defence referred to the Dover Castle case.[55] The defence for the defendant Eck, the commander of the U-Boat, who gave the order, also invoked the defence of operational necessity.[56] The facts of the case are very similar to the Llandovery Castle case.[57] The defence of reliance on superior orders was rejected because the order was manifestly unlawful.[58] With regard to operational necessity the Prosecutor argued that it would have been much more effective to save the ship and his crew by removing the boat as fast as possible instead of taking five hours to sink the wreckage.[59]

The Peleus Trial is often referred to for its famous quote from the summing up of the Judge Advocate: "It is quite obvious that no sailor and no soldier can carry with him a library of international law, or have immediate access to a professor in that subject who can tell him whether or not a particular command is a lawful one".[60]

In two other cases before British Military Courts, the *Buck* trial and the *Almelo* trial, it is questionable whether the defendants actually acted under mistake of law. The cases give some insight in the treatment of this defence before British Military

52 The Commission refers to Article 8 of the Nuremberg Charter, Article 6 of the Tokyo Charter, Article II(4)(b) of the Allied Control Council Law No. 10, "Regulation 9 of the US Mediterranean regulations, Regulation 16(f) of the Pacific regulations, September 1945, regulation 5 (d), (6) of the Pacific regulations, December 1945, and Regulation 16(f) of the China Regulations", the 'Norwegian Law of 13th December, 1946, on the Punishment of Foreign War Criminals' and other domestic regulations. Trial of Sawada 1946, pp. 19–20.

53 The Commission refers to e.g. Article 15 of the Canadian War Crimes Act of 31st August, 1946; Article 43 Dutch Criminal Code; The United States Basic Field Manual F.M. 27-10 (Rules of Land Warfare), para 345. Trial of Sawada 1946, pp. 20–22.

54 Peleus Trial 1945, p. 2.

55 Peleus Trial 1945, p. 9.

56 Peleus Trial 1945, p. 4.

57 *See also* Peleus Trial 1945, p. 19 (the motive of both commanders (Patzig and Eck) was different. Patzig's motive was concealment of criminal acts and Eck's was operational necessity (UNWCC, p. 19), the latter is arguably a justification. The prosecutor based its case on this case (Llandovery Castle) (UNWCC, pp. 10–11).

58 *See also* Vogeley 2003, p. 80.

59 Peleus Trial 1945, p. 12.

60 Peleus Trial 1945, p. 12.

Courts. Notwithstanding the general rule, that ignorance of the law is no excuse, it was accepted, in principle, that there are circumstances, i.e. superior orders concerning violations of international law, in which the defence of mistake of law must lead to an acquittal.

In *Buck* (1946) all 11 defendants except one were found guilty, "charged with committing a war crime, in that they, in violation of the laws and customs on war, were concerned in the killing of six British prisoners of war, four American prisoners of war and four French nationals".[61] The defence claimed that all of the accused had acted under superior orders. The purport of the so-called Leader Order of 18 October 1942 was that all "members of so-called Commando detachments who were parachuted from the air behind the German Lines to do acts of sabotage and interference" were not to be treated as POWs but were to be shot.[62] With regard to the defence of superior orders "the Judge Advocate expressed the view that an accused would be guilty if he committed a war crime in pursuance of an order, first if the order was obviously unlawful, secondly if the accused knew that the order was unlawful, or thirdly if he ought to have known it to be unlawful had he considered the circumstances in which it was given".[63] The defence claimed that the accused acted under mistake of fact, they "had no other information on the matter than that the prisoners had been tried and condemned, and had acted on that assumption".[64] The Prosecutor, however, held that "the obliteration of all traces of the crime and the steps taken by the accused to suppress all knowledge of the crime belied any contention that they thought that they were performing a legal execution".[65] With regard to the defence of mistake of law the Court considered that "it is a rule of English law that ignorance of the law is no excuse [...] There are some indications that this principle when applied to the provisions of international law is not regarded universally as being in all cases strictly enforceable".[66] The Judge Advocate summed up what the requirements of mistake of law are. What did the defendants know about the rights of prisoners of war? Their knowledge is not to be compared to the knowledge of legal experts. Their knowledge should be compared with what an ordinary soldier, like the defendants, know as a general fact of military life about the rights of prisoners of war. The Judge Advocate held that such a reasonable soldier is, or should be, aware of the fundamental right of a prisoner of war to security of his person.[67] Hence, although accepted in theory, both the defence of mistake of law and that of superior orders were denied on the facts of this case.

---

61 Buck Trial 1946, p. 39.
62 Buck Trial 1946, p. 42.
63 Buck Trial 1946, p. 43.
64 Buck Trial 1946, p. 43.
65 Buck Trial 1946, p. 43.
66 Buck Trial 1946, p. 44.
67 Buck Trial 1946, p. 44.

In the *Almelo* trial (1945), the accused were charged with committing a war crime in that they, in violation of the laws and usages of war, killed a British prisoner of war and a Dutch civilian. "The Judge Advocate asked whether there was any evidence upon which the court could find that, these three men or any of them honestly believed that this British officer had been tried according to law, and that they were carrying out a lawful execution. If the court was satisfied that this was not so, then it would be clearly quite right to reject any defence that might have been put up under that heading."[68] The first prerequisite for a successful plea of mistake is obviously that the defendant was honestly mistaken. His plea must be credible. The Judge Advocate continues: "On the other hand, if the court felt that circumstances were such that a reasonable man might have believed that this officer had been tried according to law, and that they were carrying out a proper judicial legal execution, then it would be open to the court to acquit the accused."[69] The mistake has to have been reasonable in order to exculpate the defendant.

One could dispute whether the mistake in this case was a mistake of law and not a mistake of fact. What were the defendants mistaken about? They believed the P.O.W.'s had been tried according to the law and the order to execute them was, thus, based on a legal decision. This is a mistake of fact, because there was no legal decision holding the verdict of execution. This mistake of fact is only subsumed by a mistake of law, when it would be a rule of international humanitarian law that prisoners of war can never be sentenced to death and the defendant was ignorant of such a rule.

In *Falkenhorst* (1946) the defendant pleaded having acted on a superior order, which he believed involved a reprisal. The annotator notes that the defence of superior order, in this case as in others, "raised with the question of reprisal, has not been strongly stressed by the defence".[70] The annotator notes how very complicated the legal principles relating to reprisals are and how in fact "[t]he whole basis of the wrongfulness of disobeying unlawful orders may fall to the ground" because reprisals precisely concern otherwise unlawful acts.[71] This case gives a foretaste of the conditions for a successful plea of superior orders, as now codified in Article 33 of the Rome Statute. According to the Notes on the case, the question is to what extent the defendant can be exonerated from responsibility for carrying out an illegitimate reprisal, if the defendant did not know about "the inadequate grounds that purported to give rise to the reprisal by his government".[72] Nevertheless, the note continues, "the laws of war demand that there must be a concurrence of a considerable number of factors before an occasion to exercise the right or reprisal arises." And "Article 2 of the Geneva Convention of

[68] Trial of Sandrock (Almelo Trial) 1945, p. 40.

[69] Trial of Sandrock (Almelo Trial) 1945, p. 41.

[70] Falkenhorst trial 1946, p. 26.

[71] Falkenhorst trial 1946, p. 27.

[72] Falkenhorst trial 1946, p. 26.

1929 forbids measures of reprisal being taken against prisoners of war."[73] One could say that an order violating this rule is manifestly unlawful. As seen before, in case of manifestly unlawful orders inference of personal knowledge is often justified.[74]

5.2.2.3 Other Countries

Reprisals have been the object of many more cases before criminal courts after the Second World War. As Best notes, not the decisions of these courts, but the Geneva Conventions of 1949 have banned reprisals (but not completely).[75] Reprisals still remain a controversial issue. The problem with reprisals is that under certain strict conditions they make legitimate what would otherwise be wrongful conduct when they are necessary and the only means to stop the adverse party in their unlawful behaviour.[76]

Controversial issues in international law will be conducive to an acquittal on the basis of mistake of law. An example of this can be found in the *Latza* trial (1948); the defendants, three German judges, were acquitted on the basis of having made a mistake of law.[77] On the 8th of February 1945 a German Standgericht was set up in Oslo, as a countermeasure to growing acts of sabotage of the Norwegian underground movement. The accused Latza acted as president of the Standgericht. On the day of the establishment of the Standgericht, five Norwegians, who were arrested earlier that same day, were sentenced to death by Latza and two other judges. The death sentences were carried out the following day. After the liberation of Norway Latza and the two other judges were "charged with having committed a war crime in that he through a denial of a fair trial and judging against their better knowledge had unlawfully caused the death of the five [...] Norwegian citizens".[78] All three accused were eventually acquitted, after two judgements by the Lagmannsrett and the Supreme Court.

In the Latza trial, the defence of mistake of law concerned the question of "the legality under international law of the enforcement of a provision punishing failure, on the part of inhabitants of occupied territory, to impart information to the occupying power regarding the activities of other inhabitants against the occupying power".[79]

One of the Norwegian defendants before the Standgericht had, pursuant to Article 3 of a German Verordnung of 12th October 1942, been sentenced to death

[73] Falkenhorst trial 1946, p. 27.

[74] *See also* Green 2003, p. 350.

[75] Best 1994, p. 313.

[76] *See also* Sect. 6.3 *infra*.

[77] Helmuth Latza and 2 others 1948.

[78] Helmuth Latza and 2 others 1948, p. 49.

[79] Helmuth Latza and 2 others 1948, p. 83.

for failure to denounce his two brothers-in-law for certain contemplated acts of sabotage. The Lagmannsrett decided that the accused had acted in an excusable mistake of law when they applied this provision of the German Verordnung, since even legal experts differed in their opinions as to whether this provision was at variance with international law.[80] The Norwegian Supreme Court upheld the decision of the Court of Appeal. It concluded that it could not be claimed that the illegality of imposing punishment for a failure to notify an occupation power of the activities of a patriotic movement had already been established as an unquestionable rule of international law.[81]

Although the defendant in this case pleaded mistake of law and he was eventually acquitted, it remains uncertain whether that acquittal was based on this defence of mistake of law or whether it was based on the dubiousness of the illegality of the German provision to begin with. The Law Reports comment that "[i]n the Latza Trial a Norwegian Lagmannsrett held that the accused had been under a pardonable misconception in incorrectly believing that a certain German law was consistent with international law, but on appeal the Norwegian Supreme Court stated that it could not find, in view of the uncertainty of international law on the point, that the German provision was in fact illegal."[82]

In the Dutch case *Wintgen* (1949), the defendant was acquitted because he did not know the concerned acts of reprisal were unlawful under international law.[83] This case is more interesting for our purposes than the Latza trial because the Court did find that the alleged acts constituted war crimes; the plea of mistake of law was, thereafter, assessed on its merits. The evaluation of Wintgen's plea of mistake of law depended on the defendant's intellectual capacities and his military position on the one hand and the gravity of the crimes on the other. In *Rauter*[84] the Special Court had already determined that the rule on superior orders applicable was not Article 43 of the Dutch Criminal Code but Article 47 of the German Military code,[85] which read:

(1) *Wird durch die Ausführung eines Befehls in Dienstsachen ein Strafgesetz verletzt, so ist dafür der befehlende Vorgesetzte verantwortlich. Es trifft jedoch den gehorchenden Untergebenen die Strafe des Teilnehmers:*

1. *wenn er den erteilten Befehl übderschritten hat; oder*
2. *wenn ihm bekannt gewesen ist, dass der Befehl des Vorgesetzten eine Handlung betraf, welche ein allgemeines oder militärischen Verbrechen oder Vergehen bezweckte.*

---

80 Helmuth Latza and 2 others 1948, pp. 69–70.

81 Helmuth Latza and 2 others 1948, pp. 82–83.

82 Law Reports of Trials of War Criminals, selected and prepared by the United Nations War Crimes Commission 1949, p. 184; Helmuth Latza and 2 others 1948, pp. 60, 69 and 82–83.

83 Wintgen 1949.

84 Rauter 1949, NJ 1949, 87, pp. 144–166.

85 Rauter 1949 NJ 1949, 87, p. 158. *See also* Röling 1961, pp. 373–374.

(2) *Ist die Schuld des Untergebenen gering, so kann von seiner Bestrafung abgesehen werden.*[86]

The Court in Wintgen then established that knowledge of unlawfulness is not an element of the alleged war crime "devastation not justified by military necessity". It found that there was some dispute about the wrongfulness of the burning of the houses. § 358 (e) US Basic Field Manual stipulated that burning of houses is a form of reprisal. Oppenheim–Lauterpacht (II, §250) interpreted Article 50 of the Hague Regulations to allow for the burning of houses by way of reprisals. The Court, however, rejects these claims and determines the acts to be war crimes. The Court then continues that this does not per se imply the defendant should be punished.[87] The defendant can claim he did not know about the wrongfulness of his acts. The Court warns that this defence should not be accepted too easily and states the terms on which its applicability should be accepted to be: the practical training the defendant received or intellectual capacities of the defendant and his military position on the one hand and the nature of the crimes committed on the other.[88] With regard to this last aspect, the Court held that "according to everyone's moral understanding the killing of defenceless prisoners or innocent civilians is far more serious than the devastation of property. In the current case, in light of the discussion about military crimes, it cannot be established that the defendant, a low ranking policeman, knew about criminal nature of his behaviour under humanitarian law."[89] The defendant was acquitted.

In an annotation to this case the famous commentator Röling noted that the German provision required knowledge that execution of the order led to a (military) crime. "In this case the defendant was acquitted because of a mistake regarding the *punishability* of the act, not because of an unavoidable mistake of law regarding the wrongfulness."[90] As seen in Chap. 2, German doctrine has changed in this respect, requiring *Unrechtsbewußtsein*, which means knowledge of the *wrongfulness* of the behaviour; a mistake about the *criminal nature* is irrelevant.[91]

---

[86] Translation (AvV):
(1) If the execution of a military order leads to the commission of a crime, the superior who issued the order is responsible for this crime. The executing subordinate is however criminally responsible as accomplice:
1. if he went beyond the scope of the order; or
2. if he knew of the fact that the order of his superior required an act which constituted a (military) crime.
(2) Is the culpability of the defendant remote, it can be decided not to punish him.

[87] Wintgen 1949, p. 984.

[88] Wintgen 1949, NJ 1949, 540, p. 985; see also Cassese 2008, pp. 296–297.

[89] Wintgen 1949, NJ 1949, 540, p. 985 (translation AvV).

[90] Wintgen 1949 NJ, 1949, 540, p. 985 (translation AvV).

[91] See also § 5 WStG which uses the term 'rechtswidrige Tat', and § 3 VStGB, *see also* Sect. 2.4.2 *supra*.

Another Dutch case in which the Court applied § 47 MStGB is *Zühlke* (1948).[92] The UNWCC Notes on the Case state that this trial offered an opportunity for the Dutch Special Court to establish their view on the defence of superior orders and Article 8 of the Nuremberg charter. The Dutch war crimes legislation did not contain a specific provision on the issue. The penal code provided for a defence of superior orders in Article 43 WvSr. The Supreme Court applied the German provision. It held that Article 8 of the Nuremberg charter only applied to major war criminals and was no rule of customary law.[93] Zühlke, a former German prison warder and member of the Waffen-SS, charged with illegal detention and ill-treatment of prisoners, was unsuccessful in his plea of superior orders. Although the defendant, as a low ranking prison warder, had only limited discretionary powers, the Court was satisfied that there existed no duty of blind obedience and that his plea of superior orders was rejected in conformity with § 47 MStGB.[94] The Court concluded with the finding that in as far as his plea of superior orders implied a plea of supposed *Befehl ist Befehl*, this plea is understood to mean a plea of duress. The facts of the case did not support this plea.[95]

In *Zimmermann* (1949), the defendant pleaded mistake of law with regard to the deportation of P.O.W.'s for forced labour in Germany.[96] In this case too, the plea was rejected on the basis of inference of knowledge on the part of the defendant from the evidence presented.[97] The Dutch Special Court referred to the public indignation in respect of similar practices in WWI. Deportation of civilians for forced labour in the German war industry must have been evidently unlawful because during WWI these acts were publicly condemned.[98] Sluiter remarks that "[t]he Court did not refer to any treaty provision in this respect."[99]

The defendant in *Lages* (1950), believed he had merely executed a lawful execution. The Court rejected his plea. It held that the executions authorised by the commander of the Sicherheitspolizei were in flagrant violation of occupation law, and Lages, a high, well-educated military officer, must have known this. According to the Court the evidence justified this inference.[100]

---

[92] Zühlke Trial 1948, NJ 1949, No. 85, pp. 129–138.

[93] Zühlke Trial 1948 Friedman, pp. 1549–1551, NJ 1949, No. 85, p. 134. *See also* Wilt 2009b. This is a debatable position, see Sect. 4.3.3 *supra*.

[94] Zühlke Trial 1948, NJ 1949, No. 85, pp. 134–135. I do not fully support the account of the reasoning of the Court given by the UNWCC in Friedman, p. 1551, where it is stated that Zülke, "who was not only a prison warder by occupation but had also been trained as a non-commissioned officer, must have known" that the detention and the ill-treatment and humiliation of the prisoners was illegal.

[95] Zühlke Trial 1948 NJ 1949, No. 85, pp. 134–135.

[96] Zimmermann 1949.

[97] *See also* Röling 1961, p. 375.

[98] Zimmermann 1949, NJ 1950, No. 9, p. 31.

[99] Sluiter 2009b, p. 982.

[100] Lages case 1950, p. 1206.

In *Arlt* (1949), the Dutch Special Court of Cassation recognised the excuse of unavoidable mistake of law in principle.[101] Arlt, a German Judge in a summary Court Martial (*Polizeistandgericht*), had sentenced a Dutch civilian to death for participating in a strike. The Special Court found that the Court Martial had been established in violation of public international law. In determining whether Arlt should be punished the Supreme Court decided it should be assessed how Arlt had discharged himself of his judicial duties within the established framework.[102] This test, referring to the established framework, seems rather lenient. It implied that it was considered a given fact that the defendant had to operate in an unlawfully established court martial. The issue was, according to the Court, whether he discharged of his duties in a proper way, respecting the basic principles of a good administration of justice,[103] that would be applicable in a legitimate court.

In the prosecution of two members of the Dutch Resistance movement, *Van E.* and his commander *B.* (1951), the Field Court Martial found both defendants not guilty on the basis of superior orders and mistake of law, respectively.[104] The particular unit of which the defendants were members was granted the status of armed forces as part of the Dutch Army by a Dutch royal decree of 1944.[105]

In April 1945 Commander B. had ordered Van E. to execute four Dutch collaborators, who previously had been taken prisoner. According to B. the execution of the prisoners was necessary because they could not take the prisoners with them, while, together with French parachutists, they had to change position. Van E. executed the order together with two others and killed the four persons. After the war both defendants were charged with manslaughter.

Commander B. was acquitted because the Court found that under the circumstances, it was very likely that the four collaborators, if released, would form a threat. They would attack the members of the B.'s unit and the French parachutists they had to protect or would tell the Germans their whereabouts. Among the members of the group and the French parachutists it was not considered to be unlawful to execute collaborators. Additionally, this unit of the Dutch Resistance Movement had been given instructions to follow all the orders of the allied forces and to do anything in their power to protect them. The defendant had to take the decision without being able to consult a superior, he found himself in a position for which he was not educated nor trained and the circumstances were such that there was no time for deliberation.[106] The Court concluded that the defendant did not

---

[101] Arlt 1949. *See also* Cassese 2008, p. 298, footnote 60.

[102] Arlt 1949, NJ 1950, no. 8, p. 29.

[103] Sluiter 2009a, p. 585.

[104] E. van E. case 1951; B. case 1951.

[105] B. case 1951, p. 522. *See also* Cassese 2008, p. 297.

[106] B. case 1951, pp. 524–525. In several cases, the courts decided obiter dicta that unlawful orders may relieve of responsibility if given on the battlefield, Cassese 2003, p. 239.

know of the unlawfulness of his acts and that, taking into account the circumstances and his personal capacities, he could not be blamed for this ignorance.[107]

In the case against Van E. the Court decided that "given the circumstances in which the order was given, the accused was entitled to assume in good faith that his commanding officer was authorized to give that order for the liquidation of the prisoners, and that this order was within the scope of his subordination".[108]

In these cases the different conditions related to the defence of superior orders and mistake of law surface. Superior orders will exculpate if the subordinate followed the order, which fell within the scope of his subordination in good faith. Mistake of law will exculpate if the mistake was unavoidable. Again, however, it is unclear whether these cases represent true cases of mistake of law.[109] The pleas could imply a plea of putative self-defence or (military) necessity, mistake of fact (did the defendant know that their victims had POW status?) or mistake of law. As noted earlier, a mistake of fact, for example as to the protected status of the victims, is subsumed by a mistake of law when had the facts been as they were perceived, this would not have justified the executions.

To conclude the discussion of Dutch cases, it should be noted that these cases have brought about discussion on alleged differences in punishment meted out to national defendants and enemy defendants. In earlier case law the Netherlands Special Court of Cassation, imposed harsh punishments for arbitrary execution. It was held that it was generally accepted that arbitrary executions are always illegal and every right-minded person knows this.[110]

In *SAH Alsagoff* (1946)[111] mistake of law as a defence was rejected. Only when the belief one has to obey superior orders is based on a mistake of fact, this may exculpate the subordinate. This mistake of fact must be made in good faith and must be reasonable. Mistake of law may only serve as mitigation of punishment. The defendants, in obeying the unlawful orders, did not act on the basis of a mistake of fact; their mistake as to the question whether their superiors were lawfully empowered to order beatings constituted a mistake of law.[112]

In the South African case *Werner* (1947)[113] mistake of law as a defence was rejected as well. The defendants held that they were given orders by a superior officer which they thought they were under a duty to obey. Reference was made to the famous case Reg. v. Smith[114] which held that in case of doubt the subordinate should obey. In this case, however, the Court held that "the so-called trial of Haensel by Major von Lubke was entirely illegal and the order given by him that Haensel

[107] B. case 1951, pp. 524–525.

[108] Cassese 2003, p. 235, note 15; E. van E. case 1951, p. 516.

[109] *See also supra* Trial of Sandrock (Almelo Trial) 1945.

[110] See Notes on the B. case by Röling, B. case 1951, pp. 525–526.

[111] R. v. SAH Alsagoff 1946, available at http://www.icrc.org/ihl-nat.nsf/WebALL!OpenView.

[112] R. v. SAH Alsagoff 1946.

[113] Werner case 1947, also available at: http://www.icrc.org/ihl-nat.nsf/WebALL!OpenView.

[114] Reg. v. Smith (17, S.C. 561).

should be executed was an unlawful order." The Court held that the defendants were not bound by these orders, because as prisoners of war they fell under the South-African command, the German command did not apply. Perhaps the defendants thought they were bound to obey all superior orders; this is a mistake of law, and mistake of law, under the law of South Africa, is not an excuse.[115] Here, the issue of mistake of law concerned the question as to if and which superior orders should be obeyed and not the contents of the particular superior order.

Gaeta discusses two Italian cases concerning the defence of superior orders, *Kappler* (1948) and *Priebke* (1998). Both cases concerned the same facts but were decided 50 years apart. The facts concerned the massacre at the Ardeatine Caves in Italy on 24 March 1944; 335 men and boys were killed as a reprisal measure in reaction to a partisan attack the day before in which 33 Germans were killed. The 335 victims were not involved in the partisan attack. The SS Lieutenant Kappler was head of the police in Rome and in charge of the summary executions.[116] In his prosecution in 1948 the Rome Military tribunal "found that it was doubtful that the accused possessed 'the conscience and the intent to obey an unlawful order'. This doubt on the existence of *mens rea* stemmed from various factors: 'the mental habit to promptly obey…(within) an organization based on extremely rigid discipline' namely the SS; 'the fact that an order with the same content had been executed in various combat zones'; and that the order 'had been issued by the Head of State and Supreme Commander of armed forces and therefore had great moral strength.' Kappler was therefore acquitted of the charge of the murder of 320 Italians out of the 335 people executed at the Fosse Ardeatine and was found guilty only of the murder of the remaining fifteen."[117] At that time, Kappler's subordinates were acquitted because they acted on superior orders; they did not knowingly execute an illegal order.[118]

Gaeta describes how in recent case law the judicial opinion changed radically. In *Priebke*, who was one of the main executioners and had evaded prosecution for several decades, the defence of superior orders was denied. Although the Germans had a right to resort to reprisals, this particular reprisal was illegitimate because it lacked proportionality and necessity. Priebke could not rely on the ordered reprisal, because the order was manifestly unlawful.[119] Gaeta has argued that "the Rome Military Court of Appeal went so far as to hold that an order to commit war crimes can never constitute a defence because such an order is always manifestly unlawful."[120] She argued that the Rome Military Court rightly applied the

[115] Werner case 1947.

[116] See M. Scharf at http://humanrightsdoctorate.blogspot.com/2008_02_01_archive.html.

[117] Gaeta 2001, p. 759; Kappler and others 1948; Hass and Priebke case 1998.

[118] Trial Watch: http://www.trial-ch.org/en/trial-watch/profile/db/spotlight/erich_priebke_579.html.

[119] ICRC: http://www.icrc.org/IHL-NAT.NSF/39a82e2ca42b52974125673e00508144/0370fc27370b3776c1256c8c0055e44d!OpenDocument.

[120] Gaeta 2001, p. 759.

Nuremberg rule.[121] She continued: “How could the order to commit such a ‘most serious crime’ relieve a subordinate of his criminal responsibility, thus giving him full impunity for that crime?”[122] It may be thought, however, that this argument is unfounded for it ignores the fact that the defence of superior orders only excuses the subordinate if certain requirements are met. It is not true, for the defence of superior orders in any (inter)national legal system, that the fact of obeying orders on its own will exculpate. If the act committed in obedience to a superior order is in fact manifestly unlawful than the defendant will not be excused. Instead of understanding Article 8 IMT Nuremberg as applicable to the *crimes* before this Court,[123] one could also argue that Article 8 IMT is applicable to the *defendants* before this Court.[124]

5.2.3 Trials Related to Other Armed Conflicts After WWII

The defendant in *U.S. v. Kinder* (1954) was prosecuted for premeditated murder of a Korean prisoner.[125] Kinder, an airman on interior guard duty, had killed the victim on a superior order. The status of the Korean prisoner was unclear, but regardless of his status, the order was unlawful under the circumstances because he did not behave violently, nor did he try to commit an offence or try to escape and he was almost unconscious from injuries previously inflicted.[126] This order was unlawful and the superior was well aware of this.

In this case mistake of law was pleaded in two aspects: (1) the defendant pleaded having acted on orders from his superior, believing them to be lawful and (2) the defendant believed he was under a duty to obey all orders of his superiors. In dealing with this plea of superior orders the Judgement of the Court referred to the Manual for Courts-Martial, United States, 1951, para 197b:

> the general rule is that the acts of a subordinate, done in good faith in compliance with his supposed duty or orders, are justifiable. This justification does not exist, however, when those acts are manifestly beyond the scope of his authority, or the order is such that a man of ordinary sense and understanding would know it to be illegal, or the subordinate wilfully or through negligence does acts endangering the lives of innocent parties in the discharge of his duty to prevent escape or effect an arrest.[127]

---

[121] Gaeta 2001, pp. 759–760.

[122] Gaeta 2001, p. 761; see also Gaeta 1999, p. 172.

[123] Gaeta 2001, p. 759.

[124] *See also* Zühlke Trial 1948, NJ 1949, No. 85, p. 134 and approvingly annotator Röling (at p. 138); McCoubrey 2001, pp. 386 + 389–390 + 393–394; Sliedregt 2003, p. 318; and Garraway 1999, p. 788. Again, this is a debatable position, see Sect. 4.3.3 *supra*.

[125] U.S. v. Kinder 1954.

[126] U.S. v. Kinder 1954, 14 CMR 769–770.

[127] U.S. v. Kinder 1954, 14 CMR 770.

Then follows a review of other authorities both civil and military, which all confirm this manifest illegality approach of the Manual for Court Martial.[128] As Osiel holds, the reasoning of the court in this case confirms that in a case of reasonable doubt a soldier should obey the superior order.[129] This implies a difference between the defence of mistake of law and the defence of superior orders. The rule with the defence of mistake of law is, in case of doubt, try to resolve your doubts if possible. In case of superior orders reasonable doubt means the order is not *manifestly* unlawful and the subordinate should follow it. The absolute necessity of discipline and hierarchy within the military organisation arguably justifies this distinction.[130]

The defence of superior orders was rejected on the facts of the case. The military court decided that there was no honest and reasonable belief that the superior order was lawful and that the evidence justified the inference that the defendant was aware of the unlawfulness of the superior order. Not only was the order itself palpably illegal, but it also had to be executed under surreptitious circumstances.[131] Moreover, the belief that one is under a duty to obey all superior orders is absolutely unwarranted and therefore neither honest nor reasonable.[132] "[N]o rational being of the accused's age [twenty], formal education [grade eleven], and military experience [two years] could have [...] considered the order lawful. Where one obeys an order to kill [...] for the apparent reason of making [the] death an example to others, the evidence must be strong, indeed, to raise a doubt that the slayer was not aware of the illegality of the order [...] The inference of fact is compelling [...] that the accused complied with the palpably unlawful order fully aware of its unlawful character."[133]

In *Sergeant W.* (1966)[134] the defendant was "a sub-officer, who at the time of the event was chasing rebels, serving in the Congolese army within the framework of military technical co-operation between Congo (DRC) and Belgium".[135] He was accused of wilfully killing a civilian. He pleaded that he had acted on a superior order to shoot at any "*élément incertain*" in the military zone which civilians were prohibited to enter. The incident did not take place within this restricted zone. The defendant held that because of the imprecise delimitation of the zone he was mistaken about this. The Brussels War Council found that this mistake of fact was by no means unavoidable (*n'était nullement invincible*); the defendant had ample opportunity to verify whether he was within the military zone. Because the order was not applicable in the first place, it could not be a

[128] U.S. v. Kinder 1954, 14 CMR 771.

[129] Osiel 1999, p. 68.

[130] *See* Chap. 4 *supra*.

[131] U.S. v. Kinder 1954, 14 CMR 773–774.

[132] U.S. v. Kinder 1954, 14 C.M.R. 775, *see* Cassese 2008, pp. 300–301.

[133] U.S. v. Kinder 1954, 14 CMR 770, pp. 773–775.

[134] Sergeant 1966, also available at: http://www.icrc.org/IHL-NAT.NSF/WebALL?openview.

[135] Henckaerts and Doswald-Beck 2005, vol. III, p. 3808, § 820.

justification for his shooting. Even if the defendant had found himself in the restricted military zone, the order he was referring to did not have the meaning he attributed to it, which was that they were not supposed to take any prisoners and they should kill every unidentifiable person that they encountered. This would have been a manifestly unlawful order. Its illegality would not have been doubtful, it would have been obvious and the defendant had the obligation to refuse to obey it.[136] In reaction to the defendant's plea that the superior orders was imprecise, the Court referred to the fact that a subordinate is permitted to ask for explications when he is uncertain about the precise scope of a superior order.[137]

One of the most notorious cases in American military history concerned the killing of more than 500 civilians by American soldiers in the Vietnamese village of My Lai. The disclosure of the horrendous events of that morning in March 1968 is said to have marked "a turning point in the public perception of the Vietnam War".[138] Lieutenant William Calley was convicted of multiple counts of murder committed during the My Lai massacre. When C Company entered the village of My Lai on the morning of 16 March 1968 it was on a search and destroy mission.[139] On entering the village, "the unit encountered only unarmed, unresisting, frightened old men, women, and children, and not the expected elements of the 48th Viet Cong Battalion".[140] "In the course of three hours more than 500 Vietnamese civilians were killed in cold blood at the hands of US troops".[141] Lieutenant Calley, a member of C Company, personally shot villagers after having pushed them into a ditch and ordered his subordinates to do the same.[142] Calley unsuccessfully contended that he was "not guilty of murder because he did not entertain the requisite *mens rea*".[143] Amongst other arguments, he held that "he genuinely thought the villagers had no right to live because they were enemy, and thus [he] was devoid of malice because he was not conscious of the criminal quality of his acts".[144] The US Army Court of Military Review rejected this contention on the following grounds. It held that in so far the alleged state of mind reflected "a mistake of fact, the governing principle is: to be exculpatory, the mistaken belief must be of such a nature that the conduct would have been lawful had the facts actually been as they were believed to be. [...]An enemy in custody may not be executed summarily".[145] In so far as the alleged state of mind constituted a mistake of law, the Court held that "[m]ere absence of a sense of

136 Henckaerts and Doswald-Beck 2005, vol. III, p. 3808, § 820.

137 Sergeant W. 1966, see at: http://www.icrc.org/IHL-NAT.NSF/WebALL?openview.

138 BBC news: http://news.bbc.co.uk/2/hi/asia–pacific/64344.stm.

139 BBC news: http://news.bbc.co.uk/2/hi/asia–pacific/64344.stm.

140 U.S. v. Calley 1973b, 46 C.M.R. 1165.

141 BBC news: http://news.bbc.co.uk/2/hi/asia–pacific/64344.stm.

142 U.S. v. Calley 1973b, 46 C.M.R. 1178.

143 U.S. v. Calley 1973b, 46 C.M.R. 1174.

144 U.S. v. Calley 1973b, 46 C.M.R. 1179, see also 1174.

145 U.S. v. Calley 1973b, 46 C.M.R. 1179.

criminality is likewise not mitigating, for any contrary view would be an excrescent exception to the fundamental rule that ignorance of the law violated is no defense to violating it. The maxim ignorantia legis neminem excusat applies to offenses in which intent is an element".[146]

Calley also based his argument of lack of *mens rea* on the plea of having acted in obedience to the superior orders of Captain Medina.[147] Calley referred to several instructions by Medina, one of which was a briefing the night before the My Lai operation. According to Calley, Medina had started the briefing by listing the men that they had lost and they were down 50 % in strength. Medina stressed the importance of neutralising My Lai, destroying everyone and everything there. Calley further said that he remembered Medina saying that all civilians had left the area and anyone there would be considered the enemy.[148] Medina, who was called as a witness, gave a different account of the briefing the night before the operation.[149] The Court of Military Review states that whether Calley "was ever ordered to kill unresisting, unarmed villagers was a contested question of fact".[150] An answer to this question cannot be found in the findings of the court martial because these have the nature of general verdict.[151] The Court continued that if the members of the court martial "found his claim of acting on superior orders to be credible, he would nevertheless not automatically be entitled to acquittal. Not every order is exonerating".[152] The Court approved of the trial judge's instructions on this matter.[153] The instructions from the Military Judge to the Court Members read:

> A determination that an order is illegal does not, of itself, assign criminal responsibility to the person following the order for acts done in compliance with it. Soldiers are taught to follow orders, and special attention is given to obedience to orders. Military effectiveness depends upon obedience to orders. On the other hand, the obedience of a soldier is not the obedience of an automaton. A soldier is a reasoning agent, obliged to respond, not as a machine, but as a person. The law takes these factors into account in assessing criminal responsibility for acts done in compliance with illegal orders. The acts of a subordinate done in compliance with an unlawful order given him by his superior are excused and impose no criminal liability upon him unless the superior's order is one which a man of ordinary sense and understanding would, under the circumstances, know to be unlawful, or if the order in question is actually known to the accused to be unlawful.[154]

---

[146] U.S. v. Calley 1973b, 46 C.M.R. 1179–1180.
[147] U.S. v. Calley 1973b, 46 C.M.R. 1180.
[148] U.S. v. Calley 1973b, 46 C.M.R. 1180.
[149] U.S. v. Calley 1973b, 46 C.M.R. 1181–1182.
[150] U.S. v. Calley 1973b, 46 C.M.R. 1180.
[151] U.S. v. Calley 1973b, 46 C.M.R. 1180.
[152] U.S. v. Calley 1973b, 46 C.M.R. 1182–1183.
[153] U.S. v. Calley 1973b, 46 C.M.R. 1183.
[154] U.S. v. Calley 1973b, 46 C.M.R. 1183; Friedman, p. 1722.

The Court of Military Review also approved the further instructions of the trial judge which held that, if the members found that Calley knew the orders to be illegal, the orders would be no defence and, if they found that Calley was unaware that the orders were illegal, they were to apply a more objective standard: Calley "must be acquitted unless the members were satisfied beyond reasonable doubt that a man of ordinary sense and understanding would have known the orders to be unlawful".[155]

The Court of Military Review concluded the discussion of the defence of absence of *mens rea* by stating that "[t]he aggregate of all his contentions against the existence of murderous *mens rea* is no more absolving than the bare claim that he did not suspect he did any wrong act until after the operation, and indeed is not convinced of it yet. This is no excuse in law".[156]

On Appeal the defence counsel's contention that the standard applied should be that of a person of "commonest understanding" instead of "ordinary sense and understanding" was rejected. The Appellate Court approved of the standard applied by the trial judge and held that: "[w]hether Lieutenant Calley was the most ignorant person in the United States Army in Vietnam, or the most intelligent, he must be presumed to know that he could not kill the persons involved here. The United States Supreme Court has pointed out that "[t]he rule that 'ignorance of the law will not excuse' [...] is deep in our law". It further referred to the palpable illegal character of the order.[157]

In this case the issues of mistake of fact, mistake of law and superior orders surfaced. A mistake of fact is not a defence if the facts, if they were as the defendant believed them to be, would not make lawful the acts the defendant is accused of. Mistake of law is never a valid excuse. Although when the defendant acted on superior orders, a mistake of law may become relevant; the jury should acquit the defendant if it is not satisfied beyond reasonable doubt that a person of ordinary sense and understanding would have known the order to be unlawful.

5.2.4 *Recent Decisions*

5.2.4.1 International Criminal Tribunal for the Former Yugoslavia

In the *Čelebići* trial (2001), on appeal, defendant Mucić's first argument in relation to the conviction for unlawful confinement of detainees in the Čelebići prison camp was that the detainees were lawfully confined.[158] The Appeals Chamber

155 U.S. v. Calley 1973b, 46 C.M.R. 1183 and Friedman, p. 1723.

156 U.S. v. Calley 1973b, 46 C.M.R. 1184.

157 U.S. v. Calley 1973a, 48 C.M.R. 29.

158 Prosecutor v. Mucić et al. 2001, § 372.

rejected this plea[159]; it was established that at least some of the prisoners were not lawfully confined.

The second argument Mucić put forward is that he lacked the requisite *mens rea* for the crime of unlawful confinement, because he did not know and could not have known "that the confinement of people at Čelebići could, or would be construed as illegal under an interpretation of an admixture of the Geneva Conventions and Article 2(g) of the Statute of the Tribunal, a Statute not then in existence".[160]

The response of the Prosecutor was that whether the defendant, thus, contends that knowledge of the law is an element of the crime or whether he raises a defence of error of law, the argument is irrelevant since "there is no general principle of criminal law that knowledge of the law is an element of the *mens rea* of a crime" and mistake of law is not available as defence under international humanitarian law.[161] The Appeals Chamber interpreted this plea of the defence as a breach of the legality principle and rejected it on the basis that the detention of those persons was at that time already illegal under the fourth Geneva Convention.[162]

The Appeals Chamber than responded to the defendant's mistake of law defence. The defence held that the Trial Chamber erred in relying upon evidence that he "had reason to know" as a basis for finding that the defendant in fact knew that the detainees were unlawfully confined. The Appeals Chamber indicated that knowledge of the rights of the prisoners is part of the required *mens rea* for unlawful confinement. As part of the required *mens rea*, knowledge of the rights of prisoners means knowledge of the existence of such rights, their social significance, not knowledge of the specific legal rules applying to prisoners. The Trial Chamber decision reflected that this knowledge could be inferred from the available evidence.[163]

However, establishing that the defendant acted with knowledge of the social meaning of the rights of prisoners, does not answer the issue of mistake of law. This issue has not been addressed by the Court. It seems to be that the Appeals Chamber agreed with the Prosecutor that mistake of law is no defence.

5.2.4.2 Special Court for Sierra Leone

Uncertainty of the law is the most obvious reason for accepting the defence of mistake of law, and it shows the relation between this defence and the principle of legality, *nulla poena sine lege previa*.[164] It must be noted that the above discussed

159 Prosecutor v. Mucić et al. 2001, § 330.

160 Prosecutor v. Mucić et al. 2001, § 373.

161 Prosecutor v. Mucić et al. 2001, § 374.

162 Prosecutor v. Mucić et al. 2001, § 374.

163 Prosecutor v. Mucić et al. 2001, §§ 380–386.

164 *See also* Chap. 3 *supra*.

decisions as to uncertainty of the law mainly concerned cases related to WWII and may now be outdated because of enhanced codification of international criminal law and international humanitarian law and the increase in number of prosecutions for international crimes. However, as recently as 2007 the Special Court for Sierra Leone (SCSL) was confronted with a question of legal uncertainty relating to an international crime. This was in AFRC trial, against amongst others defendant *Kanu* (2007), a senior member of the Armed Forces Revolutionary Council.[165]

The Trial Chamber first establishes, as the Appeals Chamber had already determined in the *Norman* case,[166] that the crimes relating to child soldiers, punishable under Article 4(c) of the statute, had crystallised as norms entailing individual criminal responsibility under customary international law at the time the alleged acts were committed.[167]

The Trial Chamber refers, in a footnote, to a dissenting opinion of Justice Robertson in the Norman case.[168] This interesting dissent deserves more attention, however, for it sheds again some light on the principle of legality. Robertson wondered whether "if it was not clear to the Secretary-General and his legal advisers that international law had by 1996 criminalized the enlistment of child soldiers, could it really have been any clearer to Chief Hinga Norman or any other defendant at that time, embattled in Sierra Leone?"[169] "The enlistment of children [...] to kill and risk being killed in conflicts not of their own making was abhorrent to all reasonable persons in 1996 [...]. But abhorrence alone does not make that conduct a crime in international law."[170] Robertson distinguishes two stages in determining when enlistment of children became a war crime: the first stage is identifying when it became a rule of international law binding on states; the second stage is "identifying when this so-called 'norm' of international law metamorphosed into a criminal law for the breach of which individuals might be punished."[171] He then continues to explain why this second stage is necessary, "even—indeed, especially—in relation to conduct which is generally viewed as abhorrent."[172] The second stage is necessary "to ensure that a defendant is not convicted out of disgust rather than evidence, or of a non-existent crime."[173]

In the AFRC trial the Trial Chamber followed the majority opinion of the Appeals Chamber. The Trial Chamber then turned to the elements of the crime of conscripting or enlisting children under the age of 15 years into armed forces or

165 Prosecutor v. Kanu 2007.

166 Prosecutor v. Norman 2004a.

167 Prosecutor v. Kanu 2007, § 728.

168 Prosecutor v. Kanu 2007, § 728, footnote 1417.

169 Prosecutor v. Norman 2004b, § 6.

170 Prosecutor v. Norman 2004b, § 9.

171 Prosecutor v. Norman 2004b, § 10.

172 Prosecutor v. Norman 2004b, § 10.

173 Prosecutor v. Norman 2004b, § 12. See also the discussion of the GBG cases in Sect. 2.3.2.4.1 *supra* and the reference there to comments by Ferdinandusse in the same vein.

groups, or using them to participate actively in hostilities. The Trial Chamber takes the Rome Statute as guideline.[174]

The defence submits that "there had been a practice by various governments in Sierra Leone of recruiting persons under the age of 15 into the military prior to the Indictment period. [...] this practice impacts on the awareness as to the unlawfulness of conscripting, enlisting or using child soldiers below the age of 15. As such conduct was not, it is submitted, on its face manifestly illegal, no conviction should be entered on Count 12 on the grounds of mistake of law".[175] Here the defence seems to argue along the lines of a superior orders defence. As seen earlier there is a difference between mistake of law per se and mistake of law when obeying superior orders. Only in the latter situation will acting on not-manifestly unlawful orders per se exculpate the mistaken defendant. However, the defendant in this case did not follow superior orders, which means that the generally more stringent rule on mistake of law applies. The defence rephrases its plea of mistake of law on appeal.

In rejecting the plea the Trial Chamber, in my opinion, confused the plea of mistake of law with the rule that international law has priority over national law, that is the rule that national law cannot make lawful what is unlawful under international law.[176] Rejecting even the possibility of invoking mistake of law, on the basis that the conduct is a crime under international customary law, the court does not enter into an assessment of the defence. It appears, therefore, that the Trial Chamber displayed a total misconception of the implications of mistake of law as an excuse; the applicability of the defence does not make the conduct lawful, but merely purports a culpability assessment.

On appeal the defence, adapting its language to the Rome Statute, held that "the Trial Chamber had erred in law in dismissing [Kanu's] argument that 'the absence of criminal knowledge on his part vitiated the requisite *mens rea* to the crimes relating to child soldiers'. He [argued] that the *mens rea* element required for the crime was in this matter negated by a mistake of law on his part. [...] [Kanu submitted] that 'he believed that his conduct [...] was legitimate'."[177] The defence too seems to have failed to capture in its plea the rationale of the defence of mistake of law. The Appeals Chamber very briefly dismissed the plea as being "frivolous and vexatious".[178]

These judgements of the Trial Chamber and Appeals Chamber of the Special Court for Sierra Leone indicate how many misconceptions surround the issue of mistake of law and how in fact the ICC Statute, at least how it has here been

---

[174] Prosecutor v. Kanu 2007, § 729.

[175] Prosecutor v. Kanu 2007, § 730.

[176] Prosecutor v. Kanu 2007, § 732. On how this principle was established in the WWII case law, *see* Vogeley 2003, pp. 84–86.

[177] Prosecutor v. Kanu 2008, § 293.

[178] Prosecutor v. Kanu 2008, § 296.

interpreted by the SCSL, has reintroduced the *ignorantia legis* rule into international criminal law.

Allowing the defence of mistake of law in this case would admittedly not have changed the ultimate result. The Court would determine the mistake to have been avoidable or unreasonable, alternatively the Court could have inferred consciousness of wrongdoing from the facts of the case (the children were being abducted and drugged etcetera). However, rejecting the defence on the basis of the unreasonableness, or the avoidability, of the mistake or inference of consciousness would have been more satisfactory, because this would specify the reproach directed at the defendant by expressing the principle of individual guilt. It is not that Kanu's mistake was irrelevant, on the contrary, it is part of what he is blamed for because he could and should have known about the wrongfulness of conscripting or enlisting children.

5.2.4.3 International Criminal Court

In *Lubanga* (2007) the International Criminal Court (ICC) Pre-Trial Chamber (PTC) inferred personal knowledge of the unlawfulness of recruiting children from the available evidence.[179] The defence held that Lubanga was unaware of the fact that, voluntarily or forcibly, recruiting children under the age of 15 entailed criminal responsibility under the statute.[180] The PTC considered that the scope of the defence of mistake of law is limited, referring to Article 32(2) first sentence. Then the PTC turned to the exceptions of Article 32(2) second sentence. It held that the defence of mistake of law can only succeed if Lubanga was "unaware of a normative objective element of the crime as a result of not realizing its social significance (its everyday meaning)".[181] There was no evidence admitted to support this. In fact, the PTC adds, there is sufficient evidence that the defendant was aware of the criminal nature of his behaviour.[182] On the one hand, the decision reveals that indeed, the scope of the mistake of law defence as provided for in Article 32(2) is limited to mistakes that negate the required mental element. On the other, it is somewhat hopeful that the PTC, in addition to rejecting this plea,

---

[179] Prosecutor v. Lubanga 2007, §§ 304–316.

[180] Prosecutor v. Lubanga 2007, § 296.

[181] Prosecutor v. Lubanga 2007, §316. The Court, thus, adopts the reading proposed by Eser, that as to legal elements the required knowledge is knowledge of the social meaning for the average person or soldier. Eser 2002, pp. 924–925. *See also* Olásolo 2008, pp. 243–244 and *critical* Weigend 2008, p. 476.

[182] Prosecutor v. Lubanga 2007, §§ 306–314 (The evidence the Court refers to is the ratification of the ICC statute (11 April 2002) before the relevant period; Geneva Conventions and two Additional Protocols (protected persons); 1989 Convention on the Rights of the Child; Appeals Chamber decision SCSL (31 May 2004); already before July 2002 awareness about the statute; testimony of Kristine Peduto that on 30 May 2003 she discussed this issue in relation to ratification of the statute with Lubanga).

holding that there were no reasons to assume that Lubanga was unaware of the social significance of this legal element, apparently found it necessary to conclude there is enough evidence to support the finding that Lubanga was aware of the wrongful, or even criminal nature of his behaviour.[183] On the basis of Article 32(2) the Court was not required to do so.

5.3 Conclusion

The first issue in assessing a plea of mistake of law concerns its credibility. In most cases where the defence of mistake of law has been raised in order to avert criminal liability for international crimes, knowledge of wrongdoing was inferred from the facts.[184] This means that the defendant must have known that his conduct violated a legal rule. Thus, in such a case, the mistake does not warrant an assessment of its avoidability or reasonableness (a should have known test). Moreover, the conclusion is that the defendant was not mistaken at all. In the case of international crimes such a conclusion is usually justified.

Several cases discussed in this chapter concerned instances of uncertainty of the law.[185] Reprisals, providing for a justification under international law for an international wrongful act, have always been a delicate issue.[186] Where the plea of superior orders concerned the lawfulness of executions,[187] frequently the mistake will have been one of fact, not of law. The case law reveals different outcomes as to the question of whether or not superior orders are merely a ground for mitigation of punishment or if superior orders provide a complete defence.[188]

In the case law after WWII there was great confusion about the legal effect of plea of superior orders.[189] According to the Law Reports, the general effect was mitigation of punishment, the only exception being the High Command case, where it was recognised that the plea could give rise to a complete defence.[190] Mitigation of punishment was of course in line with the Charter of the IMT and Control Council Law No. 10. This rule, however, was not generally recognised in

---

[183] Prosecutor v. Lubanga 2007, § 306.

[184] *See e.g.* Zimmermann 1949; Lages case 1950; U.S. v. Kinder 1954; and Prosecutor v. Lubanga 2007.

[185] *See e.g. Von Leeb (The High Command Trial)* 1948; Helmuth Latza and 2 others 1948; and Arlt 1949.

[186] *See e.g.* Wintgen 1949; and Falkenhorst trial 1946.

[187] *See e.g.* Buck Trial 1946; Trial of Sandrock (Almelo Trial) 1945; B. case 1951; and E. van E. case 1951.

[188] *See e.g.* Llandovery Castle case 1921; Peleus Trial 1945; Trial of Sawada 1946; List (The Hostages Case) 1948; R. v. SAH Alsagoff 1946; Zühlke Trial 1948; Kappler and others 1948; and Hass and Priebke case 1998.

[189] Röling 1961, p. 372.

[190] Von Leeb (The High Command Trial) 1948, UNWCC vol. XII, p. 98.

(inter)national law.[191] As the case law here under discussion shows, it was recognised in many different courts and tribunals that the plea of superior orders could provide for a complete defence. In this respect it is interesting to refer to the Dutch case *Zülhke*, where the Special Court of Cassation held that Law No. 10 did only apply in trials against major war criminals; in other trials the plea of superior orders could, under certain strict conditions, lead to an acquittal.[192]

The case law discussed in this chapter indicates that superior orders are, in principle, recognised as a ground for excluding criminal responsibility for international crimes, although acquittal only follows under very strict conditions. Only when the illegality of the order was not known to the subordinate, and the order was not manifestly unlawful, will the defendant be successful in his plea.[193] To a certain extent the subordinate has a right to assume that the orders of his superior are in conformity with international law,[194] especially when the order's unlawfulness under international law is uncertain.[195] In the case of a manifestly unlawful order, however, the subordinate is no longer entitled to assume lawfulness and he is criminally responsible for the crimes committed in obedience.[196] In such a case knowledge of wrongdoing is imputed to the defendant.[197]

As stated in the introduction, an obstacle in finding cases concerning the plea of mistake of law has been that the different defences, mistake of law, superior orders, duress and mistake of fact, are often intertwined. As seen, the case law sometimes mixes *superior orders—duress* and *superior orders—mistake of law*.[198] Where the IMT Nuremberg stated that, in a case of the defence of superior orders, the real issue is whether the defendant had a moral choice to behave differently, the court referred to *superior orders—duress*.[199] It seems that, the

[191] Röling 1961, p. 373.

[192] Zühlke Trial 1948, NJ 1949, No. 85, p. 134; *see also* Röling 1961, p. 373. For an interesting perspective on the actual scope/meaning of the Charter and CCL No. 10 provisions see McCoubrey 2001, p. 386 + 389–390 + 393–394 (holding that the "ought to have known" test also underlied these WWII provisions and the Rome Statute did, thus, not radically change the rule governing superior orders as some argue).

[193] *See also* Osiel 1999, p. 42.

[194] *See e.g.* Von Leeb (The High Command Trial) 1948; Peleus Trial 1945; and U.S. v. Kinder 1954.

[195] *See e.g.* Von Leeb (The High Command Trial) 1948.

[196] *See e.g.* Llandovery Castle case 1921; Von Leeb (The High Command Trial) 1948; U.S. v. Kinder 1954; and Buck Trial 1946.

[197] *See* Dinstein 1965, p. 200.

[198] I find it remarkable that in most cases concerning superior orders the requirement was that the defendant acted under mistake of law, while this did not imply that the particular case actually concerned a situation of *superior orders—mistake of law*. The requirement of mistake of law also seem to apply in case of *superior orders—duress*. This is remarkable, because the two defences, mistake of law and duress, although they arguably are based on the same rationale, namely that no moral choice was possible, are separate defences. Mistake of law is not a requirement of the defence of duress.

[199] *See also* Lippman 1996, p. 55.

same rationale underlies the defence of *superior orders—mistake of law*. In the case of duress, the pressure of the threat is so high that no one can be expected to be a hero and resist it. In case of a mistake of law, one can say that the defendant who does not know the law and could not have known the law, cannot choose for the lawful conduct. In both cases, the rationale of the defence is that he who had no moral choice between actions is not blameworthy.

As anticipated, the case law has not delivered many clear examples of mistake of law in the area between the two outer limits of the spectrum, legal uncertainty and manifestly illegal superior orders. In Chap. 6, after an analysis of the elements of international crimes, there are examples of situations in the intermediate area in which an excuse on the basis of mistake of law seems warranted, but where Article 32(2) ICC Statute does not apply.

References

Ambos K (2004) Der Allgemeine Teil des Völkerstrafrechts. Ansätze einer Dogmatisierung, 2nd edn. Duncker & Humblot, Berlin

Bantekas I, Nash S (2007) International criminal law, 3rd edn. Routledge-Cavendish, London

Best G (1994) War & Law since 1945. Clarendon Press, Oxford

Cassese A (2003) International criminal law. Oxford University Press Inc, Oxford

Cassese A (2008) International criminal law, 2nd edn. Oxford University Press, Oxford

Cassese A (ed) (2009) The Oxford companion to international criminal justice. Oxford University Press, Oxford

Dinstein Y (1965) The defence of 'obedience to superior orders' in international law. A.W. Sijthoff, Leiden

Eser A (2002) Mental elements—mistake of fact and mistake of law. In: Cassese A, Gaeta P, Jones JRWD (eds) The Rome Statute of the International Criminal Court: a commentary, vol I. Oxford University Press, Oxford, pp 889–948

Gaeta P (1999) The defence of superior orders: the statute of the International Criminal Court versus customary international law. Eur J Int Law 10:172–191

Gaeta P (2001) War crimes trials before Italian criminal courts: new trends. In: Fischer H (ed) International and national prosecutions of crimes under international law, current developments. Spitz, Berlin, pp 751–768

Garraway CHB (1999) Superior orders and the International Criminal Court: justice delivered or justice denied. Int Rev Red Cross 81(836):785–794

Green LC (2003) Fifteenth Waldemar A. Solf Lecture in international law, superior orders and command responsibility. Mil Law Rev 175:309–384

Henckaerts JM, Doswald-Beck L (2005) Customary international humanitarian law, vol 3. International Committee of the Red Cross, Cambridge University Press, Cambridge

Kalshoven F (2005) Belligerent reprisals, vol 11. International humanitarian law series, 2nd edn. Martinus Nijhoff Publishers, Leiden

Kalshoven F, Zegveld L (2001) Constraints on the waging of war: an introduction to international humanitarian law, 3rd edn. International Committee of the Red Cross, Geneva

Lippman MR (1996) Conundrums of armed conflict: criminal defenses to violations of the humanitarian law of war. Dickinson J Int Law 15:1–112

Lippman MR (2001) Humanitarian law: the development and scope of the superior orders defense. Penn State Int Law Rev 20:153–251

McCoubrey H (2001) From Nuremberg to Rome: restoring the defence of superior orders. Int Comp Law Q 50:386–394
Nill-Theobald C (1998) "Defences" bei Kriegsverbrechen am Beispiel Deutschlands und der USA: zugleich ein Beitrag zu einem Allgemeinen Teil des Völkerstrafrechts, vol Band S 72. Beiträge und Materialien aus dem Max-Planck-Institut für ausländisches und internationales Strafrecht, Freiburg i.Br., iuscrim edn. Max-Planck-Institut für ausländisches und internationales Strafrecht, Freiburg im Breisgau
Olásolo H (2008) Unlawful attacks in Combat situations; from the ICTY's case law to the Rome Statute. Martinus Nijhoff Publishers, Leiden
Osiel MJ (1999) Obeying orders. Transaction Publishers, New Brunswick
Röling BVA (1961) The law of war and the national jurisdiction since 1945. A. W. Sythoff, Leiden
Sliedregt E van (2003) The criminal responsibility of individuals for violations of international humanitarian law. T.M.C. ASSER Press, The Hague
Sluiter GK (2009a) Arlt. In: Cassese A (ed) The Oxford companion to international criminal justice. Oxford University Press, Oxford, pp 585–586
Sluiter GK (2009b) Zimmermann. In: Cassese A (ed) The Oxford companion to international criminal justice. Oxford University Press, Oxford, pp 981–982
Solis GD (1999) Obedience of orders and the law of war: judicial application in American forums. Am Univ Int Law Rev 15:481–525
Swart AHJ (2002) Algemene leerstukken van materieel strafrecht in de rechtspraak van de ad hoc-tribunalen. In: Joegoslavië- en Rwanda-tribunalen: impact op het Nederlandse strafrecht. Cahiers 'Van Hamel'. Universiteit van Amsterdam, Amsterdam
Vogeley S (2003) The mistake of law defense in international criminal law. In: Yee S (ed) International crime and punishment. University Press of America, Inc, Oxford, pp 59–99
Weigend T (2008) Intent, mistake of law, and co-perpetration in the *Lubanga* decision on confirmation of charges. J Int Crim Justice 6:471–487
Wilt HG van der (2009b) Zühlke. In: Cassese A (ed) The Oxford companion to international criminal justice. Oxford University Press, Oxford, p 982

Supreme Court of Leipzig

Dover Castle case (1921), German Reichsgericht, Supreme Court of Leipzig, 16 Am. J. Int'l L. 704 (1922)
Llandovery Castle case (1921), German Reichsgericht, Supreme Court of Leipzig, 16 Am. J. Int'l L. 708 (1922)

US Military Tribunals at Nuremberg

I.G. Farben Trial (1948), US Military Tribunal at Nuremberg, Judgement, 14 August 1947–29 July 1948
US Military Tribunals at Nuremberg, Case No. 6, Military Tribunal VI, N.M.T., vols. 7–8
List (The Hostages Case) (1948), US Military Tribunal at Nuremberg, UNWCC, vol. VIII; TWC vol. XI
US v. Otto Ohlendorf et al. (Einsatzgruppen case) (1948), United States Military Tribunals at Nuremberg, Case No. 9, TWC, vol. IV, pp. 1–596
Von Leeb (The High Command Trial) (1948), US Military Tribunal at Nuremberg, Friedman, The Law of War, vol. II, pp. 1421–1470; UNWCC, vol XII, pp. 1–127

The UNWCC Trials - Law Reports of Trials of War Criminals, selected and prepared by the United Nations War Crimes Commission (1949). vol. XV, Digest of Laws and Cases. London: His Majesty's Stationary Office, 1949

Dostler trial (1945), United States Military Commission, Rome, UNWCC, vol. I, pp. 28–34
Peleus Trial (1945), British Military Court, Hamburg, UNWCC, vol. I, pp. 1–21
Trial of Sandrock (Almelo Trial) (1945), British Military Court for the Trial of War Criminals, held at the Court House, Almelo, Holland, UNWCC, vol. I, pp. 35–45
Buck Trial (1946), British Military Court, Wuppertal, Germany, UNWCC, vol. V, pp. 39–44
Falkenhorst trial (1946), British Military Court, Brunswick, Norway, UNWCC, vol. XI, pp. 18–30
Trial of Sawada (1946), United States Military Commission, Shanghai, UNWCC, vol. V, pp. 1–24
Helmuth Latza and 2 others (1948), Eidsivating Lagmannsrett (Court of Appeal) and the Supreme Court of Norway, UNWCC, vol. XIV, pp. 49–85
Zühlke Trial (1948), Special Court in Amsterdam, The Netherlands, NJ 1949, No. 85; UNWCC, vol. XIV; Friedman, The Law of War (1972), vol. II, pp. 1543–1554
Rauter (1949), Special Court of Cassation, The Netherlands, NJ 1949, No. 87, at 144–61; UNWCC, vol. XIV; Annual Digest 1949, 526–45

International Criminal Tribunal for the Former Yugoslavia

Prosecutor v. Mucić et al. (2001), ICTY Appeals Chamber, Case No. IT-96-21-A, Judgement, 20 February 2001

Special Court for Sierra Leone

Prosecutor v. Norman (2004a), SCSL Appeals Chamber, Case No SCSL-2004-14-AR72(E), Decision on Preliminary Motion Based on Lack of Jurisdiction (Child Recruitment), 31 May 2004
Prosecutor v. Norman (2004b), SCSL Appeals Chamber, Case No SCSL-2004-14-AR72(E), Decision on Preliminary Motion Based on Lack of Jurisdiction (Child Recruitment), 31 May 2004, Dissenting Opinion of Justice Robertson
Prosecutor v. Kanu (2007), SCSL Trial Chamber, Case No. SCSL-04-16-T, Judgement, 20 June 2007
Prosecutor v. Kanu (2008), SCSL Appeals Chamber, Case No. SCSL-2004-16-A, Judgement, 22 February 2008

International Criminal Court

Prosecutor v. Lubanga (2007), ICC Pre-Trial Chamber, Case No. ICC-01/04-01/06, Decision on the confirmation of charges, 29 January 2007

National Case Law

United States

U.S. v. Kinder (1954), 14 C.M.R. 742 (1954)
U.S. v. Calley (1973a), U.S. Court of Military Appeals, 1973 WL 14894 (CMA), 48 C.M.R. 19
U.S. v. Calley (1973b), U.S. Army Court of Military Review, 1973 WL 14570, 46 C.M.R. 1131; Friedman, The Law of War (1972), vol. II, pp. 1703–1728

The Netherlands

Arlt (1949), Special Court of Cassation at Arnhem, The Netherlands, NJ 1950, no. 8, pp. 27–29; Summary in Annual Digest 1949, 462–4
Wintgen (1949), Special Court of Cassation, The Netherlands, NJ 1949, 540, 981-5; Excerpts in Annual Digest 1949, 484–6
Zimmermann (1949), Special Court of Cassation, The Netherlands, NJ 1950, No. 9, 30-2; Annual Digest 1949, 552–3
Lages case (1950), Special Court of Cassation, The Netherlands, NJ, 1950, No. 680, pp. 1201–1209
B. case (1951), Special Court of Cassation, The Netherlands, NJ 1952, No. 247, pp. 516–526
E. van E. case (1951), Special Court of Cassation, The Netherlands NJ 1952, No. 246, pp. 514–16

Other Countries

R. v. SAH Alsagoff (1946), Court of Assizes, Singapore, 2 MC 191
Werner case (1947), Appeal Division, South Africa, 20 May 1947, 1947 (2) South African Law Reports 828(A)
Kappler and others (1948), Rome Military Tribunal, Italy (Tribunale militare territoriale), Fore penale, 1948 603–22
Sergeant W. (1966), Brussels War Council, Belgium; Military Court, Revue juridique du Congo, 1970, 236 8; Revue de droit pénal et de criminologie, 1970, 806–10; 46 Revue juridique du Congo, 1970, 238–9; Revue de droit pénal et de criminologie, 1972–3, 807–9, 810–11
Hass and Priebke case (1998), Military tribunal of Rome; Military Appeals Court; Supreme Court of Cassation, Italy, L'Indice penale, 1998, 959–1000

Chapter 6
Applying the Theory of Mistake of Law: An Analysis of Elements of Crimes and a Survey of Dilemmas on the Battlefield

6.1 Introduction

The conclusion of Chap. 4, holding that the second sentence of Article 32(2) ICC Statute, in fact, does not cover the issue of mistake of law, was partially based on the premise that in general a mistake of law does not negate the mental element required by international crimes. Section 6.2 of the current chapter aims at validating this premise. On the basis of the crime definitions and the Elements of Crimes, it is sought to determine what the mental element requirements for war crimes and crimes against humanity are.[1]

The question is whether the provision on mistake of law in the ICC Statute correctly limits the scope of this defence to mistakes that negate the mental element or, alternatively, whether this article, thus, unjustifiably excludes from international criminal law other conceivable mistakes of law.

In Chap. 5, the analysis of (inter)national case law showed that mistake of law per se has only rarely been accepted as a ground for excluding criminal responsibility for international crimes. The purpose of the current chapter is to show that what is at stake "is not a theoretical argument, but an essential guarantee of criminal justice".[2] Thus, Sect. 6.3 of the current chapter contains a survey of situations in which the defendant acts under an understandable and relevant mistake of the law. This part of the chapter is divided into three categories of mistakes of law. The first category (Sect. 6.3.1) concerns mistakes as to the prohibition as such. This category contains examples of violations of international humanitarian law (IHL), which are not *malum in se*, but which are so-called *mala prohibita*. Not every rule of IHL can be traced back to a moral conviction and the growing complexity of (international) criminal law justifies allowing the defendant

---

[1] The international crime of genocide is excluded from this analysis, not because I believe the defence of mistake of law should categorically be excluded in case of genocide, but because the specific intent required for this crime, the intent to destroy a group, seriously complicates formulating an example of good faith belief that this was lawful.

[2] Jescheck 2004, p. 44.

A. van Verseveld, *Mistake of Law*, DOI: 10.1007/978-90-6704-867-5_6,

to invoke mistake of law.[3] With regard to this first category it is important to note that the scope of this category is influenced by the fact that many States do not live up to their obligation under the Geneva Conventions and Additional Protocols to disseminate these rules of IHL among their citizens.[4] The first category contains examples of mistakes as to justificatory circumstances and normative elements that are part of the crime definition. The second category (Sect. 6.3.2) concerns putative justifications. Grounds for excluding criminal responsibility are likely to be less clear[5] than the crime definition itself. The existence and scope of justifications is often unknown to the average person.[6] This category of mistakes of law, therefore, seems to be the most relevant in international criminal law. The third category (Sect. 6.3.3), closely related to the second, contains mistakes as to the existence of justifications not under criminal law, but under public international law. The defendant may believe there exists a ground of justification under public international law which makes the, otherwise, wrongful act legitimate. The most telling example is the right to reprisal. The Court may be able to respond to such a plea of justification on the basis of Articles 31(3) and 21 of the ICC Statute.

6.2 Subjective Requirements of Criminal Responsibility

It appears that the theoretical accounts in Chaps. 3 and 4 form a firm basis for the proposition that the correct theoretical approach dictates mistake of law to be treated as an excuse. The discussion in these chapters showed that the current codification of mistake of law as a ground for excluding criminal responsibility does not cover all possible mistakes, such as mistakes as to grounds of justification and mistake as to the prohibition as such. There will be exceptional cases where a mistake of law does negate the mental element, but, as the theory of mistake of law proved, most of the time mistake of law functions as an excuse. Consequently, the defendant who acted in the mistaken belief that his acts were lawful, acted with the required intent.[7] The following is an account of those exceptional cases where mistake of law does negate the mental element required for criminal responsibility for war crimes and crimes against humanity.

6.2.1 Elements of Crimes

On the basis of Article 9 of the ICC Statute, the elements of crimes (EOC), a document drafted by the Preparatory Commission, assists the Court in the

[3] Ambos 2006, p. 668.

[4] *See* Boister 2005, pp. 32–33.

[5] Wise 1998, p. 52.

[6] Ambos 2006, p. 668.

[7] Ambos 2006, p. 668.

interpretation of Articles 6–8. The EOC is arguably not binding on the Court,[8] but it forms an important insight in the drafters' understanding of the crime definitions in the Statute. It will, therefore, provide a useful basis to the following analysis of the required mental element.

As seen in Chap. 4, Article 30 of the ICC Statute provides for a default rule on the required mental element. The first paragraph provides that the material elements of a crime must be committed with intent and knowledge. The term "material elements" refers to the definitional elements of the crimes enumerated in Articles 6–8.[9] Article 30 does not mention the requirement of *Unrechtsbewußtsein*. Since Article 32(2) only recognizes the potential relevance of a mistake of law if it negates the mental element, the elementary issue is, when do the definitional elements require knowledge of wrongdoing?

The second and third paragraphs of Article 30 distinguish three types of material elements, relating to the conduct, the consequences and the circumstances that qualify the definition.[10] In order to determine the scope of mistake of law, as defined by Article 32(2), it has to be determined which material elements lend themselves to be negated by mistakes of law. Many circumstantial elements concern facts, but some are more of a legal character,[11] containing legal connotations or value judgements.[12] Consequences too can contain legal elements. In theory, a mistake of law concerning these elements may negate the required mental element. Many legal elements, like for example 'protected person', cannot be understood without legal knowledge.[13] This would mean that a mistake in this respect would negate the mental element; which may lead to the undesirable result of culpable mistakes remaining unpunished. As Ambos holds, it was not a good idea, however, to try to limit this undesired result by blurring the distinction between fact and law, as Article 32 does, because now mistake of law has been transposed to the same level as mistake of fact.[14] To avoid the undesired result, the General Introduction to the EOC, and, as we will see, the elements of war crimes and crimes against humanity, attempted to exclude the relevance of a mistake of law as to the legal elements. Paragraph 4 of the General Introduction of the Elements of Crimes provides:

> With respect to mental elements associated with elements involving value judgement, such as those using the terms "inhumane" or "severe", it is not necessary that the perpetrator personally completed a particular value judgement, unless otherwise indicated.

---

[8] Hebel 2001, p. 3. *But see* Weigend 2008, pp. 472–474 (reflecting on the debate about the status of the EOC and describing how the ICC Pre-Trial Chamber has confirmed its status to be "as 'law' to be applied by the Court, with a rank equal to the Statute itself").

[9] *See also* Eser 2002, pp. 909–910; Ambos 2004, p. 764; and Sliedregt 2003, pp. 56–57 and 307.

[10] Piragoff 1999, p. 529. *See also* Kelt and Hebel 2001b, p. 14.

[11] Kelt and Hebel 2001b, p. 15.

[12] Kelt and Hebel 2001a, pp. 27 + 34.

[13] Ambos 2004, p. 813.

[14] Ambos 2004 p. 814.

Clark points out that this Paragraph "endeavours to capture the majority position in *Finta* that it is not necessary to prove that the perpetrator completed the value judgement".[15] Paragraph 4 excludes the relevance of the perpetrator's personal value judgement of elements using terms like 'severe' or 'inhumane'.[16] There are some exceptions to this 'no personal value judgement required' paragraph. An example can be found in Article 8(2)(b)(iv), element 3, footnote 37: "it is required that the perpetrator realizes that the harm caused by his or her attack was unmistakably out of proportion to the expected military advantage".[17]

Ambos finds that here, in para 4, the EOC are in conflict with the Statute, more specifically with Article 32(2) second sentence.[18] Heller agrees and rejects the 'solution' offered by authors and the Elements of Crimes to apply the *Parallelwertungslehre*, which purports that the perpetrator needs only to be aware of the social meaning of his acts.[19]

It can be argued though that, although in violation of the Statute, this statement is 'correct'; as we saw in Chaps. 2 and 3, under most national law systems a legal evaluation is not required for the establishment of criminal responsibility. As we learn from Kelt and Von Hebel, the same was intended to apply for the Statute; they recall that it "was generally felt that Article 30 should not lead to the result that a perpetrator's knowledge of a legal term, or his or her value judgement, would be determinative for the inference of individual criminal responsibility. It should be enough that the perpetrator was aware of[20] the factual circumstances that formed the basis for a certain conclusion as to a legal circumstance or a certain value".[21] Further, "[t]he principle of *mens rea* coverage cannot be said to require that the perpetrator was aware that the act was criminalized. This is one of the fundamental principles of criminal law recognized in most national legal systems and in international law".[22] Indeed, it is not the belief of the defendant that determines the law. Moreover, whether he knew the act to be *criminalized* is irrelevant, even to the finding of the required *Unrechtsbewußtsein*.[23] But we cannot (yet) dispose of the provision as being completely irrelevant, because para 4 of the General Introduction says "unless otherwise indicated". What are the material elements that allow a mistake of law to negate the required mental element, i.e. those situations that Article 32(2) *does* cover?

---

[15] Clark 2001, p. 323.

[16] *See also* Kelt and Hebel 2001a, p. 34.

[17] *See also* Werle and Jessberger 2005, footnote 44, at p. 43.

[18] Ambos 2002a, p. 783. *See also* Heller 2008, p. 434.

[19] Heller 2008, p. 439. See for a discussion of his arguments Sect. 4.2.2 *supra*.

[20] Or should have been aware of (footnote in the original text, AvV).

[21] Kelt and Hebel 2001a, p. 34.

[22] Kelt and Hebel 2001a, p. 36.

[23] *See also* Sect. 2.3.2.3, (1) *supra*.

6.2.1.1 Elements of Crimes Against Humanity

The introduction to elements of crimes against humanity provides that the defendant should have had knowledge of the general context of his conduct, namely the widespread or systematic attack against a civilian population. According to Article 30(3) the intent must also extend to this context.[24] The issue is to determine what the object of the required knowledge is. Is it the existence, the nature or the political and ideological principles of the conflict?[25] Or, alternatively, general knowledge of the attack based on a policy in a broad sense?[26]

Robinson explains that during the negotiations "[i]t was argued on both sides that as a practical matter, the approach taken would make little difference since in virtually all cases the widespread or systematic character would be obvious, and therefore knowledge of it would be easily inferred. The compromise reached, as proposed by the US, was to refer in the contextual element to knowledge of the widespread or systematic attack, but then to provide in the Introduction that this 'should not be interpreted as requiring proof that the perpetrator had knowledge of all characteristics of the attack'.[27]

Again, the scope remains uncertain, but it is unlikely that this knowledge requirement extends to the legal characterisation of the attack. In this respect para 4 of the general introduction applies. The required knowledge is at least only factual; which facts are relevant to this knowledge remains doubtful. For our purposes it suffices to conclude that no proof of legal knowledge on the side of the perpetrator is needed for establishing that he acted with the required knowledge relating to the context of his behaviour. A mistake of law in this respect does not negate the mental element.

Turning now to some specific elements of crimes against humanity, an important question is whether or not these elements perhaps require legal knowledge or an intent to violate the law.

6.2.1.1.1 Specific Elements: Deportation, Torture and Persecution

The crime against humanity of deportation or forcible transfer of the population (Article 7(1)(d)) is defined by Article 7(2)(d) to mean the 'forced displacement of the persons concerned by expulsion or other coercive acts from the area in which they are lawfully present, without grounds permitted under international law'. The crime against humanity of torture also contains a so-called 'unlawfulness' element, stating that torture shall not include "pain or suffering arising only from, inherent

---

24 *See also* Werle and Jessberger 2005, pp. 49–50.

25 Ambos 2003, p. 27. *See also* Robinson 2001, p. 72.

26 Ambos 2003, pp. 31–32. *See also* Robinson 2001, p. 73.

27 Robinson 2001, p. 72.

in or incidental to, lawful sanctions".[28] And the definition of persecution refers to "the intentional and severe deprivation of fundamental rights contrary to international law".[29] The element belonging to the 'contrary to international law' element contains a footnote stating that this requirement is without prejudice to para 6 of the General Introduction to the Elements of Crimes. Paragraph 6 states that normally the elements will not repeat the elements of the crime definition that refer to the unlawfulness of the behaviour. It is difficult to understand this reference to para 6, or, indeed, the meaning of para 6 itself. Perhaps we can draw a parallel to para 5 of the General Introduction: "Grounds for excluding criminal responsibility or the absence thereof are generally not specified in the elements of crimes listed under each crime". The idea behind this paragraph was that the EOC were meant to provide a list of elements that needed proof in every case.[30]

The elements of crime do not state a specific mental element in relation to these 'unlawfulness' elements. This would mean that the default rule of Article 30 applies.[31] However, does the element 'without grounds permitted under international law' for example fall under 'material elements' as to which the perpetrator should have acted with the required mental element? The analyses in Chaps. 2 and 3 of 'unlawfulness' as an element of the crime definition, seems to justify the conclusion that most of the time this is not the case. Generally, this part of the crime definition merely indicates that there are circumstances under which international law allows the forcible transfer of the civilian population. As part of the definition the unlawfulness of the transfer requires proof. What does not need proof is knowledge or awareness on the part of the defendant as to the unlawfulness of this transfer. As indicated in Chap. 2, Roxin holds that when the legal element is equal to or constitutes the wrongfulness of the act, a mistake as to this element does not negate the required intent.[32] This does not mean that a mistake of law as to the grounds on which transfer is permitted under international law is irrelevant to the establishment of perpetrator's culpability. The issue of mistake of law is addressed at a later stage, after it has been established that the crime definition has been fulfilled. In Sect. 6.3 of this chapter we will return to this example.

6.2.1.2 Elements of War Crimes

For the purposes of this section the following elements of war crimes are relevant.

Introduction to War Crimes

With respect to the last two elements listed for each crime:

---

[28] Article 7(2)(e) ICC Statute.

[29] Article 7(2)(g) ICC Statute.

[30] *See* Kelt and Hebel 2001a, p. 38.

[31] *See* para 2 of the general introduction to the EOC.

[32] Roxin 2006, p. 489, Rn 105. *See also* Sect. 2.3.2.3 *supra.*

- There is no requirement for a legal evaluation by the perpetrator as to the existence of an armed conflict or its character as international or non-international;
- In that context there is no requirement for awareness by the perpetrator of the facts that established the character of the conflict as international or non-international;
- There is only a requirement for awareness of the factual circumstances that established the existence of an armed conflict that is implicit in the terms "took place in the context of and was associated with.

Common Elements for Article 8(2)(a)

Such person or persons were protected under one or more of the Geneva Conventions of 1949. The perpetrator was aware of the factual circumstances that established that protected status. (Footnote 32: This mental element recognizes the interplay between Articles 30 and 32. This footnote also applies to the corresponding element in each crime under Article 8 (2) (a), and to the element in other crimes in Article 8 (2) concerning awareness of the factual circumstances that establish the status of persons and property under the relevant international law of armed conflict.) (Footnote 33: With respect to nationality, it is understood that the perpetrator needs only to know that the victim belonged to an adverse party to the conflict. This footnote also applies to the corresponding element in each crime under Article 8 (2) (a).) The conduct took place in the context of and was associated with an international armed conflict. (Footnote 34: The term "international armed conflict" includes military occupation. This footnote also applies to the corresponding element in each crime under Article 8 (2) (a).)
The perpetrator was aware of the factual circumstances that established the existence of an armed conflict.

Common Elements for Article 8(2)(b)

The conduct took place in the context of and was associated with an international armed conflict.
The perpetrator was aware of factual circumstances that established the existence of an armed conflict.

Common Elements for Article 8(2)(c)

Such person or persons were either hors de combat, or were civilians, medical personnel or religious personnel taking no active part in the hostilities. (Footnote 56: The term "religious personnel" includes those non-combatant military personnel carrying out a similar function.)
The perpetrator was aware of the factual circumstances that established this status.
The conduct took place in the context of and was associated with an armed conflict not of an international character.
The perpetrator was aware of factual circumstances that established the existence of an armed conflict.

Common Elements for Article 8(2)(e)

> The conduct took place in the context of and was associated with an armed conflict not of an international character.
> The perpetrator was aware of factual circumstances that established the existence of an armed conflict.

As to the contextual elements of war crimes, the last two elements for each of the war crimes under 8(2)(a) and (b) and (c) and (e) the EOC provide "[t]he perpetrator was aware of the factual circumstances that established the existence of an armed conflict". The introduction to war crimes gives a further explanation: no legal evaluation is required and it is not required that the perpetrator was aware, even as to the factual matter, of the circumstances that established the character of the conflict as international or non-international. What is required is that the perpetrator knew of the factual circumstances which establish the existence of an armed conflict. Thus, as Ambos notes, the perpetrator is not even required to have been aware of the facts relevant to the distinction between the two types of armed conflict.[33] It could be argued that the requirement of only factual knowledge as to existence of an armed conflict is justified, because the perpetrator has no influence on the presence of these contextual elements.

Another requirement is that the perpetrator must have been aware of the facts relating to the status of the victim as a protected person. Dörmann holds that these elements indicate that the 'circumstance element' in war crimes related to the character of the armed conflict and the protected status of the person are not covered by the *mens rea* requirement of Article 30. Instead a mental element to the requirement of protected status was added, according to which "[t]he perpetrator was aware of the factual circumstances that established the protected status".[34] One could also argue that Article 30 applies, requiring knowledge of these circumstance elements, and that the EOC stipulate that the required knowledge is only factual knowledge.

In footnote 32 (under common elements for Article 8(2)(a)) the drafters state that this mental element, awareness of the factual circumstances that established the protected status, recognizes the interplay between Articles 30 and 32 of the Statute. According to Dörmann this footnote emphasizes "the general rule that while ignorance of the facts may be an excuse, ignorance of the law (in this case of the Geneva Conventions and its definitions of protected persons or property) is not".[35] It is probable that in this footnote the drafters recognize that, in general, only mistakes of fact negate the mental element but that mistakes of law do not. Perhaps unconsciously, the drafters have revealed that they intended Article 32(2) to have a very limited scope, only applying to one limited category of mistakes of

[33] Ambos 2003, p. 15. *But see* Olásolo 2008, p. 28 (arguing that it must be established the perpetrator was aware "of the facts that established the character of the conflict as international or non-international").

[34] Dörmann 2003, p. 118.

[35] Dörmann 2003, p. 118.

law. The general or common mental element requirements for war crimes relating to the existence of an armed conflict and the protected status of the victims will not be affected by a mistake of law.

6.2.1.2.1 Specific Elements: Improper use of a flag, Insignia or Uniform

Another provision where the Elements make reference to the interplay between Articles 30 and 32 is Article 8(2)(b)(vii). This article concerns the war crime of "making improper use of a flag of truce, of the flag or of the military insignia and uniform of the enemy or of the United Nations, as well as of the distinctive emblems of the Geneva Conventions, resulting in death or serious personal injury". The elements to this crime are discussed separately in the EOC. With regard to the war crime of making improper use of the flag of truce, of the flag or of the military insignia and uniform of the enemy and of the distinctive emblems of the Geneva Conventions the elements require that the defendant *knew or should have known* of the prohibited nature, that is of the illegality, of such use. With regard to making improper use of a flag, military insignia or uniform of the United Nations, the elements require that the defendant *knew* of the prohibited nature of such use. This seems to be the only crime within the Statute that requires knowledge of unlawfulness as an element of the crime; in case of improper use of a flag, military insignia or uniform of the UN *actual knowledge* of the prohibited nature of the conduct is required. According to footnote 41 the reason for this is "the variable and regulatory nature of the relevant prohibitions".[36] Here any mistake, even an unreasonable one, will exculpate the defendant.[37] The other elements to crimes of improper use of a flag, insignia or uniform, which require that the defendant *knew or should have known* about the illegality of such a use, limit the exculpatory effect of mistakes of law to reasonable mistakes. According to Cottier, here the EOC seems to deviate from Article 30 by providing for criminal responsibility for negligence.[38] Heller wonders whether such a deviation can be provided for in the EOC; he concludes that 'unless otherwise provided' in Article 30 refers to otherwise provided by the Statute.[39]

---

[36] I agree with Cottier that the 'should-have-known'-test also allows for these factors being taken into account, *see* Cottier 2008, p. 355.

[37] This actually depends on the system applied. As we saw in Chap. 2 supra the Anglo-American system does not require reasonableness in case of crimes of intent or recklessness, and some civil law system require reasonableness in all cases. *See* Sliedregt 2003, in footnote 402 on p. 316. I think the reasonableness standard in case of crimes of intent can be explained by the objective and normative application of the intent requirement. Whether the defendant acted with the required intent is determined by applying an objective standard. This standard is in this sense also normative, but not to the same extent as the negligence standard. It is not an issue of *should have known*, but rather of *must have known*. *See also* Wilt 2000, pp. 127–129, and Hullu 2006, pp. 216–217.

[38] Cottier 2008, p. 354.

[39] Heller 2008, pp. 436 + 444. *See also* Ambos 2004, p. 789; and Weigend 2004, p. 327.

How should we interpret the reference here to the interplay between Articles 30 and 32? As stated above, in the discussion of the requirement of knowledge of the protected status of the victims, the interplay was understood as to emphasize that generally mistakes of fact do negate the required mental element and mistakes of law do not. How should this explanation be applied here, since this provision seems to grant a mistake of law mental-element-negating effect? This is an exception to the interplay between Articles 30 and 32. Cottier explains the reference to the interplay as a specification of the cases in which a mistake of law constitutes a ground for excluding criminal responsibility.[40] The fact that footnote 41 also refers to this interplay, however, negates the argument that the drafters recognize the reasonableness or avoidability requirement in case of mistake of law, because in this case any mistake negates the required intent.

It is not clear as to what this 'interplay' means. As seen in the preceding chapters, Article 30 provides only for a default rule on the required mental element. Mistake of law is almost never related to this mental element but is rather concerned with the actor's culpability. What these element requiring knowledge of the prohibited nature of the conduct *do* make clear, however, is that the elements here, and only here, specifically provide for such a requirement. Reasoning *a contrario* this indicates that where the elements do not provide for this, i.e. in all other crimes, knowledge of wrongfulness is not an element of the required intent.

To conclude, a final remark should be made as to the should have known standard sometimes provided for in the elements. An example can be found in the above mentioned provision on the improper use of a flag, insignia and uniforms. Another example is located in the provision on the war crime of conscripting and enlisting child soldiers, Articles 8(2)(b)(xxvi) and 8(2)(e)(vii). Element 3 requires that the perpetrator knew or should have known the persons were under the age of 15. Werle and Jessberger find that elements like these actually expand the liability under Article 30 into the realm of negligence.[41] They argue that the elements here, by requiring that the defendant is also responsible if he should have known that they were minors, expand the liability under Article 30(3), which requires the defendant to have had actual knowledge of the soldier's minor status. I do not agree with the thesis that the EOC here turn a crime of intent into a crime of negligence.[42] The element of the crime definition relating to the age of the child soldier should, it is submitted, be regarded as a so called 'objectified' element or attendant circumstance.[43] The required mental element remains intent, but this mental element does not cover the attendant circumstance. If it were otherwise and the required intent would cover the age of the child soldier, this would arguably lead to an insufficient protection of legally protected interest. It is therefore submitted that a mistake about the age of the person does not negate the perpetrator's

[40] Cottier 2008, p. 354.

[41] Werle and Jessberger 2005, p. 48.

[42] *See also* Weigend 2008, p. 485.

[43] *See also* Weigend 2008, p. 485 (Weigend speaks of an 'accompanying circumstance').

intent. Such a mistake is, however, not completely irrelevant either, since this would imply a rule of strict liability. The reasonableness of the mistake should be taken into account in assessing the perpetrator's culpability. This is not incompatible with Article 30, because Article 30 does not cover the issue of culpability. Article 30 is only concerned with establishing whether the actor acted with the required intent.[44] The crime is a still a crime of intent but for a part of the definition negligence suffices.[45]

6.2.1.3 Conclusion

The elements of crimes against humanity and war crimes purport that the only elements that, potentially, could be covered by a mistake of law, the normative elements, are in fact excluded from the scope of this defence. Article 32 provides that mistakes of law are relevant when they negate the mental element. A crime definition consists of factual and normative elements. In general the factual elements are covered by the mental element, that is to say, if the perpetrator lacks intent or knowledge relative to one of the factual elements, the required mental element is lacking. In general, because so called 'objectified' factual elements are not covered by the required intent. The EOC stipulate that in general the normative elements are *not* covered by the mental element, meaning that, in order to establish the required mental element, it is irrelevant what the defendant knew, thought or believed relative to these normative elements. Only if the perpetrator had no knowledge of the factual circumstances underlying this normative element, will he lack the required intent.

The normative element will be established ex post, it is for the judges to decide whether the act was 'severe' or 'unlawful' or 'excessive'. It is not up to the perpetrator to determine the law. His decision to act (which may be based on a mistaken evaluation of the law) will be normatively assessed. Criminal intent is not required; it is not a requirement of criminal responsibility that the perpetrator acted with the intent to violate the law. This is not an element of the crime definition that requires proof in every single case. This is not a strange or exceptional position; as we saw in Chaps. 2 and 3, in a threefold system, especially, this is a very common and logical approach. As stated, this does not imply however that a mistake of law is always irrelevant. In fact, the excuse mistake of law justifies a finding that no criminal intent is required. If the defendant is without fault unaware of the wrongfulness of his behaviour, he lacks the required culpability for criminal punishment.

---

44 *See* Sect. 4.2.2 *supra*.

45 To the contrary Heller 2008, p. 444 (Heller resists the incorporation of should have known elements also because of "a widespread disposition to avoid responsibility based on either negligence or recklessness").

What Article 32(2), taken together with the elements, shows is that the drafters seem to have left out a whole range of otherwise relevant mistakes. These mistakes can only be taken into account in a system that recognizes the establishment of guilt, in the sense of reproachability, as a requirement separate from the required intent, but, included as part of a comprehensive system of liability, as an inextricable element of criminal responsibility.

Another question is whether or not it is likely that a defendant will be mistaken about the lawfulness of his behaviour, when his acts amount to war crimes or crimes against humanity. Because most international crimes are *malum in se*, we are inclined to answer this question in the negative; it is not likely that anyone can reasonably claim mistake of law in these cases. In such cases a plea of mistake of law will, most of the time, be implausible and a presumption of knowledge of wrongdoing will be justified. Fulfilment of the intent requirement of the crime definition will justify the inference that the perpetrator also acted with the required *Unrechtsbewußtsein*. However, does this mean that we must abolish the defence a priori? No matter how abhorrent most international crimes may be, some circumstances may justify a violation of the law nevertheless. These circumstances are covered by justificatory circumstances, and it is plausible that a defendant makes a mistake as to the legal scope of these circumstances because this scope is often far from settled.

6.3 Dilemmas on the Battlefield

As argued before, not all norms of international criminal law, including justifications, have fully crystallized and the fact that perpetrators are likely to be less familiar with international crimes than with domestic crimes, seems to warrant not excluding the defence of mistake of law a priori.

Weigend argues that it is unlikely that an 'isolated' mistake of law ever arises in connection with the crimes enumerated in the ICC Statute.[46] Saland noted that, at the Rome Conference, it was argued that "it would be hard to conceive of a situation of mistake of law, given the nature of the crimes within the jurisdiction of the Court".[47]

But, as Boister asks himself, "can it be fairly assumed that all those who may enter combat in 'civilized' states know all of the rules, and what about those in 'uncivilized' states, or states that have failed?".[48]

Each section below discusses a situation in which a perpetrator of an international crime, could invoke mistake of law as an excuse for his unlawful behaviour. The first section (Sect. 6.3.1) outlines a situation in which the mistake of law is

[46] Weigend 2004, p. 332.

[47] Saland 1999, p. 210.

[48] Boister 2005, p. 38.

relevant because of the uncertainty of the international offence the perpetrator is accused of. This may be uncertainty of the prohibition as such or uncertainty about the meaning of a legal or justificatory element of the crime definition. The second section (Sect. 6.3.2) outlines a case in which the defendant was mistaken as to the legal scope or existence of a ground of justification. The third section (Sect. 6.3.3) concerns mistakes about defences under public international law. These all concern situations which are not covered by Article 32 ICC Statute.

6.3.1 Mistakes About the Prohibition

First, it is necessary to examine international crimes that are not *malum in se*. In the rare case of international crimes that are *mala prohibita*, the perpetrator's ignorance of wrongfulness will be credible. An example we already encountered in the previous part is the *improper use of a flag, insignia or uniform*. Fletcher mentions the war crime of Article 8(2)(b)(xii), declaring that no quarter will be given, as an example of an offence *malum prohibitum*.[49] It may be doubted as to whether or not this is a good example, because every military officer will recognize that this is a prohibited order, especially those in command positions, who are the only persons who can potentially be liable for this crime.[50]

It is likely that other examples given by Fletcher and Ambos are more convincing. Ambos refers amongst other things to the war crimes of causing 'widespread, long-term and severe damage to the natural environment'[51] and the vague element of the crimes against humanity of Article 7(1)(k) referring to 'other inhumane acts'.[52] As Ambos holds, a mistake of law as to these normative elements will be irrelevant to the finding of intent, but must in the final analysis be addressed when assessing the defendant's culpability.[53]

A mistake about a normative element will only negate the required intent if the defendant is not even aware of the social meaning of the element in question. A mistake about the legal significance is irrelevant to the finding of intent, no legal knowledge is required. A mistake about the legal significance that leads the defendant to be mistaken about the wrongfulness of his behaviour is, nevertheless, relevant to the establishment of the defendant's culpability.[54] Article 32(2) does not cover these mistakes however. Under the proposed supplement to the Statute,

---

49 Fletcher 2007, p. 31.

50 See element 3 in the EOC.

51 Article 8(2)(b)(iv) ICC Statute. According to Werle and Jessberger the defendant's beliefs are relevant on the basis of Element 3, footnote 37 EOC, Werle and Jessberger 2005, footnote 44, at p. 43.

52 Ambos 2004, p. 818. *See also* Fletcher 2007, p. 85.

53 Ambos 2004, p. 818.

54 *See also* Sect. 2.3.2.3, (2) *supra*.

this mistake would be relevant; the issue of culpability would revolve around the question of the avoidability of the defendant's mistake.

The next section explores the consequences of mistake of law as to justificatory definitional elements, such as 'civilians taking direct part in hostilities' and 'military objectives'.[55]

6.3.1.1 Military Objectives

It is a war crime to intentionally direct attacks against civilians, not taking direct part in hostilities and against civilian objects, that is objects which are not military objectives.[56] These war crimes emanate from one of the four fundamental general principles of humanitarian law, that is the principle of distinction. A distinction should be made between the civilian population and combatants and between civilian objects and military objectives.[57] A person or an object can only be a legitimate target of military action if it is a military objective. Civilians and civilian objects can never be a legitimate target; Articles 51 and 52 AP I grant them a protected status in international armed conflicts (IAC). Articles 51(3) AP I provides that civilians enjoy protection, unless and for such time as they take a direct part in hostilities.

The Law of Armed Conflict (LOAC) applicable in IAC distinguishes between combatants and civilians. The notion of 'combatant' is, however, unknown in the LOAC applicable in non-international armed conflicts (NIAC) and the notion of 'civilian' is nowhere defined in the applicable treaty law.[58] The principle of distinction is arguably nevertheless applicable in NIAC as a rule of customary international humanitarian law.[59] The protection against violence and inhuman treatment as provided for in Common Article 3 of the Geneva Conventions (CA 3) and Article 4 AP II applies to all persons not taking active part in the hostilities. Article 13(2) AP II provides that civilians enjoy protection against direct attack, unless and for such time as they take a direct part in hostilities.

The definition of 'direct participation in hostilities' is however contested, as Ducheine en Pouw illustrate.[60] The Interpretative Guidance on the Notion of Direct Participation in Hostilities (IGDPH) of the ICRC states the following on the this issue: "For the purpose of the principle of distinction in non-international

---

[55] See e.g. Article 8(2)(b)(i) and (ii) ICC.

[56] See Article 8(2)(b)(i), (e)(i) and (b)(ii) ICC.

[57] Article 48 AP I. The other principles are: military necessity, humanity and proportionality, see e.g. The Manual of the Law of Armed Conflict 2004, pp. 21–26. *See also* Gill and Sliedregt 2005, p. 29, footnote 2 and accompanying text. On the principle of distinction see also Olásolo 2008, pp. 13–14 + 104–105.

[58] Melzer 2009, p. 27. *See also* Kleffner 2008, p. 69.

[59] *See* Henckaerts and Doswald-Beck 2005a, Rule 1, pp. 5–8. *See also* Ducheine and Pouw 2010, pp. 88–89; and Kleffner 2008, p. 70.

[60] Ducheine and Pouw 2010, pp. 89–100; and Pouw 2009, pp. 24–25.

armed conflict, all persons who are not members of State armed forces or organized armed groups of a party to the conflict are civilians and, therefore, entitled to protection against direct attack unless and for such time as they take a direct part in hostilities. In non-international armed conflict, organized armed groups constitute the armed forces of a non-State party to the conflict and consist only of individuals whose continuous function is to take a direct part in hostilities ("continuous combat function")".[61] Hence, in a NIAC the protection against direct attack does not apply to (1) members of State armed forces; (2) members of organised armed groups of a party to the conflict, who assume a continuous combat function; and (3) civilians who take a direct part in hostilities, for the time they take such direct part.

With respect to the second category, Ducheine and Pouw discern a problem with the norm ISAF uses to determine whether persons involved in the Afghan drug industry can be directly attacked. According to ISAF such individuals can be attacked when there is a "clearly established link with the insurgency".[62] According to Ducheine and Pouw this norm suggests that the established link is sufficient to determine these persons to be legitimate military objectives. However, before this conclusion can be drawn, it has to be established that the link with the insurgency consists of a continuous combat function.[63] Individuals who are not members of State armed forces only lose the protection against direct attack when they participate directly in hostilities. For members of organised armed groups, this direct participation is established when they assume continuous combat functions (CCF). The members are legitimate targets for the time they assume these functions.[64] Civilians lose the protection against direct attack when they take part in hostilities on an *ad hoc* basis, whilst participating. Civilians do not lose their *status* as civilians and as soon as they cease their hostile acts they regain their protection against direct attack. This is referred to as the 'revolving door' of civilian protection.[65]

To determine whether a specific act constitutes a direct participation in hostilities the ICRC discerns three constitutive elements. First, the harm likely to result from a specific act must attain a certain threshold.[66] Second, there must be a direct causal link between the act "and the harm likely to result from that act, or from a coordinated military operation of which the act constitutes an integral part".[67] Thirdly, the "act must be specifically designed to directly cause the required

[61] Melzer 2009, p. 27. As Pouw notes, the IGDPH is clearly not a binding text, but "it is currently the single most comprehensive document on the notion of direct participation in hostilities", Pouw 2009, p. 18.

[62] See NATO 2010. *See also* Ducheine and Pouw 2010, pp. 92–93; and Pouw 2009, pp. 8–9 + 11.

[63] Ducheine and Pouw 2010, p. 93; and Pouw 2009, p. 27.

[64] Melzer 2009, pp. 71–73. *See also* Pouw 2009, p. 25.

[65] Melzer 2009, pp. 70–71.

[66] Melzer 2009 p. 47. *See also* Pouw 2009, pp. 31–32.

[67] Melzer 2009, p. 51. *See also* Pouw 2009, pp. 32–33.

threshold of harm in support of a party to the conflict and to the detriment of another".[68] These three requirements apply both in the determination of the CCF of members of organised armed groups and in determining the direct participation in hostilities on an *ad hoc* basis by civilians.

As the example offered by Ducheine and Pouw indicates, ISAF, in directly attacking persons involved in the Afghan drug industry without establishing the CCF of the targeted individuals or their direct participation as civilians, violates the principle of distinction, at least so far as this principle is interpreted by the ICRC. If the ICRC is followed[69] and a violation found to have occurred, this violation may be based on a misinterpretation of the law. This misinterpretation consists of the statement that a link with the insurgency is enough to establish direct participation in hostilities. This is an example of a mistake of law concerning the application of the principle of distinction, a fundamental principle of IHL. This is not a mistake about the prohibition as such (of directly attacking civilians), but a mistake about the interpretation of a justificatory norm (those who directly take part in hostilities in a NIAC, are (no longer) protected against direct attack). This mistake is not covered by Article 32, since it does not negate the required intent; only an understanding of the social significance of the term civilian is required.

As stated above, the principle of distinction does not only apply to individuals but also to objects. Article 48 AP I proscribes that a distinction should be made between civilian objects and military objectives. But what if soldiers are inside a civilian object? And what if the object of an intended military attack has a dual use, both military and civilian? How do you then determine whether this object is a legitimate military target?[70]

If we look at the definition of military objectives in Article 52(2) of the Additional Protocol I,[71] we see that this is not a purely factual question but involves a normative assessment. The definition holds the requirement that a military objective is only that object which by its nature, location, purpose or use makes an effective contribution to military action and whose destruction in whole or in part in the circumstances ruling at the time offers a 'definite military advantage'. Once it has been established that the attack is aimed at a military objective, the attack will still be prohibited if it is expected to cause incidental death or injury to civilians and/or damage to civilian objects "which would be

---

[68] Melzer 2009 p. 58. *See also* Pouw 2009, pp. 33–34.

[69] Which is to be awaited because the notion of direct participation in hostilities is a "highly contentious and paradoxic subregime of LOAC", Pouw 2009, p. 17.

[70] *See also* Rogers 2005.

[71] "Attacks shall be limited strictly to military objectives. In so far as objects are concerned, military objectives are limited to those objects which by their nature, location, purpose or use make an effective contribution to military action and whose total or partial destruction, capture or neutralization, in the circumstances ruling at the time, offers a definite military advantage", Article 52(2) API.

excessive in relation to the concrete and direct military advantage anticipated".[72] In some cases it is inevitable that civilians are the unintended victims of the attack on a military objective. The principle of proportionality[73] addresses the issue whether the military advantage gained by the attack weighs up to this 'collateral damage'.

In its report to the Office of the Prosecutor of the ICTY the committee of experts established to investigate the NATO bombardments in the Kosovo crisis (OTP committee) says the following on the principle of proportionality:

> The main problem with the principle of proportionality is not whether or not it exists but what it means and how it is to be applied. It is relatively simple to state that there must be an acceptable relation between the legitimate destructive effect and undesirable collateral effects. [...] The questions which remain unresolved once one decides to apply the principle of proportionality include the following:
>
> (a) What are the relative values to be assigned to the military advantage gained and the injury to non-combatants and or the damage to civilian objects?
> (b) What do you include or exclude in totalling your sums?
> (c) What is the standard of measurement in time or space? and
> (d) To what extent is a military commander obligated to expose his own forces to danger in order to limit civilian objects?
>
> It may be necessary to resolve them on a case by case basis, and the answers may differ depending on the background and values of the decision maker. [...] [I]t is unlikely that military commanders with different doctrinal backgrounds and differing degrees of combat experience or national military histories would always agree in close cases.[74]

The bombardment of the Serb Radio and Television Station (RTS) in Belgrade, which resulted in the death of 10–17 civilians[75] is such an event about which diverse opinion exists as to the primary issue (to be addressed before the proportionality) as to whether this was a military objective.[76] The OTP committee and Human Rights Watch (HRW) present opposite views on this issue.[77] The first considered the RTS to be a legitimate target. HRW did not. Both reports agree that a radio or TV station can be a military objective when it incites to violence, as was the case with Radio Milles Collines in Rwanda. This was, however, not the case with the RTS in Belgrade. The station was used for propaganda, but this alone does

---

[72] Article 51(5)(b) API and Article 57(2)(a)(iii) API.

[73] The use of the term "proportionality" is debateable. As Kalshoven indicates, the term does not figure in Protocol I, Kalshoven 2003, p. 498.

[74] OTPICTY 2000, § 48–50.

[75] OTPICTY 2000, §71.

[76] *See also* W. Fenrick in reaction to C. Garraway in: Duyx et al. 2000, p. 99.

[77] HRW 2000.

not make it a military objective. The ICTY report finds that it appears however that the primary reasons for NATO to decide to bomb the RTS were to cut out the Serbian command and control system that was operating via the RTS.[78] The ICTY report then states that, assuming the RTS was a legitimate target, "the civilian casualties were unfortunately high but do not appear to be clearly disproportionate".[79] The ICTY report admits that the effect of the bombing was only temporarily; within a few hours the broadcasting was recovered and could be continued from another location. The issue that than arises is whether the military advantage is substantial enough to justify the anticipated civilian casualties. According to the ICTY report one should not only judge the proportionality of this attack on this specific target on itself. In addition, one has to see the bigger picture of the whole military campaign. After examining proportionality from this perspective they concluded that the attack was not disproportionate.[80] HRW sees it differently. It does not only regard the attack as disproportionate, but it also denies that the RTS was a military objective to begin with. As NATO had anticipated, the broadcasting resumed from a different location within several hours after the attack. According to HRW the attack did not yield a 'definite military advantage', which would imply that the object of attack did not fulfil the requirements of military objective.[81]

On the one hand, one could characterise a mistake about whether something is a military objective as a mistake of fact. In most cases, it will be a mistake of fact. A good example is the bombing of the Chinese Embassy in Belgrade.[82] This was clearly a factual mistake; NATO intended to hit and believed itself to be bombing the Yugoslav Federal Directorate for Supply and Procurement.[83] On the other, the case of the bombardment of the RTS is not such a case of mistake of fact. NATO intended to hit the RTS. Arguably NATO was mistaken about the legitimacy of this target as a military objective, a mistake of law.

These reports show the nature of dispute about the legitimacy of certain targets. Important parameters are the 'effective contribution to military action' and 'definite military advantage'. The next important parameter is the proportionality of targeting the military objective. The question in determining the legitimacy of the target is: how far do you go back (or forth) in time and space? Best, for example, warns for the dangers of interpreting 'definite military advantage' as to include a psychological advantage. "It moves the standard of judgment from the purportedly rational and objective towards the probably irrational and admittedly subjective".[84] The difference between the outcomes of the two reports is based on a

[78] OTPICTY 2000, § 76.

[79] OTPICTY 2000, § 77.

[80] OTPICTY 2000, § 78. *See also* Olásolo 2008, pp. 130–131.

[81] HRW 2000, p. 15, footnote 80 and accompanying text.

[82] *See also* Rogers 2005, p. 174.

[83] Rogers 2005, p. 174.

[84] Best 1994, p. 275.

different view as to whether the 'definite military advantage' must be temporally or geographically related to the object of the attack.[85] In case of objects of dual-use in particular the question of whether these are military objectives, in which case the civilian damage is collateral, may be a complex one.[86]

Again a mistake of law as to the legitimacy of a target does not negate the required intent, Article 32 does not apply. The mistake should be taken into account in the assessment of the defendant's culpability.

6.3.2 *Putative Justifications*

Mistakes about the grounds for justification, or putative justifications, are of particular importance to the scope of a 'mistake of law' defence. Fletcher argues these mistakes are, in fact, the only real cases of mistake of law.[87] Criteria of justification are supposed to function not only as ex post decision rules, but ex ante as conduct rules.[88] Ignorance of these criteria in respect of lawful conduct may indicate a lack of *Unrechtsbewußtsein*. This makes putative justification a valid excuse, especially in international criminal law, where grounds of justifications are as yet not well developed.[89]

Acting on unlawful superior orders, believing it to be your duty to do so because you are under the mistaken impression they are lawful, can be categorised as a putative justification. You are mistaken about the justification of lawful orders. This special case of putative justification, and whether or not it deserves a separate provision from mistake of law, has been discussed in Chaps. 2 and 4. In the current section two other cases of putative justification are addressed: a mistake as to the right to self-defence and a mistake as to necessity.

6.3.2.1 Mistake of Self-Defence

Self-defence is an almost universal defence which exists in some form in every national criminal law system.[90] In systems that apply an objective test, requiring the defensive action to have been necessary and proportionate, the defence can be qualified as a justification.[91] This is the case with the ICC provision on self-

---

85 See also footnote 36 under element 2 of Article 8(2)(b)(iv) EOC (according to this footnote the advantage may or may not be temporally or geographically related to the object of the attack).

86 *See also* Rogers 2005.

87 Fletcher 1998, p. 167.

88 Fletcher 1985, p. 976.

89 *See also* Eser 2008, pp. 865–866.

90 Sliedregt 2003, pp. 264–266.

91 Sliedregt 2003 pp. 264–265.

defence, Article 31(1)(c). This provision requires the defendant to have acted in response to an imminent and unlawful use of force against himself or another person, or in case of war crimes, against an attack against property essential to his survival or the survival of the other person or property which is essential to the accomplishment of a military mission. The provision also requires the defendant to have acted proportionally.[92]

It should be kept in mind however that, as noted by Van der Wilt, "the margins for invoking self-defence as a justification to counter a charge of war crimes are extremely small. […] the justification is not available for military inter se, in view of the reciprocal right to kill and to be killed. Neither would it apply in the context of civilians taking up arms against a military adversary, as the former would lose their status as protected person and would qualify as combatants as well".[93]

Nonetheless, Ambos offers the two following examples of mistaken self-defence: a soldier believes he can commit a crime against humanity to defend the property of his military unit, while Article 31(1)(c) only allows war crimes under these circumstances.[94] Alternatively, if the soldier commits a war crime, but the property he is protecting is not essential to the accomplishment of the military mission and he is aware of this, he makes a mistake as to the scope of self-defence in the sense of Article 31(1)(c).[95] If the defendant was mistaken about the legal scope of the justification, this mistake can be qualified as a mistake of law. Since it does not negate the required intent, Article 32(2) does not apply.[96]

6.3.2.2 Necessity

Necessity, in most national law systems,[97] refers to a situation where the defendant, under the pressure of the circumstances has to choose between two conflicting interests. Necessity is a justification, based on the weighing of two

[92] Other related and (theoretically) interesting issues that will not be addressed here are: the requirement of knowledge of the attack (see on this issue, e.g. Fletcher 1998, pp. 101–106; Eser 2008, p. 883; Ambos 2002b, p. 1035; Ambos 2008b, p. 177) and the distinction between individual self-defense and collective self-defense or the right of self-defense under public international law, *see e.g.* Ambos 2002b, p. 1034; Sliedregt 2003, pp. 254–255; Eser 2008, pp. 879–880; Fletcher and Ohlin 2008; and a symposium on this book in the JICJ, July 2009.

[93] Wilt 2009a, p. 539.

[94] Eric Pouw pointed out to me that this example is purely theoretical because it unjustly presumes that a soldier knows what constitutes a crime against humanity.

[95] Ambos 2004, p. 819.

[96] Ambos 2004, p. 819.

[97] Van Sliedregt sees "a growing awareness [in American codes] of the distinction between duress and choice of evils as one between excuse and justification", as the distinction is known is civil law systems, in particular the German system; she warns, however, that the majority of American states still seem to adhere to the common law, Sliedregt 2003, pp. 270–271. For the civil law distinction between choice of evils as a justification and duress as an excuse, see Sliedregt 2003, pp. 276–279. On this defense in the Dutch legal system see Dolman 2006.

colliding interests; the act is justified if the least costly interest is violated to protect the higher interest.[98] A mistake of law occurs when the defendant is mistaken for example about the existence of a conflict of duties.[99]

Although it can be argued convincingly, as Ambos has, that necessity is not available in case of international crimes because there can never be a balancing of interest, no interest would be high enough to justify committing an international crime, I would submit that a mistake as to the applicability of this justification is not inconceivable.

Let us look at the following 'ticking bomb' scenario: The defendant, a military interrogator, is confronted with a high value detainee, who is suspected of having placed a very destructive bomb somewhere in a densely populated area. In fact, the suspect admits this and tells that the bomb will go off in two hours; he is the only person who knows where the bomb is located and he is determined not to reveal the location. The interrogator is aware of the prohibition on torture, but believes this is a situation of necessity; if he acts in violation of the law and tortures the detainee into revealing the location of the bomb, this act will be justified because it will safe the lives of perhaps tens of people. However, the prohibition on torture is absolute[100]; the interrogator is mistaken about the applicability of a ground of justification. The issue of his culpability, and thus of whether he should be punished for torturing the detainee, should revolve around the question whether he could have avoided his mistake of law.[101]

Another example of a possible situation of necessity was presented by Justice Robertson in his dissent to an appeal decision in the Norman trial. Robertson suggested that there may be a defence of necessity available under circumstances where a family or community is under murderous and unlawful attack. As he holds, the scope of such a defence is to be determined by court, deciding a specific case.[102] One can imagine that under such circumstances the defendant may well make a mistake of law as to the proper scope of the justification of necessity.

Sands convincingly describes 'the path' to the approval of abusive interrogation techniques, constituting torture, to be applied by the US military in the 'war on terror'. Sands' investigation reveals that the lawyers responsible for the memo's that redefined the definition of torture, argued amongst other things, that the criminal law defence of necessity was "available to prevent a direct and imminent threat to the US and its citizens".[103] They herewith of course flagrantly repudiated

---

[98] *See also* Ambos 2008b, p. 183 (on the difference between justifying necessity and excusing duress).

[99] This can also happen on the basis of a mistake of fact.

[100] See for a recent case on such a ticking bomb scenario, a case before the Israeli Supreme Court, H.C. 5100/94 1999. *See also*, Jessberger 2005 and Gaeta 2004.

[101] Or perhaps whether this was a situation of duress.

[102] Prosecutor v. Norman 2004b, § 46. On this dissent *see also* Sect. 5.2.4.2 *supra*.

[103] Sands 2008, p. 89.

the absolute character of the prohibition on torture as provided for in the 1984 Torture Convention.[104] After Secretary of Defence Rumsfeld approved of the memo, the new techniques were applied in Guantanamo and eventually also ended up in the Abu Ghraib prison in Iraq. Although these new techniques also violated the US Field Manual 34–52,[105] it seems likely that in the field of the 'war on terror' the idea had arisen that the 'new enemy' asked for new rules,[106] that necessity justified balancing the interest of the US citizens against the rights of the 'unlawful combatants' not to be tortured and to be treated humanely. It is not inconceivable that the soldiers in the field might be confused about the alleged necessity of applying torture techniques when even the administration's lawyers were confused.[107] The prohibition on torture is absolute,[108] and the definition on what constitutes torture cannot be changed unilaterally. The main responsibility for this total misconception, that there could be circumstances under which a violation of this prohibition could be justified, lies with the policy makers. A plea of mistake of law of a low level executioner may bring this to light.

6.3.3 Mistaken Defences Under Public International Law

Military necessity and reprisals are international defences. This means that an individual can raise this defence only in his public capacity and not in his private capacity. As Van Sliedregt stated with regard to military necessity, it "is an interest of a State or another party to an armed conflict. [...] If military necessity can be a justification under the laws of war, it can only exonerate an individual as an instrument of his State".[109] When a defence of reprisal or military necessity applies, there is no violation of international humanitarian law (IHL).[110] These international justifications allow for a breach of international obligations under very limited circumstances.

6.3.3.1 Military Necessity

A clear distinction should be made between general principles of IHL, justifications under public international law and justifications under criminal law. Military necessity is both a general principle (all military actions must be militarily

[104] Sands 2008, p. 86.
[105] Sands 2008, p. 90.
[106] Sands 2008, p. 192.
[107] Sands 2008, p. 108.
[108] *See* Jessberger 2005, p. 1068.
[109] Sliedregt 2003, p. 296.
[110] *See also* Sliedregt 2003, pp. 293–294.

necessary) and a justification under public international law (some violations of IHL are justified by military necessity). A violation of a rule of IHL (e.g. deportation or excessive destruction of property), can only be justified by military necessity if the violated rule of IHL provides for this justification.[111] Military necessity is thus not a general justification,[112] unlike criminal law justifications.

It must be said that "[r]arely, if ever, is the judgment of a field commander in battle—balancing military necessity and advantage—subject to legal challenge, let alone criminal sanction".[113] Van Sliedregt refers to The High Command trial; the defendant Reinecke was exculpated from spoliation on the basis of military necessity. She states this case and the Hostages case, which dealt with military necessity as a justification for destruction and devastation, were exceptions, rather than rules; the defence of military necessity was rejected in most cases.[114] Dörmann and Lippman also refer to the Hostages Trial[115] in which defendant Rendulic was acquitted because of his good faith mistake about the military necessity of destruction and devastation of the province of Finnmark, Finland.[116] The question is, however, whether this mistaken justification was based on a mistake of fact or law. The acquittal was based on the honest judgement on the basis of the conditions prevailing at the time that urgent military necessity for the devastation and destruction existed. At the end of 1944 the retreating Germans expected a Soviet offensive. The offensive never came, the judgement about military necessity was based on a mistake of fact.

More recent cases referred to demonstrate the unsuccessfulness of pleas of military necessity are the judgments of Trial Chamber of the ICTY in the cases against Krstić,[117] and against Blagojević and Jokić.[118] Indeed, in these cases the plea of military necessity was rejected; no pleas of mistake of law seem to have been submitted.

A mistake of law may occur when the actor believes his violation of the law of armed conflict is justified on the basis of military necessity. The crime definition

111 *See also* Ambos 2008b, pp. 98–99.

112 *See also* Kalshoven 2005, p. 366; Lippman 1996, pp. 59 + 64; Dörmann 2008, p. 312.

113 Hampson 2007, p. 298.

114 Sliedregt 2003, p. 297.

115 Dörmann 2008, p. 313, footnote 126; Lippman 1996, p. 62.

116 Lippman 1996, pp. 62 + 64, List (The Hostages Case) 1948, TWC XI, p. 1297.

117 Prosecutor v. Krstić 2001, § 527 ("The evacuation [of the Bosnian Muslim population from the Srebrenica enclave] was itself the goal and neither the protection of the civilians nor imperative military necessity justified the action."). This reasoning recognizes the two grounds of justification for forcible transfer; the justifications were denied on the facts of the case. *See* Zahar and Sluiter 2008, p. 432

118 Prosecutor v. Blagojević and Jokić 2005, §§ 598–602 (§ 601: "The fact that no step is taken by the perpetrator to secure the return of those displaced, when the circumstances that necessitated the evacuation have ceased, is among the factors that may prove an intent to permanently displace the victims rather than the intent to secure the population through a lawful—and therefore temporary—evacuation"). *See* Dörmann 2008, pp. 316–318. (This case also concerns destruction of property not justified by military necessity, §615.)

concerned may or may not contain a 'not justified by military necessity'-clause.[119] I take the example of a mistake as to the lawfulness of an operation transferring the population from a certain area during an armed conflict. Van Baarda points out how the terms evacuation and deportation are used indiscriminately. Following his suggestion, that evacuation refers to lawful forcible transfer and deportation to unlawful forcible transfer,[120] deportation can amount to a war crime and a crime against humanity. Robinson recalls how states were very cautious in defining the concept of deportation in the Rome Statute because many of them carry out legitimate acts of deportation, which are then called acts of evacuation, on a frequent basis.[121] The ICC crime definitions of deportation refer to 'unlawful deportation' and 'deportation without grounds permitted under international law'.[122]

The relevant IHL provisions are Article 49 of the Fourth Geneva Convention and Article 17 of Additional Protocol II.[123] They provide that forcible transfer is permitted if the security of the population or imperative military reasons so demand. Van Baarda points out how Article 49 and Article 17 are actually self-contradictory.[124] Both provisions first state that forcible transfers are prohibited, regardless of their motive (Article 49) or if they are ordered for reasons related to the conflict (Article 17). Subsequently, however, these provisions provide that an exception to this rule applies when 'the security of the population or imperative military reasons so demand'. This second exception refers to the 'military necessity' justification.[125] As Van Baarda asks himself, how can a transfer based on military necessity not be related to the conflict? The same ambiguity can be found in Article 8(2)(e)(viii) ICC Statute.[126] Van Baarda demonstrates that the grounds for forcible transfer permitted under international law, turning deportation into evacuation, are unsettled.[127] His conclusion is that while Articles 49 and 17 seem to provide for two separate justifications for forcible transfer (security and military necessity), the second justification cannot exist without the first. On the basis of a case law study and the taxonomy of IHL Van Baarda concludes that 'military necessity' in this context can only mean the necessity to evacuate the

---

119 See an example by Nill-Theobald, Nill-Theobald 1998, p. 131 (mistake as to military necessity in case of the destruction of a village).

120 Baarda 2002, pp. 61–62.

121 Robinson 2001, p. 86. *See also* Saland 1999, p. 209.

122 See the war crimes of: (Article 8(2)(a)(vii)(unlawful deportation), 8(2)(b)(viii)(deportation), 8(2)(e)(viii)(ordering the displacement for reasons related to the conflict, unless security or imperative mil. reasons); and the crime against humanity of: (Article 7(1)(d) jo (2)(d), deportation without grounds permitted under international law).

123 If it concerns an internal armed conflict.

124 Baarda 2002, p. 73.

125 Baarda 2002, pp. 71–72 (referring to Article 147 GC IV, which prohibits deportation as a 'grave breach' unless 'justified by military necessity').

126 Baarda 2002, p. 74.

127 Baarda 2002, pp. 73–74. According to Jescheck deportation of the civilian population cannot be justified by military necessity, Jescheck 2004, p. 51.

civilian population in order to guarantee their safety, unlike other provisions of the Geneva Conventions and the Additional Protocols, where 'military necessity' relates to the necessity to gain victory promptly.[128]

Considering this divergence between the text of Articles 49 and 17 and its legal interpretation as outlined by Van Baarda, it is not inconceivable that a soldier participates in the war crime of deportation, while believing he is evacuating the civilian population of a particular area. Even forcible transfer can be lawful. It may be very difficult, from within or without, to distinguish between a lawful and an unlawful case of forcible transfer. The impact of such a transfer might be just as grave, and the opposition by the civilian population against it just as fierce, in both cases. A mistake in this respect may amount to a mistake of fact or a mistake of law. It is a mistake of law when the subordinate follows the order to forcibly transfer a civilian population, while knowing this transfer is ordered for imperative military reasons and not in the interest of the security of the civilian population.

6.3.3.2 Reprisals

Zegveld and Kalshoven demonstrate how the prohibition on reprisals against civilians and civilian objects in Articles 51 et seq. of AP I can arguably not be regarded as rules of customary international law.[129] The same has been argued by Greenwood.[130] This is even more so in case of an internal armed conflict, since AP II contains no provision at all on reprisals.[131]

According to Jescheck reprisals cannot be a justification for the international crimes of the ICC statute since Article 31 does not provide for reprisals as a ground for excluding criminal responsibility.[132] Saland and Ambos however refer to Article 31(3) and the history of negotiations leading up to this provision and Article 21, which leaves room to consider defences like military necessity and reprisals.[133]

The fact that international humanitarian law contains numerous prohibitions on targeting civilians, does not mean that these prohibitions imply a prohibition on reprisals against civilians as well. It may confirm, however, that the conditions under which recourse to reprisal is legitimate are very stringent.[134]

Although Van Sliedregt acknowledges that it is unlikely that the ICC will allow resort to the defence of reprisal, she concedes that reprisals may be useful, at least

---

128 Baarda 2002, pp. 81–85.

129 Kalshoven and Zegveld 2001, pp. 143–146. *See also* Osiel 2009, pp. 35–36+55; and Kalshoven 2003, pp. 492+505.

130 Greenwood 2006b, pp. 322–324; Greenwood 2006a, pp. 332, 336, 342–351.

131 Kalshoven 2003, p. 504. Greenwood 2006a, p. 339.

132 Jescheck 2004, p. 52.

133 Saland 1999, p. 209; Ambos 2002b, p. 1028; Ambos 2008b, p. 174, Rn. 84; Ambos 2004, p. 829. *See also* Sliedregt 2003, p. 291; Greenwood 2006a, p. 332.

134 *See also* Kalshoven 2003, p. 509.

when the following requirements are adhered to: "the requirement of proportionality, [of] express warning in advance, and [of] termination as soon as the adversary has discontinued its unlawful attacks" and "when the decision is made at the highest level of government".[135] Ambos points out how reprisals against certain protected persons and property are absolutely prohibited. In so far as the prohibition on reprisals is not regarded as customary international law, its use is at least limited by strict conditions.[136] Greenwood lists as requirements:

1. it must be a response to a prior violation of international law which is imputable to the state against which the reprisal is directed [...];
2. it must be reasonably proportionate;
3. it must be undertaken for the purpose of putting an end to the enemy's unlawful conduct and preventing future illegalities and not for mere revenge; and
4. since reprisals are a subsidiary means of redress, no other effective method of redress must be available.[137]

The fact that the scope of legitimate or justifiable[138] resort to reprisals is to a certain extent unclear, and arguably significantly wider to States that are not party to Additional Protocol I,[139] means that a mistake may be easily made. That the decision to resort to reprisals will usually be taken at the higher levels of command or at government level, does not exclude the relevance of such a mistake to the lower echelons, the executing soldiers. They may well believe that the violation of law they are committing is justified by legitimate recourse to reprisals. In individual criminal proceedings the soldier, who in his official capacity executed the reprisal ordered from the highest level of government, should be able to invoke this defence under international law; or at least the excuse of mistake of law, for making a mistake in participating in an unlawful resort to reprisals.

Kalshoven's severe criticism on a decision and a judgement in two cases before the ICTY shows how even today the scope of the prohibition of reprisals against civilians remains uncertain. From his criticism we learn that the Trial Chamber's conviction that reprisals against civilians are categorically prohibited under today's (customary) international law is unsubstantiated.[140] The first decision of a ICTY Trial Chamber discussed by Kalshoven is a decision in a "Rule 61 procedure" against Milan Martić.[141] On the issue of reprisals against civilians the Trial

[135] Sliedregt 2003, p. 292; as to the last requirement Greenwood comments that this is more a matter of military discipline than international law, Greenwood 2006b, p. 300, footnote 16.

[136] Ambos 2008b, p. 99.

[137] Greenwood 2006b, p. 299.

[138] Kalshoven finds this term more accurate because it reflects that reprisals are "imperfect means of supporting international law", Kalshoven 2005, p. 24.

[139] Greenwood 2006b, pp. 324–325.

[140] Kalshoven 2003, p. 492. *See also* on the same decisions of the ICTY: Greenwood 2006a, p. 332 (both authors find the findings of the Trial Chamber inaccurate and unnecessary).

[141] Prosecutor v. Martić 1996.

Chamber concluded that "the rule which states that reprisals against the civilian population as such, or individual civilians, are prohibited in all circumstances, even when confronted by wrongful behaviour of the other party, is an integral part of customary international law and must be respected in all armed conflict".[142] The Trial Chamber mainly based this conclusion on the following arguments. First, it referred to Article 1 Common to all Geneva Conventions, which requires the High Contracting Parties to ensure respect for the Conventions in all circumstances.[143] Second, it referred to General Assembly resolution 2,675, which states that "[c]ivilian populations, or individual members thereof, should not be the object of reprisals [...]".[144] The final argument of the Trial Chamber is that, although Protocol II does not contain a provision similar to Article 51(6) AP I, holding a prohibition of reprisals against civilians in an international armed conflict, such a prohibition of reprisals against civilians in an internal armed conflict must be inferred from Article 4 APII.[145] Kalshoven is not at all convinced by these arguments. He states that Common Article 1, or for that matter the 1949 Geneva Conventions in general, do not "deal with the protection of the civilian population against the effects of hostilities, or *a fortiori* with the issue of reprisals in that context".[146] Further, he states that Article 51(6) API is the result of GA resolution 2,675; protocol II does not contain a similar clause. Article 4 APII "is irrelevant to the matter of reprisals against the civilian population in a situation of internal armed conflict [...]".[147] This article "belongs to the realm of Geneva-style "humane treatment", not to that of the Hague-style protection of civilian populations "against the dangers arising from military operations"."[148] He concludes that the "Trial Chamber has not convincingly shown that reprisals against the civilian population are banned as a matter of customary international law, nor that the treaty prohibition of reprisals against the civilian population applies outside international armed conflicts".[149]

The other decision of the ICTY Trial Chamber Kalshoven critizes is the Kupreškić Judgement.[150] In this case the defendants, who are Bosnian Croats, were being prosecuted for their part in the attack by the HVO (Croatian Defence Council) on the Muslims in Ahmići on 16 April 1993. As part of its argument about the protection of the civilian population in armed conflict, the Trial Chamber also addressed the issue of reprisals against civilians.[151] The Trial Chamber

---

142 Prosecutor v. Martić 1996, § 17.

143 Prosecutor v. Martić 1996, § 15.

144 Prosecutor v. Martić 1996, § 16.

145 Prosecutor v. Martić 1996, § 16.

146 Kalshoven 2003, p. 491. *See also* Greenwood 2006a, pp. 348–349.

147 Kalshoven 2003, p. 491.

148 Kalshoven 2003, p. 492.

149 Kalshoven 2003, p. 492.

150 Prosecutor v. Kupreškić et al. 2000.

151 Prosecutor v. Kupreškić et al. 2000, §§ 527–536, Kalshoven 2003, p. 500.

referred to Article 51(6) and 52(1) AP I, which prohibits reprisals against the civilian population and civilian objects respectively. The Trial Chamber concluded that these prohibitions transformed into general rules of international law, despite the lack of *usus*. As a result of the Martens clause, the Chamber continues, *opinio iurus sive necessitates* may play a much greater role than *usus*.[152] Kalshoven notes how the Court does not mention that APII is silent on the matter of reprisals against civilians.[153] Kalshoven points out that several questions remain unanswered in the Trial Court's reasoning. First of all, the question "whether this presumed general rule binds states that expressly or implicitly have rejected it".[154] And second, the more important question "whether it should also be deemed to apply in situations of internal armed conflict—for which [...] no rule comparable to Article 51(6) and 52(1) of Protocol I has been included in Protocol II".[155] In relation to the first question, about dissident states, Kalshoven refers to the express reservation to the ratification of Protocol I made in 1998 by the United Kingdom. "This spells out in clearest possible terms the strict legal conditions under which that country, in the face of "serious and deliberate attacks" by an adverse party on civilians or civilian objects, "will regard itself as entitled to take measures otherwise prohibited" by Articles 51–55".[156] Kalshoven also refers to a statement in the same tenor made by Italy in 1986 on ratifying the Protocol,[157] and to the fact to France, not yet a party to the Protocol, tried "frantically and ultimately [...] to find agreement on a formula that would specify the conditions for a legitimate recourse to reprisals against an enemy civilian population".[158]

In relation to the second question, the issue of reprisals against civilians in internal armed conflict, Kalshoven notes that the Trial Chamber has circumvented "the problem posed by the silence of Protocol II by just not referring to it".[159] The Trial Chamber refers to a statement by the International Law Commission on Common Article 3 in relation to the Draft Articles on State Responsibility. The Trial Chamber reads into this statement a prohibition of reprisals against civilians in the combat zone.[160] Kalshoven rejects this conclusion, "as with the rest of the 1949 Conventions, common Article 3 does not govern the conduct of hostilities".[161] "The conclusion the Chamber draws from the Commission's opinion, [...], is therefore unfounded, and completely disregards the fact that a quarter-century after 1949, all attempts to include a prohibition on reprisals in Protocol II,

152 Prosecutor v. Kupreškić et al. 2000, § 527.
153 Kalshoven 2003, p. 500.
154 Kalshoven 2003, p. 502.
155 Kalshoven 2003, p. 502.
156 Kalshoven 2003, p. 502.
157 Kalshoven 2003, p. 502.
158 Kalshoven 2003, p. 503, fn. 75.
159 Kalshoven 2003, p. 504.
160 Prosecutor v. Kupreškić et al. 2000, § 534.
161 Kalshoven 2003, p. 504.

in the provisions protecting the civilian population from the dangers of actual combat, failed miserably".[162]

After having argued at length that reprisals against the civilian population in armed conflicts are prohibited under all circumstances both under treaty law and general international law, the Trial Chamber surprisingly[163] concludes this issue by stating that reprisals, even when considered lawful, are restricted by last resort, prior warning, high-level decision, proportionality, termination when goal is achieved, and 'elementary considerations of humanity'.[164]

By way of final comment Kalshoven notes that, in both decisions, the discussion of the issue of reprisals against civilians was unnecessary. Neither the facts of the decision in the Martić case, nor the defence in the Kupreškić case warranted this discussion.[165]

Kalshoven explains how in determining the lawfulness of a resort to reprisals a belligerent can easily be mistaken. Some "rules are of doubtful validity and, while wholeheartedly accepted by some, are just as emphatically rejected by others (for instance: rules on contraband, on air warfare, on the use of nuclear weapons, and so on)".[166] The acts which give rise to the reprisal might have been lawful, which would make the reprisal itself unlawful and could then give cause for contra-reprisals.[167] Again, it is thus not unimaginable that at the deciding level the decision to take reprisals is based on a mistake of law. On the one hand, it does not seem likely that the executioner of the unlawful reprisal will be prosecuted for this violation of the law of war; he does not have the deciding responsibility and can therefore not be liable for a wrong decision. On the other, reprisals entail acts that are otherwise violations of the law of war. The executioner commits war crimes; only if the reprisal is justified will the wrongfulness of these acts be negated. If a mistake of law is easily made at the highest level of authority, it is only understandable, and probably excusable, if the low-level executioner follows this order by mistake.

6.4 Conclusion

Section 6.2 of this chapter revealed that only a very limited number of mistakes of law will indeed negate the required mental element. The defence of mistake of law provided for in Article 32(2) of the Rome Statute does not apply to mistakes as to the prohibition as such or to putative justification (under criminal or public

[162] Kalshoven 2003, p. 504.

[163] Kalshoven 2003, p. 505.

[164] Prosecutor v. Kupreškić et al. 2000, § 535; Kalshoven 2003, p. 505.

[165] Kalshoven 2003, pp. 493–494 and 505.

[166] Kalshoven 2005, p. 41.

[167] Kalshoven 2005 p. 41.

international law).[168] This means that the mistaken defendants in the examples given in Sect. 6.3 of this chapter will not be able to invoke this defence. Under the supplement proposed in Chap. 4, however, these relevant cases of mistake of law will find their proper place, namely in the assessment of whether the perpetrator could have avoided committing the wrongful act, in the assessment of the actor's culpability. However rare the case of prosecution of the soldier executing an order mistakenly based on military necessity may be, and however even rarer a successful plea of mistake of law in such a case may be, this does not mean that the defence of mistake of law should be excluded a priori. In those exceptional cases where this excuse may be raised, it serves as an essential component in the establishment of the individual's culpability.

References

Ambos K (2002a) Der Allgemeine Teil des Völkerstrafrechts. Ansätze einer Dogmatisierung. Duncker & Humblot, Berlin

Ambos K (2002b) Other grounds for excluding criminal responsibility. In: Cassese A, Gaeta P, Jones JRWD (eds) The Rome Statute of the International Criminal Court: A commentary, vol I. Oxford University Press, pp 1003–1048

Ambos K (2003) Some preliminary reflections on the *mens rea* requirements of the crimes of the ICC statute and of the elements of crimes. In: Vohrah LCea (ed) Man's Inhumanity to Man. Kluwer Law International, The Hague, pp 11–40

Ambos K (2004) Der Allgemeine Teil des Völkerstrafrechts. Ansätze einer Dogmatisierung. 2nd edn. Duncker & Humblot, Berlin

Ambos K (2006) Remarks on the general part of international criminal law. J Int Crim Justice 4:660–673

Ambos K (2008b) Internationales Strafrecht. 2nd edn. C.H. Beck, München

Baarda TA van (2002) Deportatie is verboden, evacuatie niet. Maar, wat is het verschil? Militair Rechtelijk Tijdschrift 94(2 + 3):61–119

Best G (1994) War & law since 1945. Clarendon Press, Oxford

Boister N (2005) Reflections on the relationship between the duty to educate in humanitarian law and the absence of a defence of mistake of law in the Rome Statute of the International Criminal Court. In: Burchill R, White ND, Morris J (eds) International conflict and security law. Essays in memory of Hilaire McCoubrey. Cambridge University Press, Cambridge, pp 32–48

Clark RS (2001) The mental element in international criminal law: the Rome Statute of the International Criminal Court and the elements of offenses. Crim Law Forum 12(3):291–334

Cottier M (2008) Article 8, para. 2(b)(vii). In: Triffterer O (ed) Commentary on the Rome Statute of the International Criminal Court, observers' notes, article by article, 2nd edn. Verlag C.H. Beck oHG, München, pp 350–362

Dolman MM (2006) Overmacht in het stelsel van strafuitsluitingsgronden. Wolf Legal Publishers, Nijmegen

Dörmann K (2003) Elements of war crimes under the Rome Statute of the International Criminal Court. sources and commentary. ICRC/Cambridge University Press, Cambridge

[168] *See also* Olásolo 2008, p. 243.

Dörmann K (2008) Article 8, para 2(a). In: Triffterer O (ed) Commentary on the Rome Statute of the International Criminal Court, observers' notes, article by article. Verlag C.H. Beck oHG, München, pp 300–323

Ducheine PAL, Pouw EH (2010) ISAF Operaties in Afghanistan: oorlogsrecht, doelbestrijding in counterinsurgency, ROE, mensenrechten & ius ad bellum. Wolf Legal Publishers, Nijmegen

Duyx P, Haveman R, Sliedregt E van (2000) War crimes law and the Statute of Rome: some afterthoughts? report of the seminar hosted by the Netherlands in Rijswijk, The Netherlands on 22 Oct 1999. Revue de Droit Militaire et de Droit de la Guerre 39 (1-2-3-4):68–122

Eser A (2002) Mental elements: mistake of fact and mistake of law. In: Cassese A, Gaeta P, Jones JRWD (eds) The Rome Statute of the International Criminal Court: a commentary, vol I. Oxford University Press, Oxford, pp 889–948

Eser A (2008) Article 31: grounds for excluding criminal responsibility. In: Triffterer O (ed) Commentary on the Rome Statute of the International Criminal Court: observers' notes, article by article, 2nd edn. C.H. Beck oHG, München, pp 863–893

Fletcher GP (1985) The right and the reasonable. Harv Law Rev 98:949–981

Fletcher GP (1998) Basic concepts of criminal law. Oxford University Press, New York

Fletcher GP (2007) The grammar of criminal law. American, comparative, and international, volume one: Foundations, vol 1. Oxford University Press, New York

Fletcher GP, Ohlin JD (2008) Defending humanity: when force is justified and why. Oxford University Press, New York

Gaeta P (2004) May necessity be available as a defence for torture in the interrogation of suspected terrorists? J Int Crim Justice 2:785–794

Gill T, Sliedregt E van (2005) Guantánamo Bay: a reflection on the legal status and rights of 'Unlawful Enemy Combatants'. Utrecht Law Rev 1(1):28–54

Greenwood C (2006a) Belligerent reprisals in the jurisprudence of the international criminal tribunal for the former Yugoslavia. In: Greenwood C (ed) Essays on war in international law. Cameron May, London, pp 331–351

Greenwood C (2006b) Twilight of the law of belligerent reprisals. In: Greenwood C (ed) Essays on war in international law. Cameron May, London, pp 295–329

Hampson F (2007) Military necessity. In: Gutman R, Rieff D, Dworkin A (eds) Crimes of war: what the public should know, 2nd edn. W.W. Norton & Company Ltd., London, pp 297–298

Hebel H von (2001) The making of the elements of crimes, introduction. In: Lee RS (ed) The International Criminal Court, elements of crimes and rules of procedure and evidence. Transnational Publishers, Inc, Ardsley, pp 3–18

Heller KJ (2008) Mistake of legal element, the common law, and Article 32 of the Rome Statute. J Int Crim Justice 6:419–445

Henckaerts JM, Doswald-Beck L (2005) Customary international humanitarian law. International Committee of the Red Cross, vol 1. Cambridge University Press, Cambridge

Hullu Jd (2006) Materieel Strafrecht. Kluwer, Deventer

Jescheck HH (2004) The general principles of international criminal law set out in Nuremberg, as mirrored in the ICC statute. J Int Crim Justice 2(1):38–55

Jessberger F (2005) Bad torture: good torture? What international criminal lawyers may learn from the recent trial of police officers in Germany. J Int Crim Justice 3:1059–1073

Kalshoven F (2003) Reprisals and the protection of civilians: two recent decisions of the Yugoslavia tribunal. In: Vohrah LCea (ed) Man's inhumanity to man. Kluwer Law International, The Hague, pp 481–510

Kalshoven F (2005) Belligerent reprisals, vol 11. International humanitarian law series, 2nd edn. Martinus Nijhoff Publishers, Leiden

Kalshoven F, Zegveld L (2001) Constraints on the waging of war: an introduction to international humanitarian law, 3rd edn. International Committee of the Red Cross, Geneva

Kelt M, H von Hebel (2001a) The making of the elements of crimes, general principles of criminal law and elements of crimes. In: Lee RS (ed) The International Criminal Court, elements of crimes and rules of procedure and evidence. Transnational Publishers, Inc, Ardsley, pp 19–40

Kelt M, H von Hebel (2001b) The making of the elements of crimes, what are elements of crimes? In: Lee RS (ed) The International Criminal Court, elements of crimes and rules of procedure and evidence. Transnational Publishers, Inc., Ardsley, pp 13–18
Kleffner JK (2008) The notions of civilians and fighters in non-international armed conflicts. In: Beruto GL, Ravasi G (eds) The conduct of hostilities revisiting the law of armed conflict: 100 years after the 1907 Hague conventions and 20 years after the 1977 additional protocols/ International Institute of Humanitarian Law. Nagard, Milano, pp 69–77
Lippman MR (1996) Conundrums of armed conflict: criminal defenses to violations of the humanitarian law of war. Dickinson J Int Law 15:1–112
Melzer N (2009) Interpretive guidance on the notion of direct participation in hostilities under international humanitarian law. International Committee of the Red Cross, Geneva
Nill-Theobald C (1998) "Defences" bei Kriegsverbrechen am Beispiel Deutschlands und der USA: zugleich ein Beitrag zu einem Allgemeinen Teil des Völkerstrafrechts, vol Band S 72. Beiträge und Materialien aus dem Max-Planck-Institut für ausländisches und internationales Strafrecht, Freiburg i.Br., iuscrim edn. Max-Planck-Institut für ausländisches und internationales Strafrecht, Freiburg im Breisgau
Olásolo H (2008) Unlawful attacks in combat situations: from the ICTY's case law to the Rome Statute. Martinus Nijhoff Publishers, Leiden
Osiel M (2009) The end of reciprocity: terror, Torture and the Law of war. Cambridge University Press, Cambridge
Piragoff DK (1999) Article 30: Mental Element. In: Triffterer O (ed) Commentary on the Rome Statute of the International Criminal Court: Observers'Notes, Article by article. Nomos Verslagsgesellschaft, Baden–Baden, pp 527–535
Pouw EH (2009) To kill or not to kill: ISAF and the search within international humanitarian law and human rights law for a legal basis to target narcotics-individuals. Paper for the International conference—human rights and the military: a duty to protect?, 28–30 August 2009, Wellington, New Zealand
Robinson D (2001) The elements of crimes against humanity. In: Lee RS (ed) The International Criminal Court, elements of crimes and rules of procedure and evidence. Transnational Publishers, Inc, Ardsley, pp 57–108
Rogers APV (2005) What is a legitimate military target? In: Burchill R, White ND, Morris J (eds) International conflict and security law. Essays in memory of Hilaire McCoubrey. Cambridge University Press, Cambridge, pp 160–184
Roxin C (2006) Strafrecht Allgemeiner teil, Band I, Grundlagen, der Aufbau der Verbrechenslehre. 4th edn. C.H. Beck, Munchen
Saland P (1999) International criminal law principles. In: Lee RS (ed) The International Criminal Court, the making of the Rome Statute, issues, negotiations, results. Kluwer Law International, The Hague, pp 189–216
Sands P (2008) Torture team. deception, cruelty and compromise of law. Allen Lane, London
Sliedregt E van (2003) The criminal responsibility of individuals for violations of international humanitarian law. T.M.C. Asser Press, The Hague
Weigend T (2004) The harmonization of general principles of criminal law; the statutes and jurisprudence of the ICTY, ICTR, and the ICC: An overview. Nouvelles Etudes Penales 19:319–335
Weigend T (2008) Intent, mistake of law, and co-perpetration in the *Lubanga* decision on confirmation of charges. J Int Crim Justice 6:471–487
Werle G, Jessberger F (2005) 'Unless otherwise provided': Article 30 of the ICC statute and the mental element of crimes under international criminal law. J Int Crim Justice 3:35–55
Wilt HGvd (2000) The duty to know: enkele beschouwingen over het leerstuk van command responsibility. In: Corstens GJM, Groenhuijsen MS (eds) Rede en recht liber amicorum voor Nico Keijzer. Gouda Quint, Deventer, pp 123–135
Wilt HG van der (2009a) Can romantics and liberals be reconciled?: Some further reflections on defending humanity. Journal of International Criminal Justice 7:529-539

Wise EM (1998) Commentary on Parts 2 and 3 of the Zutphen intersessional draft: General principles of criminal law. Nouvelles Etudes Penales 13bis:43–53
Zahar A, Sluiter GK (2008) International criminal law, a critical introduction. Oxford University Press, Oxford

Miscellaneous

HRW (2000) The crisis in Kosovo. Civilian deaths in the NATO air campaign, February 2007. Human Rights Watch
The Manual of the Law of Armed Conflict (2004) UK Ministry of Defence. Oxford University Press, Oxford
NATO (2010) NATO's role in Afghanistan. available at: http://www.nato.int/cps/en/natolive/topics_8189.htm, last visited: 7 July 2010
OTPICTY (2000) Final report to the prosecutor by the committee established to review the NATO bombing campaign against the federal republic of Yugoslavia. vol 2000

Table of Cases

International Case Law

US Military Tribunals at Nuremberg

List (The Hostages Case) (1948), US Military Tribunal at Nuremberg, UNWCC, vol. VIII; TWC vol. XI

International Criminal Tribunal for the Former Yugoslavia

Prosecutor v. Martić (1996), ICTY Trial Chamber, Case No. IT-95-11-R61, Decision 8 March 1996
Prosecutor v. Kupreškić et al. (2000), ICTY Trial Chamber, Case No. IT-95-16-T, Judgement, 14 Jan 2000
Prosecutor v. Krstić (2001), ICTY Trial Chamber, Case No. IT-98-33-T, Judgement 2 Aug 2001
Prosecutor v. Blagojević and Jokić (2005), ICTY Trial Chamber, Case No. IT-02-60-T, Judgement 17 Jan 2005

Special Court for Sierra Leone

Prosecutor v. Norman (2004b), SCSL Appeals Chamber, Case No SCSL-2004-14-AR72(E), Decision on Preliminary Motion Based on Lack of Jurisdiction (Child Recruitment), 31 May 2004, Dissenting Opinion of Justice Robertson

National Case Law

Other Countries

H.C. 5100/94 (1999), The Supreme Court of Israel

Chapter 7
Concluding Remarks

7.1 Introduction

Mistake of law may excuse the perpetrator of an international crime. The provision in the ICC Statute, nevertheless, does not provide for this excuse. Based on the common law approach towards mistake of law, Article 32 is limited to a failure-of-proof defence. Only when the mistake negates the required intent will the defendant be exculpated. In truth, however, mistake of law does not concern the issue of intent; mistake of law concerns the culpability of the defendant. The result of the current codification is twofold. First, some mistakes, namely mistakes as to the prohibition as such and mistakes about justifications, are unduly not covered by the Statute. Second, under the current codification there is no room for differentiation according to the culpability of the defendant in making the mistake.

Chapters 2 and 3 demonstrated how in a twofold structure there is actually no principled solution to deal with issues of mistake of law. Applying a strict rule of *ignorantia non excusat* led to unjust results in case of reasonable mistakes of law. An answer was found in requiring knowledge of the law when a crime definition's mental element is termed 'wilfully' or 'knowingly', turning mistake of law into a failure-of-proof defence. However, in a failure-of-proof defence there is no room for the requirement of reasonableness, at least not in case of intentional crimes. In a threefold structure, the key to the solution was found in requiring *Unrechtsbewußtsein* as an element of criminal responsibility besides the required intent. This element of *Unrechtsbewußtsein* is an element of culpability and is presumed when the crime definition has been fulfilled. The presumption is rebuttable. A mistake of law, or better, a mistake of *Recht*, will negate the defendant's culpability if it was an unavoidable mistake. A mistake of *Recht*, because no legal knowledge is required. Legal elements in a crime definition are subjected to the *Parallelwertungslehre*; only if the defendant does not even know the social, everyday meaning of a legal element will his intent be negated. If he recognises this social meaning, but nevertheless believes his conduct to be lawful, this will not negate the required mental element, but may negate his culpability when he

A. van Verseveld, *Mistake of Law*, DOI: 10.1007/978-90-6704-867-5_7,

unavoidably lacked *Unrechtsbewußtsein*. The requirement of *Unrechtsbewußtsein* facilitates and at the same time justifies the rule that no criminal intent is required.

Essential to the German solution has been the recognition of the distinction between justification and excuse, wrongdoing and attribution, defeasible and comprehensive rules and conduct rules and decision rules. As seen in Chap. 3 these distinctions also have important implications for issues like criminal intent, putative justifications and the meaning of an element of unlawfulness or wrongfulness in the crime definition.

Chapter 4 confirmed that the ICC Statute is based on a twofold system of crimes, which has serious implications for issues of defences like mistake of law. Many authors have recognised this and have tried to repair the 'damage' by suggesting for example that an avoidability test should be applied to cases of mistake of law. It was argued, however, that this is not an option if the drafters have deliberately left out the avoidability requirement. The solutions offered perhaps reveal a feeling of having to make do with what one has got. Alternatively, a 'way out' was offered by suggesting that the ICC Statute does not provide for, nor reject, the excuse of mistake of law. In that case, Articles 31(3) and 21 would offer a tool to incorporate a mistake of law defence. But if these solutions do not deliver a principled answer to the issue, adding a new provision to the Statute is inevitable. I proposed the following provision:

> If it is concluded that the defendant acted in the mistaken belief that his conduct was lawful, or that he was mistaken about a fact extrinsic to the required mental element, and if this mistake was unavoidable, the defendant shall not be convicted in respect of such a wrongful act.

This provision would recognise the true character of this defence as an excuse, requiring a culpability assessment: Could the defendant have avoided making the mistake and thus be blamed for committing the wrongful act? The proposed provision would also allow abandoning the separate provision on superior orders. I accept the standard will actually be higher than under some national laws and international case law, because under the new provision even the reasonableness or avoidability of obedience to a non-manifestly unlawful order will be assessed. On the other hand, the provision would apply to all international crimes and the standard of assessment will be more subjective or personal, taking into account the subordinate's personal (in)capacities and the opportunities he had under the circumstances to behave differently.

The case law discussed in Chap. 5 revealed that mistake of law per se has only rarely been invoked; superior orders has been a more common defence. Because it was difficult to disentangle the mixed defences, of mistake of law, mistake of fact, superior orders and duress, this investigation did not reveal the (theoretical) reasons for rejecting or accepting pleas of mistake of law. To make sure that mistake of law, after all the theoretical reflections on it in the preceding chapters, did not end up as being seen as merely a lawyer's concoction, Chap. 6 sketched a few practical scenarios. The aim was to demonstrate that, although only rarely and under strict conditions, mistake of law may be a valid excuse. The sketched scenarios of mistake of law do not fall under the current ICC provision; in these cases there is a risk of conviction of non-culpable perpetrators.

Most pleas of mistake of law encountered in this study have been rejected on the basis of inference of consciousness of wrongdoing; the plea was regarded as incredible, the defendant must have known his conduct violated a(n international) legal rule. In the case of international crimes this inference of consciousness will almost always be justified. This would probably also be our conclusion in the case outlined in the Introduction; the plea of torturing on superior orders, because you thought you were just doing your job, or even a good job, is simply implausible. Or is it? Does the fact that, as may now be stated with certainty,[1] the US government was responsible for allowing, no, even promoting interrogation techniques that include torture when the detainee is a so-called 'unlawful enemy combatant', change the credibility of the pleas of superior orders and mistake of law? Perhaps we need to be careful not to let our moral indignation speak out of turn. An assessment of the avoidability of mistakes may bring to light circumstances that would otherwise remain undisclosed; circumstances that may affect the culpability of the perpetrator, but also circumstances that may implicate the responsibility of others. The excuse mistake of law, being both essential to the finding of the perpetrator's culpability and to the establishment of the full facts of the case, constitutes an indispensable component of the general part of international criminal law.

References

Bybee (2002) Memorandum for Alberto Gonzales, Counsel to the President, Re: Standards of Conduct for Interrogation under 18 U.S.C. §§ 2340–2340A ('The Torture Memos'), available at www.findlaw.com

Gourevitch P, Morris E (2008) Standard operating procedure. The Penguin Press, New York

Hersch SM (2004) Chain of command; The road from 9/11 to Abu Ghraib. Allen Lane, New York

Sands P (2008) Torture team. Deception, cruelty and compromise of law. Allen Lane, London

---

1 See amongst other sources: Bybee 2002; Sands 2008; Hersch 2004; Gourevitch and Morris 2008.

Bibliography

Ambos K (1999) General principles of criminal law in the Rome Statute. Criminal Law Forum 10:1–32

Ambos K (2002a) Der Allgemeine Teil Des Völkerstrafrechts. Ansätze einer dogmatisierung. Duncker & Humblot, Berlin

Ambos K (2002b) Other grounds for excluding criminal responsibility. In: Cassese A, Gaeta P, Jones JRWD (eds) The Rome Statute of the International Criminal Court: a commentary, vol 1. Oxford University Press, Oxford, pp 1003–1048

Ambos K (2003) Some preliminary reflections on the mens rea requirements of the crimes of the ICC Statute and of the elements of crimes. In: Vohrah LC et al (ed) Man's inhumanity to man. Kluwer Law International, The Hague, pp 11–40

Ambos K (2004) Der allgemeine Teil des Völkerstrafrechts. Ansätze einer Dogmatisierung. 2nd edn. Duncker & Humblot, Berlin

Ambos K (2006) Remarks on the general part of International Criminal Law. J Int Crim Justice 4:660–673

Ambos K (2007) Towards a universal system of crime: comments on George Fletcher's *Grammar of Criminal Law*. Cardozo Law Rev 28(6):2647–2673

Ambos K (2008a) Amicus Curiae brief, ECCC, criminal case file no. 001/18-07-2007-ECCC/OCIJ (PTC 02), 27 Oct 2008

Ambos K (2008b) Internationales Strafrecht, 2nd edn. C.H. Beck, München

Ambos K (2008c) May the state torture suspects to save the life of innocents? J Int Crim Justice 6:261–287

Arnold J, Karsten N, Kreicker H (2003) The German border guard cases before the European Court of Human Rights. Eur J Crime Crim Law Crim Justice 11(1):67–92

Artz G (1986) The problem of mistake of law. Brigham Young Univ Law Rev 3:711–732

Ashworth A (2006) Principles of criminal law, 5th edn. Oxford University Press, Oxford

Ashworth AJ (1974) Excusable mistake of law. Criminal Law Rev 652–662

Baarda TAv (2002) Deportatie is verboden, evacuatie niet. Maar, wat is het verschil? Militair Rechtelijk Tijdschrift 94(2+3):61–119

Bantekas I, Nash S (2007) International Criminal Law, 3rd edn. Routledge-Cavendish, London

Bassiouni MC (ed) (1998) The statute of the International Criminal Court, a documentary history. Transnational Publishers, Ardsley

Best G (1994) War & Law since 1945. Clarendon Press, Oxford

Boister N (2005) Reflections on the relationship between the duty to educate in humanitarian law and the absence of a defence of mistake of law in the Rome Statute of the International Criminal Court. In: Burchill R, White ND, Morris J (eds) International Conflict and Security Law. Essays in memory of Hilaire McCoubrey. University Press, Cambridge, pp 32–48

A. van Verseveld, *Mistake of Law*, DOI: 10.1007/978-90-6704-867-5,

Boot M (2002) Nullum Crimen Sine Lege and the Subject Matter Jurisdiction of the International Criminal Court: Genocide, Crimes Against Humanity, War Crimes. Intersentia, Antwerp
Cassese A (2003) International Criminal Law. Oxford University Press, Inc., Oxford
Cassese A (2008) International Criminal Law, 2nd edn. Oxford University Press, Oxford
Cassese A (ed) (2009) The Oxford Companion to International Criminal Justice. Oxford University Press, Oxford
Clark RS (2001) The mental element in International Criminal Law: the Rome Statute of the International Criminal Court and the elements of offenses. Crim Law Forum 12(3):291–334
Cottier M (2008) Article 8, para. 2(b)(vii). In: Triffterer O (ed) Commentary on the Rome Statute of the Interantional Criminal Court, observers' notes, article by article, 2nd edn. Verlag C.H. Beck oHG, München, pp 350–362
Cryer R (2005) Superior orders and the International Criminal Court. In: Burchill R, White ND, Morris J (eds) International Conflict and Security Law. Essays in memory of Hilaire McCoubrey. University Press, Cambridge, pp 49–67
Dan-Cohen M (1984) Decision rules and conduct rules: on acoustic separation in criminal law. Harvard Law Rev 97(3):625–677
Delmas-Marty M, Spencer JR (eds) (2002) European criminal procedures. Cambridge University Press, Cambridge
Desportes F, Le Gunehec F (2000) Le nouveau droit pénal. Tome 1, Droit pénal général. Enseignement et pratique, 7th edn. Economica, Paris
Desportes F, Le Gunehec F (2007) Droit pénal général, 14th edn. Economica, Paris
Dinstein Y (1965) The defence of 'obedience to superior orders' in international law. A. W. Sijthoff, Leiden
Dinstein Y (2000) Defences. In: McDonald GK, Swaak-Goldman O (eds) Substantive and procedural aspects of International Criminal Law. The experience of international and national courts. Commentary, vol 1. Kluwer Law International, The Hague, pp 369–388
Dolman MM (2006) Overmacht in het stelsel van strafuitsluitingsgronden. Wolf Legal Publishers, Nijmegen
Dörmann K (2003) Elements of war crimes under the Rome Statute of the International Criminal Court. Sources and commentary. ICRC. Cambridge University Press, Cambridge
Dörmann K (2008) Article 8, para. 2(a). In: Triffterer O (ed) Commentary on the Rome Statute of the Interantional Criminal Court, observers' notes, article by article. Verlag C.H. Beck oHG, München, pp 300–323
Ducheine PAL, Pouw EH (2010) ISAF Operaties in Afghanistan: oorlogsrecht, doelbestrijding in counterinsurgency, ROE, mensenrechten & ius ad bellum. Wolf Legal Publishers, Nijmegen
Duff RA (2002) Rule-violations and wrongdoings. In: Shute S, Simester AP (eds) Criminal Law Theory: doctrines of the general part. Oxford University Press, Oxford, pp 47–74
Duyx P, Haveman R, Sliedregt E van (2000) War Crimes Law and the Statute of Rome: some afterthoughts? Report of the seminar hosted by the Netherlands in Rijswijk, The Netherlands on 22 October 1999. Revue de Droit Militaire et de Droit de la Guerre 39 (1–):68–122
Elliott C (2000) The French Law of Intent and Its Influence on the Development of International Criminal Law. Crim Law Forum 11:35–46
Enschedé CJ (2008) Beginselen van Strafrecht. Kluwer, Deventer
Eser A (2002) Mental elements—mistake of fact and mistake of law. In: Cassese A, Gaeta P, Jones JRWD (eds) The Rome Statute of the International Criminal Court: a commentary, vol 1. Oxford University Press, Oxford, pp 889–948
Eser A (2008) Article 31: grounds for excluding criminal responsibility. In: Triffterer O (ed) Commentary on the Rome Statute of the International Criminal Court: observers' notes, article by article, 2nd edn. C.H, Beck oHG, München, pp 863–893
Ferdinandusse WN (2006) Direct application of International Criminal Law in national courts. T.M.C. Asser Press, The Hague
Fletcher GP (1978) Rethinking criminal law, Oxford University Press, Oxford (reprinted in 2000)
Fletcher GP (1985) The right and the reasonable. Harvard Law Rev 98:949–981

Fletcher GP (1998) Basic concepts of criminal law. Oxford University Press, New York
Fletcher GP (2007) The grammar of criminal law: American, comparative, and international. Foundations, vol 1. Oxford University Press, New York
Fletcher GP, Ohlin JD (2008) Defending humanity; when force is justified and why. Oxford University Press, New York
Fletcher GP, Sheppard S (2005) American law in a global context, the basics. Oxford University Press, Oxford
Frowein JA (1990) Im Zweifel für den vielleicht tödlichen Schuß? In: Festschrift für Peter Schneider zum 70. Geburtstag. E. Denninger, pp 112–121
Gaeta P (1999) The defence of superior orders: the statute of the International Criminal Court versus Customary International Law. Eur J Int Law 172–191
Gaeta P (2001) War crimes trials before Italian criminal courts: new trends. In: Fischer H (ed) International and national prosecutions of crimes under international law, current developments. Spitz, Berlin, pp 751–768
Gaeta P (2004) May necessity be available as a defence for torture in the interrogation of suspected terrorists? J Int Crim Justice 2:785–794
Garraway CHB (1999) Superior orders and the International Criminal Court: justice delivered or justice denied. Int Rev Red Cross 81(836):785–794
Gill T, Sliedregt E van (2005) Guantánamo Bay: a reflection on the legal status and rights of 'unlawful enemy combatants'. Utrecht Law Rev 1(1):28–54
Gourevitch P, Morris E (2008) Standard operating procedure. The Penguin Press, New York
Grace BR (1986) Ignorance of the law as an excuse. Columbia Law Rev 86:1392–1411
Green LC (1999) Essays on the modern law of war, 2nd edn. Transnational Publishers, Inc., New York
Green LC (2003) Fifteenth Waldemar A. Solf Lecture in International Law, Superior Orders and Command Responsibility. Milit Law Rev 175:309–384
Greenwood C (2006a) Belligerent reprisals in the jurisprudence of the International Criminal Tribunal for the former Yugoslavia. In: Greenwood C (ed) Essays on war in International Law. Cameron May, London, pp 331–351
Greenwood C (2006b) Twilight of the law of belligerent reprisals. In: Greenwood C (ed) Essays on war in international law. Cameron May, London, pp 295–329
Hampson F (2007) Military necessity. In: Gutman R, Rieff D, Dworkin A (eds) Crimes of war: what the public should know, 2nd edn. W.W. Norton & Company Ltd., London, pp 297–298
Hebel H von (2001) The making of the elements of crimes, introduction. In: Lee RS (ed) The International Criminal Court, elements of crimes and rules of procedure and evidence. Transnational Publishers, Inc., Ardsley, pp 3–18
Heller KJ (2008) Mistake of legal element, the common law, and article 32 of the Rome Statute. J Int Crim Justice 6:419–445
Henckaerts JM, Doswald-Beck L (2005a) Customary International Humanitarian Law, International Committee of the Red Cross, vol 1. Cambridge University Press, Cambridge
Henckaerts JM, Doswald-Beck L (2005b) Customary International Humanitarian Law. International Committee of the Red Cross, vol 3. Cambridge University Press, Cambridge
Hersch SM (2004a) Chain of command; the road from 9/11 to Abu Ghraib. Allen Lane, New York
Hersch SM (2004b) Torture at Abu Ghraib. *The New Yorker*, 10 May 2004
Hullu J de (2006) Materieel strafrecht. Kluwer, Deventer
Husak D, Hirsch A von (1993) Culpability and mistake of law. In: Shute S, Gardner J, Horder J (eds) Action and value in criminal law. Clarendon Press, Oxford, pp 157–174
Jefferson M (2003) Criminal law, 6th edn. Longman/Pearson Education, Harlow
Jescheck HH (2004) The general principles of International Criminal Law set out in Nuremberg, as mirrored in the ICC Statute. J Int Crim Justice 2(1):38–55
Jescheck HH, Weigend T (1996) Lehrbuch des Strafrechts. Allgemeiner Teil. Duncker & Humblot GmbH, Berlin

Jessberger F (2005) Bad torture–good torture? What international criminal lawyers may learn from the recent trial of police officers in Germany. J Int Crim Justice 3:1059–1073
Kahan DM (1997) Ignorance of the law is an excuse–but only for the virtuous. Mich Law Rev 96:127–154
Kalshoven F (2003) Reprisals and the protection of civilians: two recent decisions of the Yugoslavia tribunal. In: Vohrah LC et al. (eds) Man's inhumanity to man. Kluwer Law International, The Hague, pp 481–510
Kalshoven F (2005) Belligerent Reprisals, vol 11. International Humanitarian Law series, 2 edn. Martinus Nijhoff Publishers, Leiden
Kalshoven F, Zegveld L (2001) Constraints on the waging of war: an introduction to International Humanitarian Law, 3rd edn. International Committee of the Red Cross, Geneva
Keijzer N (1977) The military duty to obey. Vrije Universiteit Amsterdam, Amsterdam
Keijzer N (1978) Military obedience. Sijthoff & Noordhoff International Publishers, Alphen aan de Rijn
Kelk C (2005) Studieboek Materieel Strafrecht, 3rd edn. Kluwer, Deventer
Kelt M, Hebel H von (2001a) The making of the elements of crimes, general principles of criminal law and elements of crimes. In: Lee RS (ed) The International Criminal Court, elements of crimes and rules of procedure and evidence. Transnational Publishers, Inc., New York, pp 19–40
Kelt M, Hebel H von (2001b) The making of the elements of crimes, what are elements of crimes? In: Lee RS (ed) The International Criminal Court, elements of crimes and rules of procedure and evidence. Transnational Publishers, Inc., New York, pp 13–18
Kleffner JK (2008) The notions of Civilians and Fighters in non-international armed conflicts. In: Beruto GL, Ravasi G (eds) The conduct of hostilities revisiting the law of armed conflict: 100 years after the 1907 Hague conventions and 20 years after the 1977 additional protocols/ International Institute of Humanitarian Law. Nagard, Milano, pp 69–77
Koopmans FAJ (2007) Het beslissingsmodel van 348/350 Sv. Kluwer, Deventer
Lensing JAW (1996) Amerikaans Strafrecht. Een vergelijkende inleiding. Gouda Quint, Arnhem
Lippman MR (1996) Conundrums of armed conflict: criminal defenses to violations of the humanitarian law of war. Dickinson J Int Law 15:1–112
Lippman MR (2001) Humanitarian law: the development and scope of the superior orders defense. Penn State International Law Review 20:153–251
Loewy AH (2000) Criminal law in a Nutshell, 3rd edn. West Group, St. Paul
May R (1999) Criminal evidence, 4th edn. Sweet & Maxwell, London
McCoubrey H (2001) From Nuremberg to Rome: restoring the defence of superior orders. Int Comp Law Quaterly 50:386–394
Melzer N (2009) Interpretive guidance on the notion of direct participation in hostilities under International Humanitarian Law. International Committee of the Red Cross, Geneva
Mitchell S (ed) (1979) Archbold, pleading, evidence, & practice in criminal cases, 40th edn. Sweet & Maxwell, London
Nill-Theobald C (1998) "Defences" bei Kriegsverbrechen am Beispiel Deutschlands und der USA: zugleich ein Beitrag zu einem Allgemeinen Teil des Völkerstrafrechts, vol Band S 72. Beiträge und Materialien aus dem Max-Planck-Institut für ausländisches und internationales Strafrecht, Freiburg i.Br., iuscrim edn. Max-Planck-Institut für ausländisches und internationales Strafrecht, Freiburg im Breisgau
Olásolo H (2008) Unlawful attacks in combat situations; from the ICTY's case law to the Rome Statute. Martinus Nijhoff Publishers, Leiden
Ormerod DC (2008) Smith and Hogan criminal law, 12th edn. Oxford University Press, Oxford
Osiel M (1999) Obeying orders. Transaction Publishers, New Brunswick
Osiel M (2009) The end of reciprocity: terror, torture and the law of war. Cambridge University Press, Cambridge

Piragoff DK (1999) Article 30: mental element. In: Triffterer O (ed) Commentary on the Rome Statute of the International Criminal Court: observers' notes article by article. Nomos Verslagsgesellschaft, Baden-Baden, pp 527–535

Pouw EH (2009) To kill or not to kill: ISAF and the search within International Humanitarian Law and Human Rights Law for a legal basis to target Narcotics-Individuals. Paper for the international conference—human rights and the military; a duty to protect?, 28–30 August 2009, Wellington, New Zealand

Pradel J (2006) Manuel de droit pénal général. Cujas, Paris

Robinson D (1999) "Defining crimes against humanity" at the Rome conference. Am J Int Law 93(1):43–57

Robinson D (2001) The elements of crimes against humanity. In: Lee RS (ed) The International Criminal Court elements of crimes and rules of procedure and evidence. Transnational Publishers, Inc., New York, pp 57–108

Robinson PH (1984) Criminal law defenses, vol 2. West Publishing Co., St. Paul

Robinson PH, Grall JA (1982–1983) Element analysis in defining criminal liability: the model penal code and beyond. Stanford Law Rev 35:681–762

Rogers APV (2005) What is a legitimate military target? In: Burchill R, White ND, Morris J (eds) International Conflict and Security Law. Essays in memory of Hilaire McCoubrey. University Press, Cambridge, pp 160–184

Röling BVA (1961) The law of war and the national jurisdiction since 1945. A. W. Sythoff, Leiden

Roxin C (1994) Strafrecht Allgemeiner Teil, Band I, Grundlagen. der Aufbau der Verbrechenslehre. C.H. Beck'sche Verlagsbuchhandlung, München

Roxin C (2006) Strafrecht Allgemeiner Teil, Band I, Grundlagen, der Aufbau der Verbrechenslehre, 4th edn. C.H. Beck, Munchen

Saland P (1999) International Criminal Law principles. In: Lee RS (ed) The International Criminal Court, the making of the Rome Statute, issues, negotiations, results. Kluwer Law International, The Hague, pp 189–216

Sands P (2008) Torture team. Deception, Cruelty and Compromise of Law. Allen Lane, London

Scaliotti M (2001) Defences before the International Criminal Court: substantive grounds for excluding criminal responsibility—part 1. Int Crim Law Rev 1:111–172

Scaliotti M (2002) Defences before the International Criminal Court: substantive grounds for excluding criminal responsibility—part 2. Int Crim Law Rev 2:1–46

Schabas WA (2004) An introduction to the International Criminal Court, 2nd edn. Cambridge University Press, Cambridge

Sliedregt E van (2003) The criminal responsibility of individuals for violations of International Humanitarian Law. T.M.C. Asser Press, The Hague

Sluiter GK (2009a) Arlt. In: Cassese A (ed) The Oxford companion to International Criminal Justice. Oxford University Press, Oxford, pp 585–586

Sluiter GK (2009b) Zimmermann. In: Cassese A (ed) The Oxford companion to International Criminal Justice. Oxford University Press, Oxford, pp 981–982

Smith ATH (1985) Error and mistake of law in Anglo-American Criminal Law. Anglo Am Law Rev 14:3–32

Solis GD (1999) Obedience of orders and the law of war: judicial application in American forums. Am Univ Int Law Rev 15:481–525

Stolwijk SAM (2009) Een inleding in het strafrecht in 13 hoofdstukken, 3rd edn. Kluwer, Deventer

Strasser S (ed) (2004) The Abu Ghraib investigations, the official reports of the independent panel and the pentagon on the shocking prisoner abuse in Iraq. Public Affairs, New York

Swart AHJ (2002) Algemene leerstukken van materieel strafrecht in de rechtspraak van de ad hoc-tribunalen. In: Joegoslavië-en Rwanda-tribunalen: impact op het Nederlandse strafrecht. Cahiers 'Van Hamel'. Universiteit van Amsterdam, Amsterdam

Travers ML (1995) Mistake of law in mala prohibita crimes. Univ Chic Law Rev 62:1301–1331

Triffterer O (2008) Article 32: mistake of law. In: Triffterer O (ed) Commentary on the Rome Statute of the International Criminal Court: observers' notes, article by article, 2nd edn. C.H, Beck oHG, München, pp 895–914

Veen TW van (1972) Facet-Wederrechtelijkheid. Nederlands Juristenblad, pp 466–469

Vogeley S (2003) The mistake of law defense in International Criminal Law. In: Yee S (ed) International crime and punishment. University Press of America, Inc., Oxford, pp 59–99

Walther S (1995) Problems in blaming and punishing individuals for human rights violations: the example of the berlin wall shootings. In: Roht-Arriaza N (ed) Impunity and human rights in international law and practice. Oxford University Press, New York, pp 99–112

Weigend T (2004) The Harmonization of General Principles of Criminal Law: the statutes and jurisprudence of the ICTY, ICTR, and the ICC: an overview. Nouvelles Etudes Penales 19:319–335

Weigend T (2008) Intent, mistake of law, and co-perpetration in the *Lubanga* decision on confirmation of charges. J Int Crim Justice 6:471–487

Werle G (2003) Völkerstrafrecht. Mohr Siebeck, Tübingen

Werle G, Jessberger F (2005) 'Unless otherwise provided': article 30 of the ICC Statute and the mental element of crimes under International Criminal Law. J Int Crim Justice 3:35–55

Wilt HG van der (1999) Commentary to the Prosecutor v. Erdemovic Appeals Judgement. In: Klip A, Sluiter GK (eds) Annotated leading cases of International Criminal Tribunals, vol 1. Intersentia, Antwerp, pp 654–656

Wilt HG van der (2000) The duty to know: enkele beschouwingen over het leerstuk van command responsibility. In: Corstens GJM, Groenhuijsen MS (eds) Rede en Recht. Liber Amicorum voor Nico Keijzer, Gouda Quint, Deventer, pp 123–135

Wilt HG van der (2009a) Can romantics and liberals be reconciled?: Some further reflections on defending humanity. J Int Crim Justice 7:529–539

Wilt HG van der (2009b) Zühlke. In: Cassese A (ed) The Oxford companion to International Criminal Justice. Oxford University Press, Oxford, p 982

Wise EM (1998) Commentary on parts 2 and 3 of the Zutphen Intersessional draft: general principles of criminal law. Nouvelles Etudes Penales 13:43–53

Zahar A, Sluiter GK (2008) International Criminal Law. A critical introduction. Oxford University Press, Oxford

Zimmermann (1949) Special court of Cassation, The Netherlands, Dutch Special Court of Cassation, NJ 1950, no 9, 30–32; Annual Digest 1949, 552–553

Zimmermann A (2002) Superior orders. In: Cassese A, Gaeta P, Jones JRWD (eds) The Rome Statute of the International Criminal Court: a commentary, vol 1. Oxford University Press, Oxford, pp 957–974

Miscellaneous

The American Series of Foreign Penal Codes, France (1999) The American Series of Foreign Penal Codes, France, vol 31

HRW (2000) The Crisis in Kosovo. Civilian Deaths in the NATO Air Campaign, February 2007. Human Rights Watch

International Committee of the Red Cross (1999) Paper relating to the mental element in the common law and civil law systems and to the concepts of mistake of fact and mistake of law in national and international law. Preparatory Commission for the International Criminal Court, Working group on Elements of Crimes, PCNICC/1999/WGEC/INF/2/Add.4, New York

International Committee of the Red Cross (2004) The Roots of Behaviour in War. Geneva, Switzerland 2004

Manual of Service Law (2011) vol 1, 31 January 2011 edn http://www.mod.uk/DefenceInternet/AboutDefence/CorporatePublications/LegalPublications/ManualOfServiceLaw/

The Manual of the Law of Armed Conflict (2004) UK Ministry of Defence, Oxford University Press, Oxford

NATO NATO's Role in Afghanistan http://www.nato.int/cps/en/natolive/topics_8189.htm, last visited: 7 July 2010

OTPICTY (2000) Final Report to the Prosecutor by the Committee Established to Review the NATO Bombing Campaign Against the Federal Republic of Yugoslavia

Table of Cases

International Case Law

Supreme Court of Leipzig

Dover Castle case (1921), German Reichsgericht, Supreme Court of Leipzig, 16 Am. J. Int'l L. 704 (1922)

Llandovery Castle case (1921), German Reichsgericht, Supreme Court of Leipzig, 16 Am. J. Int'l L. 708 (1922)

US Military Tribunals at Nuremberg

I.G. Farben Trial (1948), US, Military Tribunal at Nuremberg, Judgement, 14 August 1947–29 July 1948, US Military Tribunals at Nuremberg, Case No. 6, Military Tribunal VI, N.M.T., vols 7–8

List (The Hostages Case) (1948), US Military Tribunal at Nuremberg, UNWCC, vol VIII; TWC vol XI

US v. Otto Ohlendorf et al. (Einsatzgruppen case) (1948), United States Military Tribunals at Nuremberg, Case No. 9, TWC, vol IV, pp.1–596

Von Leeb (The High Command Trial) (1948), US Military Tribunal at Nuremberg, Friedman, The Law of War, vol II, p. 1421–1470; UNWCC, vol XII, p. 1–127

The UNWCC Trials—Law Reports of Trials of War Criminals, selected and prepared by the United Nations War Crimes Commission (1949). vol XV, Digest of Laws and Cases. London: His Majesty's Stationary Office, 1949

Dostler trial (1945), United States Military Commission, Rome, UNWCC, vol I, pp. 28–34

Peleus Trial (1945), British Military Court, Hamburg, UNWCC, vol I, pp. 1–21

Trial of Sandrock (Almelo Trial) (1945), British Military Court for the Trial of War Criminals, held at the Court House, Almelo, Holland, UNWCC, vol I, pp. 35–45

Buck Trial (1946), British Military Court, Wuppertal, Germany, UNWCC, vol V, pp. 39–44

Falkenhorst trial (1946), British Military Court, Brunswick, Norway, UNWCC, vol XI, pp. 18–30

A. van Verseveld, *Mistake of Law*, DOI: 10.1007/978-90-6704-867-5,

Trial of Sawada (1946), United States Military Commission, Shanghai, UNWCC, vol V, pp. 1–24

Helmuth Latza and 2 others (1948), Eidsivating Lagmannsrett (Court of Appeal) and the Supreme Court of Norway, UNWCC, vol XIV, pp. 49–85

Zühlke Trial (1948), Special Court in Amsterdam, The Netherlands, NJ 1949, No. 85; UNWCC, vol XIV; Friedman, The Law of War (1972), vol II, pp. 1543–1554

Rauter (1949), Special Court of Cassation, The Netherlands, NJ 1949, No. 87, at 144–61; UNWCC, vol XIV; Annual Digest 1949, 526–45

European Court of Human Rights

Case of K.-H. W. v. Germany (Application no. 37201/97) (2001), ECtHR, 22 March 2001

International Criminal Tribunal for the Former Yugoslavia

Prosecutor v. Martić (1996), ICTY Trial Chamber, Case No. IT-95-11-R61, Decision 8 March 1996

Prosecutor v. Erdemović (1997a), ICTY Appeals Chamber, Case No. IT-96-22-A, Judgement 7 October 1997, Separate and dissenting opinion of Judge Cassese

Prosecutor v. Erdemović (1997b), ICTY Appeals Chamber, Case No. IT-96-22-A, Judgement 7 October 1997

Prosecutor v. Kupreškić et al. (2000), ICTY Trial Chamber, Case No. IT-95-16-T, Judgement, 14 January 2000

Prosecutor v. Mucić et al. (2001), ICTY Appeals Chamber, Case No. IT-96-21-A, Judgement, 20 February 2001

Prosecutor v. Krstić (2001), ICTY Trial Chamber, Case No. IT-98-33-T, Judgement 2 August 2001

Prosecutor v. Blagojević and Jokić (2005), ICTY Trial Chamber, Case No. IT-02-60-T, Judgement 17 January 2005

Special Court for Sierra Leone

Prosecutor v. Norman (2004a), SCSL Appeals Chamber, Case No SCSL-2004-14-AR72(E), Decision on Preliminary Motion Based on Lack of Jurisdiction (Child Recruitment), 31 May 2004

Prosecutor v. Norman (2004b), SCSL Appeals Chamber, Case No SCSL-2004-14-AR72(E), Decision on Preliminary Motion Based on Lack of Jurisdiction (Child Recruitment), 31 May 2004, Dissenting Opinion of Justice Robertson

Prosecutor v. Kanu (2007), SCSL Trial Chamber, Case No. SCSL-04-16-T, Judgement 20 June 2007

Prosecutor v. Kanu (2008), SCSL Appeals Chamber, Case No. SCSL-2004-16-A, Judgement 22 February 2008

International Criminal Court

Prosecutor v. Lubanga (2007), ICC Pre-Trial Chamber, Case No. ICC-01/04-01/06, Decision on the confirmation of charges, 29 January 2007

National Case Law

United States

People v Weiss (1938), New York Court of Appeals, 276 NY 384, 12 NE2d 514, 114 ALR865

Long v. State (1949), Supreme Court of Delaware, 5 Terry 262, 65 A.2d 489

U.S. v. Kinder (1954), 14 C.M.R. 742 (1954)

Lambert v. People of the State of California (1957), Supreme Court of the United States, 355 U.S. 225, 78 S.Ct. 240

Reyes v. United States (1958), United States Court of Appeals, Ninth Circuit, 258 F.2d 774

U.S. v. International Minerals & Chemical Corp. (1971), Supreme Court of the United States, 402 U.S. 558, 91 S.Ct. 1697

U.S. v. Calley (1973a), U.S. Court of Military Appeals, 1973 WL 14894 (CMA), 48 C.M.R. 19

U.S. v. Calley (1973b), U.S. Army Court of Military Review, 1973 WL 14570, 46 C.M.R. 1131; Friedman, The Law of War (1972), vol II, pp. 1703–1728

Liparota v. U.S. (1985), Supreme Court of the United States, 471 U.S. 419, 105 S.Ct. 2084

Cheek v. U.S. (1991), Supreme Court of the United States, 498 U.S. 192, 111 S.Ct. 604

Ratzlaf v. U.S. (1994), Supreme Court of the United States, 510 U.S. 135, 114 S.Ct. 655

U.S. v. Curran (1994), United States Court of Appeals, Third Circuit, 20 F.3d 560

U.S. v. Obiechie (1994), United States Court of Appeals, Seventh Circuit, 38 F.3d 309

U.S. v. Rogers (1994), United States Court of Appeals, Fourth Circuit, 18 F.3d 265

Bryan v. U.S. (1998), Supreme Court of the United States, 524 U.S. 184, 118 S.Ct. 1939

United Kingdom

Regina v. Morgan (1975), 2 W.L.R. 923

Germany

Bundesgerichtshof, 18-03-1952 (1952), GSSt 2/ 51 (Lexetius.com/1952,1)
BGHSt 35, 379 (1988)

Mauerschützen I (1992), BGHSt 39, 1, BGH 5 StR 370/92, 3 November 1992

Mauerschützen II (1993), BGHSt 39, 168, BGH 5 StR 418/92, 25 March 1993

Mauerschützen III (1995), BGHSt 41, 101, BGH 5 StR 111/94, 20 March 1995

BVerfGE 95, 96, 24 October 1996 (1996), 2 BvR 1851, 1853, 1875 und 1952/94

BVerfGE 95, 96, 24 October 1996 (1997), 18 Human Rights Law Journal (1997) No. 1–4, pp. 65–78

The Netherlands

Arlt (1949), Special Court of Cassation at Arnhem, The Netherlands, NJ 1950, no. 8, pp. 27–29;
Summary in Annual Digest 1949, 462–4

Wintgen (1949), Special Court of Cassation, The Netherlands, NJ 1949, 540, 981–5; Excerpts in Annual Digest 1949, 484–6

Lages case (1950), Special Court of Cassation, The Netherlands, NJ, 1950, No. 680, pp. 1201–1209

B. case (1951), Special Court of Cassation, The Netherlands, NJ 1952, No. 247, pp. 516–526

E. van E. case (1951), Special Court of Cassation, The Netherlands, NJ 1952, No. 246, pp. 514–16

Other countries

R. v. SAH Alsagoff (1946), Court of Assizes, Singapore, 2 MC 191

Werner case (1947), Appeal Division, South Africa, 20 May 1947, 1947 (2) South African Law Reports 828(A)

Kappler and others (1948), Rome Military Tribunal, Italy (Tribunale militare territoriale), Fore penale, 1948, 603–22

Sergeant W. (1966), Brussels War Council, Belgium; Military Court, Revue juridique du Congo, 1970, 236–8; Revue de droit pénal et de criminologie, 1970, 806–10; 46 revue juridique du Congo, 1970, 238–9; Revue de droit pénal et de criminologie, 1972–3, 807–9, 810–11

Hass and Priebke case (1998), Military tribunal of Rome; Military Appeals Court; Supreme Court of cassation, Italy, L'Indice penale, 1998, 959–1000

H.C. 5100/94 (1999), The Supreme Court of Israel

MIX
Papier aus verantwortungsvollen Quellen
Paper from responsible sources
FSC® C105338

If you have any concerns about our products,
you can contact us on
ProductSafety@springernature.com

In case Publisher is established outside the EU,
the EU authorized representative is:
Springer Nature Customer Service Center GmbH
Europaplatz 3, 69115 Heidelberg, Germany

Printed by Libri Plureos GmbH
in Hamburg, Germany